THE S. S. HUEBNER FOUNDATION FOR INSURANCE EDUCATION

Lectures

Life Insurance Trends and Problems
Life Insurance Trends at Mid-Century
Investment of Life Insurance Funds
Accident and Sickness Insurance
Pensions: Problems and Trends
The Beneficiary in Life Insurance
Life Insurance Sales Management
All Lines Insurance
Risk Management

Studies

An Analysis of Government Life Insurance
Group Life Insurance
Group Health Insurance
Group Annuities
The Economic Theory of Risk and Insurance
Life Insurance Housing Projects
Life Insurance Investment in Commercial Real Estate
Total Disability Provisions in Life Insurance Contracts
Insurance and Economic Theory
Transition to Multiple-Line Insurance Companies
Compulsory Temporary Disability Insurance
    in the United States
Development of Comprehensive Insurance
    for the Household
Savings Bank Life Insurance
Rights of Creditors in Life Insurance Policies
Regulation of Blue Cross and Blue Shield Plans
Subrogation in Insurance Theory and Practice
Corporate Self-Insurance and Risk Retention Plans
Participating Life Insurance Sold by Stock Companies
Ratemaking for Homeowners Insurance

RATEMAKING
for
HOMEOWNERS
INSURANCE

By

GERALD R. HARTMAN
Assistant Professor of Insurance
University of Pennsylvania

Published for

THE S. S. HUEBNER FOUNDATION
FOR INSURANCE EDUCATION
University of Pennsylvania

by

RICHARD D. IRWIN, Inc., Homewood, Illinois

© 1967

The S. S. Huebner Foundation for Insurance Education
University of Pennsylvania

First Printing, November, 1967

Library of Congress Catalog Card No. 67-21002

Manufactured in the United States of America

To My Mother

Bessie Priest Hartman

THE S. S. HUEBNER FOUNDATION
FOR INSURANCE EDUCATION

The S. S. Huebner Foundation for Insurance Education was created in 1940, under the sponsorship of the American Life Convention, the Life Insurance Association of America (then the Association of Life Insurance Presidents), and the Institute of Life Insurance, and operated under a deed of trust until 1955 at which time it was incorporated as a Pennsylvania nonprofit corporation. Its primary purpose is to strengthen and encourage insurance education at the collegiate level. Its activities take three principal forms:

a) The providing of fellowships to teachers in accredited colleges and universities of the United States and Canada, or persons who are contemplating a teaching career in such colleges and universities, in order that they may secure preparation at the graduate level for insurance teaching and research.

b) The publication of research theses and other studies which constitute a distinct contribution directly or indirectly to insurance knowledge.

c) The collection and maintenance of an insurance library and other research materials which are made available through circulating privileges to teachers in accredited colleges and universities desirous of conducting research in the insurance field.

Financial support for the Foundation is provided by contributions from more than one hundred and twenty life insurance companies and proceeds from the sale of Foundation publications.

The program of activities is under the general direction of a Board of Trustees representing the life insurance institution. Actual operation of the Foundation has been delegated to the University of Pennsylvania under an administrative plan submitted by the University and approved by the Board of Trustees. The University discharges its responsibilities through an Administrative Board consisting of five officers and faculty members of the University of Pennsylvania and four academic persons associated with other institutions. Active management of the Foundation is entrusted to an Executive Director, appointed by the University of Pennsylvania.

Foreword

Ratemaking is often viewed by laymen and students as a process that involves such complicated data and intricate mathematical procedures that only those with extensive, specialized training could hope to have more than a general understanding of the process. This attitude and the situation it reflects are both unfortunate since the calculation of rates is a basic and obviously significant aspect of insurance. In fact, ratemaking has been referred to as the heart of the insurance transaction. Thus, those who would know insurance must, of necessity, know about ratemaking.

While the ratemaking process is appropriately known as having high intellectual demands, those with the potential for undertaking studies and eventual responsibilities in ratemaking have been deterred more than occasionally from seriously considering this type of work because of a distorted opinion of the actuary's role. Some individuals with mathematical orientations mistakenly believe that actuarial procedures are esoteric, while others harbor the equally inaccurate view that the actuary is confined both in the nature of his work and the recognition accorded his efforts. The old saw about actuaries being issued green shades and elastic arm bands is probably not too far removed from the general view of actuaries and their type of work. The now widespread knowledge that actuaries are highly compensated, particularly after obtaining a professional designation, has seemingly not helped to alter the actuary's image. Few observers recognize the involvement of actuaries in the policy making of insurance companies, for example, or, alternatively, the impact of company policy on the work of actuaries.

Some of the misconceptions about ratemaking and actuaries have been perpetuated because of the dearth of reference materials that describe the ratemaking function in its entirety and in other than rudimentary terms. This is much more of a problem in property and liability insurance than in life insurance, no doubt because of the diverse lines of insurance included in the former coverages. The different types of data involved in property and liability insurance ratemaking; the dissimilar methods for collecting and analyzing such data; the varying degrees of reliability of the information available; the complications introduced by regulatory requirements, both statutory and administrative; and the impact of competitive forces are undoubtedly among the considerations that have discouraged attempts to describe the rate making process in property and liability insurance in detail and also in language familiar to the layman.

Problems such as these are among the factors that underlie the writing of this volume. The bulk of the manuscript was submitted originally by its author, Dr. Gerald R. Hartman, as a doctoral dissertation at the University of Pennsylvania. The data have since been up-dated and certain changes have been made, in part as a consequence of a review of the dissertation by several prominent actuaries. This volume is the twentieth in the Huebner Foundation's "Studies Series," and the twenty-ninth volume to be published under the auspices of the Foundation's publication program.

Dr. Hartman was raised in Chicago and graduated from the Illinois Institute of Technology where he majored in Fire Protection and Safety Engineering, a program which cultivated his interest in property insurance. It is of interest to note that Dr. Hartman held a Western Actuarial Bureau Scholarship during the time of his undergraduate studies. Dr. Hartman received a Master of Science degree in Hydraulic Engineering from the University of Iowa, after having written a thesis on "Flood Insurance." He subsequently was awarded a Huebner Foundation Fellowship to undertake a doctoral program of study in Business and Applied Economics with a specialization in Insurance at the University of Pennsylvania. Dr. Hartman received his Ph.D. degree in 1964.

Dr. Hartman's first faculty appointment was at Georgia State College, where he was a member of the Insurance Department from 1963 until 1966. In the fall of 1966 Dr. Hartman assumed his current position as an Assistant Professor of Insurance on the faculty of the Wharton School of Finance and Commerce at the University of Pennsylvania.

The policies of the S. S. Huebner Foundation preclude the endorsement of statements made by authors of volumes published under the auspices of the Foundation's Publication Program, but this fact should not detract in any way from the findings and conclusions contained in this volume.

ROBERT D. EILERS

PHILADELPHIA
October, 1967

Preface

Few subjects of concern to the nonlife insurance industry have caused more repercussions within the industry than multiple line underwriting, and probably no other subject within the multiple line area has created more controversy than rating. While a great deal has been written about most features of multiple line insurance, these writings are generally rather narrow in scope. The purpose of this study is to present a comprehensive analysis of ratemaking for homeowners insurance and three of its important forerunners. An attempt has been made to place multiple line rating problems, as exemplified by homeowners rating, in proper perspective by first examining the fundamentals of property and liability insurance rating and reviewing the historical development of rating bureaus and rate regulation in this country.

I first became interested in insurance rating when I studied the Dean Analytic System as part of the Fire Protection and Safety Engineering curriculum at Illinois Institute of Technology (IIT). During my undergraduate summers and for three years after graduating from IIT, I was employed by the Michigan, Tennessee, and Iowa fire insurance rating bureaus. After working with multiple line rating problems in the Rating and Research Department of the Insurance Company of North America (INA) during the summers of 1961 and 1962, I, as a S.S. Huebner Fellow at the University of Pennsylvania, decided to write my doctoral dissertation on multiple line ratemaking. The personnel of INA's Rating and Research Department were exceedingly cooperative during the entire course of the project. The dissertation was completed while I was a faculty member at Georgia State College. I am deeply appreciative of the encouragement and help I received from my Georgia State colleagues.

In 1965, INA awarded me a research fellowship which greatly facilitated extensive revision and updating of the dissertation for publication in its present form. I am grateful to H. P. Abbott, B. W. Cork, Acis Jenkinson, 3rd, and R. C. Kern for helping to arrange the fellowship and for providing secretarial assistance. I am thankful to INA's Actuarial Department for bringing the fellowship to fruition.

My indebtedness is extended to many other individuals and organizations for the cooperation and help they gave me in this endeavor. It would not be practical to mention herein all of those who have helped me, since they number in the hundreds. To each and every one of these individuals and organizations I am grateful. Special credit, however, is due the following individuals who reviewed one or more sections of the manuscript or made other valuable contributions to the study through lengthy interviews or correspondence: J. W. Wieder, Jr., Aetna Casualty and Surety Company; C. C. Hewitt, R. P. White, Allstate Insurance Company; E. S. Overman, American Institute for Property and Liability Underwriters; A. B. Kelley, Factory Mutual Insurance Companies; R. M. Beckwith, P. R. Bechtolt, J. Crane, K. H. Parker, Fire Insurance Research and Actuarial Association; R. C. McCullough, General Reinsurance Corporation; Kenneth Black, Jr., J. W. Hall, Georgia State College; R. J. Icks, Illinois Bureau of Casualty Underwriters; R. B. Taylor, H. L. Wayne, Inland Marine Insurance Bureau; W. H. Crandall, R. Dunn, H. R. Heilman, W. B. Pugh, Jr., E. Rondepierre, R. E. Salzmann, J. S. Schmidt, Insurance Company of North America; C. N. Wight, Middle Department Association of Fire Underwriters; F. Caso, H. Pierson, Multi-Line Insurance Rating Bureau; R. G. Wegenke, National Association of Independent Insurers; H. L. Tollack, National Association of Insurance Commissioners; W. S. Gillam, National Bureau of Casualty Underwriters; J. H. Boyajian, J. H. Finnegan, L. J. Simon, National Insurance Actuarial and Statistical Association; the late C. O. Shaver, Nationwide Mutual Fire Insurance Company; R. C. Hayden, R. M. Kennedy, New York Fire Insurance Rating Organization; N. G. Alford, Jr., F. Cardi, F. Harwayne, J. Malmuth, H. Sohmer,

A. Trupin, New York Insurance Department; W. Kedrow, L. M. Michel, H. A. Miller, K. Rathert, Reliance Insurance Company; R. L. Gatewood, Southeastern Underwriters Association; P. G. Buffinton, State Farm Fire and Casualty Company; W. H. Rodda, Transportation Insurance Rating Bureau; R. L. Johe, J. Moseley, United States Fidelity and Guarantee Company; C. A. Williams, Jr., University of Minnesota; H. S. Denenberg, J. C. Phillips, J. S. deCani, University of Pennsylvania; T. Lenhart, R. Schoneman, E. N. Searl, and the late J. Hommes Western Actuarial Bureau.

Although I take full responsibility for the inevitable errors that remain in the text, I wish to express my sincere appreciation to the following individuals who read entire drafts of earlier versions of the book and whose penetrating comments and corrections were of considerable help in shaping the final version: R. L. Hurley, Fire Insurance Research and Actuarial Association; E. J. Hobbs, F. J. Hunt, Jr., L. H. Longley-Cook, R. K. Syfert, Insurance Company of North America; H. F. Perlet, L. R. Plast, Multi-Line Insurance Rating Bureau; the late T. O. Carlson, National Bureau of Casualty Underwriters; R. D. Eilers, C. M. Kahler (my understanding and inspiring faculty adviser), D. M. McGill, University of Pennsylvania.

I am indebted to the S.S. Huebner Foundation for providing me with financial assistance during the three years that I was a graduate student at the University of Pennsylvania and for undertaking the publication of this volume. Miss Mildred A. Brill, Administrative Assistant of the Huebner Foundation, deserves special recognition for her excellent editorial assistance.

Finally, I wish to thank my wife, Iris, and my daughters, Bessie Pam and Sheri Helene, for the many sacrifices they made on the book's behalf during this long experience.

GERALD R. HARTMAN

PHILADELPHIA, PA.
October, 1967

Table of Contents

List of Tables

CHAPTER I

Introduction

DEFINITION OF MULTIPLE-LINE INSURANCE POLICIES

Monoline System

It is not possible to appreciate fully the problems created by multiple-line underwriting without understanding the development of insurance in this country on a monoline basis. For about 100 years prior to the passage of multiple line legislation in the late 1940's, the insurance laws of many states limited the kinds of insurance which an insurer could write to only the types of insurance in one of three broad duo-classifications: life and health, fire and marine, and casualty and surety.[1] The various kinds of insurance were rather arbitrarily and inconsistently allocated by the state legislatures and/or insurance departments to each of these duo-classifications. In a loose and broad sense each duo-classification comprises a line of insurance. The three main lines were commonly referred to as life, fire, and casualty lines.

This system, which compartmentalized the insurance business, was known as the monoline system. The exact etymology of the word "line" as used in the expression "line of insurance" is

---

[1] Provision was also made for the writing of title insurance and insurance of life of property, neither of which is germane to this study. Title insurance may be written only by insurers that specialize in writing this insurance exclusively. Apparently no insurance of life of property has been written in this country.

1

unknown; however, it very likely is derived from the fact that the underwriting experience for various kinds of insurance is reported on separate *lines* of the annual statement.[2]   However, since the various types of insurers were empowered later in the monoline era to write kinds of insurance which were, and still are, reportable on more than one line of the annual statement, the expression "monoline" is a misnomer.

The operation of the monoline system may be understood by illustrating how it functioned in New York. Section 46 of the New York Insurance Law, *"Kinds of Insurance Authorized,"* lists and defines 23 kinds of insurance:

1. Life	14. Property damage liability
2. Annuities	15. Workmen's compensation and
3. Accident and health	employer's liability
4. Fire	16. Fidelity and surety
5. Miscellaneous property	17. Credit
6. Water damage	18. Title
7. Burglary and theft	19. Motor vehicle and aircraft
8. Glass	20. Marine
9. Boiler and machinery	21. Marine protection and indemnity
10. Elevator	nity
11. Animal	22. Life of property
12. Collision	23. Substantially similar to one of
13. Personal injury liability	the above kinds of insurance

Under the monoline system, just prior to the passage of full multiple-line legislation in New York, the kinds of insurance were allocated as follows:

A. Life and accident and health insurers: 1, 2, and 3.

B. Casualty insurers and surety companies: 3, 6, 7, 8, 9, 10, 11, 12, 13, 14, 15, 16, and 17.

C. Fire and marine insurers: 4, 5, 6, 12, 19, 20, and 21.

---

[2] For a sample annual statement see *Insurance Accounting Fire and Casualty,* edited by W. Rogers Hammond with the collaboration of Gerald R. Hartman, a project of the Insurance Accounting and Statistical Association (2nd ed.; Philadelphia: Chilton Co., 1965), Appendix.   In the 1905 annual statement the lines other than life and health were merely fire, marine, inland marine, and casualty. See John A. Diemand, "Historical Development of Multiple Line Underwriting," in H. Wayne Snider (ed.), *Readings in Property and Casualty Insurance* (Homewood, Ill.: Richard D. Irwin, Inc., 1959), p. 524.

Under this system an insurer generally would start out in business by being licensed to write one, or perhaps a few, of the kinds of insurance listed under either A or B or C above. Eventually a life insurer, for example, might write life, annuities, and accident and health insurance, but such an insurer was prohibited from writing any other kind of insurance. There was some overlapping between the life and accident and health insurers, on the one hand, and the casualty insurers and surety companies, on the other, in the writing of Number 3, accident and health insurance.

There was also some overlap between casualty insurers and surety companies and the fire and marine insurers in the writing of Numbers 6 and 12, water damage and collision. In many states, however, casualty insurers were not allowed to write the form of water-damage insurance known as sprinkler-leakage insurance. The areas of overlapping during the monoline era varied among the states and within a given state over time. In many states fire insurers were permitted to write certain explosion coverage but not steam-boiler insurance, in which explosion is a principal peril. Fire insurers were allowed to write fire legal *liability* insurance but generally not other types of liability insurance.[3]

Multiple-Line Legislation

Beginning in the late 1940's and lasting until the mid-1950's the state insurance laws were amended to permit individual insurers meeting certain financial requirements to write all kinds of insurance that were included in the fire and casualty lines, categories B and C above. The amendments were known as multiple-line legislation and in effect permitted a single financially qualified insurer to write every kind of insurance except life, annuities, title, and life of property.

Actually multiple-line legislation was enacted by degrees in several states. As a prelude to full multiple-line underwriting,

---

[3] Milton W. Mays, "Significant Contrasts and Comparisons between Life Insurance and the Various Property and Casualty Insurance Fields," in Snider, *op. cit.*, p. 38.

a committee (commonly referred to as the Diemand Committee)[4] appointed by the National Association of Insurance Commissioners (NAIC) recommended that all states allow any financially qualified fire, marine, casualty, or surety company to write the following kinds of coverage:

1. All kinds of insurance or reinsurance other than life or annuities on risks *outside* the United States.
2. Reinsurance on any kind of insurance other than life or annuities.
3. Any and all kinds of automobile insurance.
4. Any and all kinds of aircraft insurance.
5. Personal-property floater policies on an all-risk basis.

As these suggestions were enacted, they became known as *partial* multiple-line legislation. The first recommendation is reflected in Section 341d of the New York Insurance Law, which was added in 1946 and provided that an insurer organized to write fire and/or marine insurance:

... may in addition, except with respect to life insurance, title insurance and contracts for the payment of annuities, *reinsure* risks of every kind or description and may, except with respect to life insurance, title insurance and contracts for the payment of annuities, write any and all kinds of insurance on risks *outside of the United States*, its territories and possessions, provided it maintains a surplus to policyholders of not less than one million five hundred thousand dollars ... [Italics added.]

Suggestions 3 and 4 as they relate to a fire and marine company are exemplified by Section 341e of the New York Insurance Law, which was amended in 1947 to permit such an insurer to:

... do the kinds of business specified in paragraph nineteen (b) of section forty-six [automobile and aircraft legal liability insurance], provided it shall have a capital of at least three hundred thousand dollars.

Full multiple-line underwriting as it relates to a fire or marine insurer is illustrated by Section 341f of the New York Insurance Law, which was added in 1949 and provided that such an insurer may write:

---

[4] "Report of the Multiple-Line Underwriting Committee," *Proceedings of the National Association of Insurance Commissioners*, 1944, p. 125.

. . . any one or more of the kinds of business provided in section forty-six except those specified in paragraphs one, two, eighteen and twenty-two thereof [i.e., life, annuities, title, and life of property insurance], provided it shall have a minimum capital of five hundred thousand dollars and surplus to policyholders equal in the aggregate to the minimum capital and minimum surplus required on organization by this section and by section three hundred eleven for all kinds of insurance business which it is to be licensed to do. . . .

Multiple-Line Insurance Policies

Full multiple-line legislation was followed, as would be expected, by sanction for individual insurers to write in a single policy coverages that were previously limited to separate contracts from the traditional fire and casualty lines. A contract which contains at least one kind of coverage from each of the traditional fire and casualty lines is customarily defined as a multiple-line insurance policy. This study is primarily concerned with the rating of those multiple-line insurance policies which were designed for noncommercial risks. These policies are known as personal multiple-line policies. Foremost among these are the homeowners policies, and consequently homeowners contracts receive primary attention in this study.

HISTORICAL BACKGROUND

The practice of limiting an insurer's underwriting powers to certain kinds of insurance was virtually unique to the United States.[5] Contrary to subsequent practice, the charters of the early American insurers were often very broad and were apparently fashioned in the liberal English tradition.

Many of the early companies, organized in the eastern part of the United States, were empowered by their charters to write not only fire and marine, but also life insurance. [Casualty insurance was virtually nonexistent at this time.] . . . In some of the newer states, such as Texas,

---

[5] J. M. Kidd, "Multiple Line Underwriting outside the U.S.A.," in Snider, *op. cit.*, p. 117.

companies were organized to conduct a general insurance business including fire, marine, casualty, and life.[6]

Restrictions upon Underwriting Powers

The exact origin of, and the reasons for, the practice of restricting insurers to a single line of insurance is a matter of speculation.[7] It seems that in many instances the distribution of kinds of insurance among the types of insurers was self-imposed by underwriting practices and that the various states subsequently formalized the divisions in their laws. For example, after the Civil War the use of glass had developed to such an extent that prudence dictated that the values be insured. Fire insurers refused to write plate-glass insurance; however, casualty insurers who were primarily concerned with liability risks agreed to write this form of property insurance. Apparently a similar situation developed in connection with burglary insurance.[8]

Some restrictions were adopted, we are told, in the interest of insureds. The division between fire and casualty insurance was likely a carry-over from the division between life and property insurance. It was first considered necessary to protect the reserve funds of life companies from the conflagration exposure; later it was considered necessary to protect the policyholders of a casualty insurer from the conflagration exposure of the fire business, and, conversely, to protect the insureds of a fire insurer from the possible catastrophe-type losses of the newer forms of casualty insurance.[9] This attitude was perhaps justified in the 1800's,

---

[6] William D. Winter, "The Multiple-Line Concept," *Examination of Insurance Companies* (New York: New York Insurance Department, 1953), Vol. I, p. 536.

[7] Spencer L. Kimball, *Insurance and Public Policy* (Madison, Wis.: University of Wisconsin Press, 1960), p. 117. Also see Benjamin N. Woodson, "All-Lines Underwriting: New Fashion or New Era?" in Snider, *op. cit.*, p. 129.

[8] Winter, *loc. cit.*, p. 535.

[9] See L. H. Longley-Cook, "All-Lines Insurance," *The Proceedings of the Conference of Actuaries in Public Practice*, Vol. XIII, p. 278, and Raymond Harris, "Provisions of the New York Insurance Law Affecting the Organization, Licensing, and Corporate Procedure of Insurers under Sections 40–46," *Examination of Insurance Companies*, Vol. II, p. 61.

when insurers generally were not nearly so strong financially as they had become by the 1940's. Also, the conflagration hazard had diminished through the years because of improved techniques of fire protection. The impact of catastrophic losses on individual insurers also had been reduced because of improved underwriting practices and reinsurance facilities, which limited the retention of risk in any geographic area.[10]

In New York, statutory classification and restriction of insurers' powers appeared in 1849, in the state's first general insurance law.[11] A large majority of states tended to follow New York in confining insurers to a single line of insurance. The Appleton Rule,[12] which in essence required all insurers who did business in New York to operate according to New York law wherever they did business, forced this practice upon virtually all insurers licensed in New York.

Trend toward Multiple-Line Insurance

The monoline concept was at no time universally enforced in the United States. Certain states were reluctant to embrace the concept.[13] Some states which enacted monoline legislation allowed insurers that had previously obtained broad charters to continue to exercise their original charter rights.[14] As the nation grew and insurance needs became more complex, each type of insurer tended to expand its scope of operation in order to meet the public's needs. Also there developed a trend for insurers to operate in groups, known as fleets, under common ownership and management, so

---

[10] Alfred M. Best, "Rating the Financial Structure of Insurance Companies," in Snider, *op. cit.*, pp. 80–83.

[11] William C. Gould, "Insurance Examinations—History and Development," *Examination of Insurance Companies*, Vol. II, p. XV.

[12] Winter, *op. cit.*, pp. 536–38.

[13] Kimball, *op. cit.*, pp. 118–19.

[14] Burton Mansfield, "Shall We Abandon the American Restrictions upon the Classes of Insurance Written by (A) a Company Doing Direct Writing, and (B) a Company Doing Reinsurance?", *Proceedings of the National Convention of Insurance Commissioners*, 1914, pp. 150–51.

that complete coverage could be written jointly by a fire and a casualty insurer often on a single piece of paper. A prime example of this was the "combination automobile policy," in which a fire insurer contracted to protect the automobile against the peril of fire and a casualty insurer contracted to provide protection against the other perils, such as liability, covered by the policy. There also was a tendency to reach into each other's established fields.[15] The complexity of desired coverages made distinction among some kinds of insurance obscure and arbitrary.

Few states defined the kinds of insurance which a given type of insurer could write in exactly the same way. Therefore, coverages an insurer was permitted to underwrite in one state were at times illegal in another. As was previously mentioned, underwriting restrictions during the monoline era were liberalized in varying degrees among the states, and some states allocated certain kinds of insurance to more than one type of insurer. Eventually sprinkler-leakage, automobile, and aircraft insurance became the subject matter of both fire and casualty insurers in several states.[16]

As the "process of mutual ingression"[17] continued, the demarcation between fire-marine and casualty-surety insurers became more illogical and arbitrary. This led to a weakening of the argument in favor of the monoline system. Bickelhaupt[18] observes that the trend to multiple-line insurance was a vacillating one. While the final impetus for change was given in 1944 by the NAIC Diemand Committee Report,[19] it was not until eleven years later that all states passed some form of multiple-line legislation.[20]

---

[15] Clarence W. Hobbs, "The Powers of Casualty Insurance Companies," address before 161st Meeting of the Insurance Society of New York, December 6, 1921 (mimeo).

[16] *Ibid.*

[17] *Ibid.*

[18] David L. Bickelhaupt, *Transition to Multiple-Line Insurance Companies* (Homewood, Ill.: Richard D. Irwin, Inc., 1961), pp. 39–40.

[19] "Report of the Multiple-Line Underwriting Committee," *Proceedings of the National Association of Insurance Commissioners*, 1944, p. 125.

[20] On September 5, 1955, Ohio became the last state to pass multiple-line legislation.

SIGNIFICANCE OF MULTIPLE-LINE INSURANCE

Premium Writings

Multiple-line insurance policies have been available in this country at least since 1950.[21] However, statistics on multiple-line policies were kept neither in a uniform manner nor in such a way that they could be separated in the aggregate from other comprehensive policies. Therefore, a precise record of multiple-line policy premiums is not available.

However, in the 1956 convention annual statement, two categories were established, homeowners multiple peril (HMP) and commercial multiple peril (CMP), which have helped to standardize the reporting of multiple-line policy statistics. Even these two categories contain data which are not homogeneous because not all multiple-peril policies are multiple-line policies. An integrated policy which includes the perils covered both in a fire policy and in the extended-coverage *endorsement* is a multiple-*peril* policy and it may be reported as HMP. Such a policy, however, is *not* a multiple-*line* policy, because it lacks the combination of casualty and fire lines of coverages. A similar situation exists in the commercial category. An offsetting practice engaged in by some insurers writing multiple-line policies was arbitrarily breaking down the premiums for such policies into components and reporting those premiums in the annual statement as other than multiple line. Although exact multiple-line policy premium data are unavailable, the two categories established in the annual statement are generally thought to consist mostly of multiple-line policy premiums and therefore are treated as such. That will be the practice herein.

---

[21] Frederic J. Hunt, Jr., "Homeowners—The First Decade," *Proceedings of the Casualty Actuarial Society*, Vol. 49, No. 91 (May, 1962), p. 12. The Insurance Company of North America, which is generally conceded to be the developer of homeowners policies in the United States, made its first formal homeowners filing in Pennsylvania on August 11, 1950. The filing was approved for use effective September 11, 1950.

Absolute Growth. A reasonable indication of the significance of multiple-line insurance policies is shown in Table 1 by the premium series attributed to multiple-peril policies since 1956.

TABLE 1

COMPARISON OF FIRE AND CASUALTY (F&C),* HOMEOWNERS
MULTIPLE PERIL (HMP), COMMERCIAL MULTIPLE PERIL
(CMP), AND COMBINED HOMEOWNERS AND COMMERCIAL
MULTIPLE PERIL (MP) INSURANCE NET PREMIUMS
WRITTEN BY STOCK AND MUTUAL INSURERS,
1956–65
(000 Omitted)

Year	F&C*	HMP	CMP	MP
1956	$10,600,079	$ 178,912	$ 17,729	$ 196,641
1957	11,530,043	240,680	28,459	269,139
1958	12,196,592	344,710	29,343	374,053
1959	13,406,151	522,604	37,872	560,477
1960	14,250,338	763,765	55,574	819,339
1961	14,728,542	883,873	81,728	965,601
1962	15,637,139	1,039,152	157,822	1,196,974
1963	16,327,852	1,229,854	263,023	1,492,878
1964	17,414,553	1,333,073	371,340	1,704,413
1965	19,050,704	1,523,204	508,993	2,032,198

* Includes multiple-peril premiums.

SOURCE: *Best's Fire and Casualty Aggregates and Averages,* 1966, pp. 141, 144, 209, and 212.

Rates of Growth. Table 2 shows that the annual rate of growth for each multiple-peril category usually exceeded the corresponding rates for the fire and casualty business (including multiple peril) as a whole. The approximate average annual rates of growth for fire and casualty and for combined multiple peril during the period under review were 7 and 30 percent, respectively.

TABLE 2

COMPARATIVE ANNUAL PERCENT INCREASE* OF FIRE AND CASUALTY
(F&C), HOMEOWNERS MULTIPLE PERIL (HMP), COMMERCIAL
MULTIPLE PERIL (CMP), AND COMBINED HOMEOWNERS AND
COMMERCIAL MULTIPLE PERIL (MP) INSURANCE
NET PREMIUMS WRITTEN BY STOCK AND
MUTUAL INSURERS,

1957–65

Year	F&C† (%)	HMP (%)	CMP (%)	MP (%)
1957	9	35	61	37
1958	6	43	3	39
1959	10	51	29	50
1960	6	46	47	46
1961	3	16	47	18
1962	6	18	93	24
1963	4	18	67	25
1964	7	8	41	14
1965	9	14	37	19
Geometric average‡	7	27	45	30

* Percent increase $= \left(\dfrac{\text{Year } (n+1)}{\text{Year } (n)} - 1\right) \times 100$; rounded to nearest percent.

† Includes multiple-peril premiums.

‡ Geometric average $= \left(\sqrt[9]{\dfrac{1965 \text{ data}}{1956 \text{ data}}} - 1\right) \times 100$; rounded to nearest percent.

SOURCE: Based on data in Table 1.

Percent of Fire and Casualty Premiums. In 1965, multiple-peril premium writings were more than $327 million greater than in 1964. Multiple-peril premiums accounted for more than 20 percent of the total increase in fire and casualty premiums in 1965. By 1965, annual written multiple-peril premiums exceeded $2 billion and represented 10.7 percent of all fire and casualty premiums. In 1956, as shown in Tables 1 and 3, multiple-peril premiums were only $196 million and accounted for 2 percent of total fire and casualty premiums.

TABLE 3

COMBINED HOMEOWNERS AND COMMERCIAL MULTIPLE PERIL (MP)
NET PREMIUMS AS A PERCENT OF ALL FIRE AND CASUALTY
(F&C)* NET PREMIUMS WRITTEN BY STOCK
AND MUTUAL INSURERS,
1956–65

Year	MP as a Percent of Total F&C*
1956	2.0
1957	2.3
1958	2.9
1959	4.2
1960	5.7
1961	6.5
1962	7.7
1963	9.1
1964	9.9
1965	10.7

* Includes multiple-peril premiums.
SOURCE: Based on data in Table 1.

Distribution between Homeowners and Commercial Premiums. The absolute growth of CMP premiums, though not as large as that of HMP premiums, has been continuous. CMP premiums should continue to show healthy increases because of continued development of several commercial multiple-line programs by rating bureaus and independent insurers. Although the full impact of these programs is yet to be shown, CMP accounted for a larger percent of MP premiums in 1965 than it did in any preceding year. Considering the developments in the commercial field, CMP can be expected to continue to account for an increasing percentage of MP premiums for several years to come.

TABLE 4

DISTRIBUTION OF MULTIPLE PERIL NET PREMIUMS WRITTEN
BY STOCK AND MUTUAL INSURERS BETWEEN HOMEOWNERS
MULTIPLE PERIL (HMP) AND COMMERCIAL
MULTIPLE PERIL (CMP),
1956–65

Year	HMP (%)	CMP (%)
1956	91	9
1957	90	10
1958	92	8
1959	93	7
1960	93	7
1961	92	8
1962	87	13
1963	82	18
1964	78	22
1965	75	25

SOURCE: Based on data in Table 1.

Insurers Writing Multiple Line

Another indication of the significance of multiple-line insurance
is shown by the increase in the number of insurers writing this
type of insurance. Between 1956 and 1965 there have been large
increases in both the absolute number and the percentage of stock
and mutual insurers writing MP coverages. These facts are shown
in Tables 5 and 6, respectively. Because, as was previously
mentioned, some insurers that were writing multiple-line policies
continued to break down premiums for such policies into their
components and report them in the annual statement as other than
multiple line, the figures in Table 5 most likely understate the
number or insurers actually writing multiple line, especially in
the earlier years.

TABLE 5

COMPARATIVE GROWTH IN THE NUMBER OF STOCK AND MUTUAL
INSURERS WRITING FIRE AND CASUALTY (F&C), HOMEOWNERS
MULTIPLE PERIL (HMP), AND COMMERCIAL
MULTIPLE PERIL (CMP) INSURANCE
1956–65

Year	Stock			Mutual		
	F&C	HMP	CMP	F&C	HMP	CMP
1956.........	750	370	214	385	172	24
1957.........	752	410	264	377	191	64
1958.........	733	409	285	375	197	89
1959.........	748	444	301	377	224	111
1960.........	767	470	320	370	254	115
1961.........	791	490	362	368	262	130
1962.........	809	505	412	353	266	160
1963.........	808	521	439	344	263	172
1964.........	804	508	435	340	261	184
1965.........	805	495	422	339	260	190

SOURCE: *Best's Fire and Casualty Aggregates and Averages,* 1957–66, *passim.*

TABLE 6

COMPARATIVE PERCENT OF STOCK AND MUTUAL INSURERS
WRITING HOMEOWNERS MULTIPLE PERIL (HMP), AND
COMMERCIAL MULTIPLE PERIL (CMP) INSURANCE
1956–65

Year	Homeowners Multiple Peril			Commercial Multiple Peril		
	Stock & Mutual %	Stock %	Mutual %	Stock & Mutual %	Stock %	Mutual %
1956.....	48	49	45	20	29	6
1957.....	63	55	51	29	35	17
1958.....	55	56	52	34	39	24
1959.....	60	60	61	37	41	30
1960.....	64	61	69	38	42	31
1961.....	65	62	71	42	46	35
1962.....	66	62	75	49	51	45
1963.....	68	64	76	53	54	50
1964.....	67	63	77	54	54	54
1965.....	66	61	79	53	53	56

SOURCE: Based on data in Table 5.

Beneficial Effects

The statistics in the foregoing tables reflect only part of the signifiance of multiple-line insurance. The real importance of multiple-line insurance lies in benefits to both insureds and insurers. These benefits may be divided into those which relate directly to insureds and those which benefit insureds only indirectly.

Direct Benefits. Direct benefits accruing to insureds as a consequence of multiple-line insurance include the following:

1. Convenience. Multiple-line insurance leads to greater convenience because it enables insureds to buy necessary insurance protection with fewer policies.

2. Expense savings. The reduction in handling costs due to multiple-line insurance benefits the insurance buyer by enabling him either to reduce his insurance costs or to buy more adequate coverage with the expense savings.

3. Reduced adverse selection. Integrated multiple-line insurance policies reduce *adverse selection* by requiring the purchase of a package of coverages rather than allowing insureds to choose only those coverages for which they have the greatest exposure. This leads to lower rates.

4. Increased insurance protection. Multiple-line insurance policies can be more complete and attractive than monoline policies because multiple-line policies may include fringe coverages without material increases in rates. Also they eliminate gaps and overlaps in an insurance program. An important aspect of the increase in multiple-line policy premiums is that it has not been due solely to a transfer of premiums from the traditional kinds of insurance,[22] i.e., the increase is not due only to a switching of monoline policies for multiple-line policies. The growth of multiple-line premiums reflects an increase in coverage due to the purchase of more insurance to value and the purchase in a

---

[22] Kent H. Parker, "Multi-Peril Development," address before the 6th Annual Arizona Insurance Day, Tucson, February 8, 1963; reported in *Weekly Underwriter*, Vol. 188, No. 7 (February 16, 1963), p. 16.

multiple-line policy of coverages that previously were only rarely bought separately.[23]

5. Reduced litigation.   Multiple-line insurance reduces litigation among insurers to decide which one is liable for a loss, because one insurer may write all the coverages.

The following statement illustrates why, and how, several of the foregoing benefits are achieved:

Now in the case of Homeowners Policy B there is one policy, instead of three.   There are no endorsements or forms, instead of three.   There is one insertion in the typewriter, instead of four to six.   There are 50 words to type, instead of 160.   There is one premium item to bill, collect and transmit, instead of three.   There is one manual that must be consulted, instead of three.   There are no extensions of rate times amount of insurance, and last of all, there are one or three premium cards to punch, instead of six to eleven.   We ... think such economies ... should be reflected in the price charged on this new coverage ... in the form of a reduced premium.

The other element affecting the cost of the package policy is to be found on the loss side of the premium dollar ... a package contract can be sold profitably at a price considerably less than the sum of all its various components when sold separately ... One of the factors that contributes to this is selling the package in a controlled amount. ... The purchaser must take all of the perils in the package, regardless of the fact that his own exposure to one of them might be somewhat remote. The selection against the insurer is limited both as to amount of insurance and the peril to be covered.[24]

The true value of multiple-line insurance policies lies in their nature as improved insurance products at generally lower prices than would otherwise be possible.

Indirect Benefits.   Several of the predicted advantages of multiple-line insurance would inure directly to the benefit of insurers but indirectly to insureds.   Whether or not these advan-

---

[23] In 1952 the Insurance Company of North America reported that of each 100 policyholders carrying fire insurance, only 98, 25, and 16 policyholders carried extended coverage, comprehensive personal liability, and theft insurance, respectively.   See T. E. Walton, Jr., "How Homeowners Policies Benefit Producers as Well as Policyholders," *Eastern Underwriter*, December 12, 1952, p. 73.

[24] Roy C. McCullough, "Multiple-Line Insurance and Its Value to the Insuring Public," address before the First Annual Baltimore Insurance Day, Baltimore, Md., February 4, 1954 (mimeo).

tages have materialized is difficult to discern; however, they appear to have been achieved to some degree.

1. Simplification of corporate structure. Multiple-line legislation made it unnecessary for insurers to operate on the fleet or group basis for the purpose of providing facilities for writing both fire and casualty coverages. Consequently, several affiliated companies were merged with their parent companies as single multiple-line insurers with considerable savings in overhead expenses.[25]

2. Improved stability. On the premise that all lines of insurance do not go "bad" at the same time, it was believed that the stability of insurers would be improved because of the wider spread of underwriting liability which would be possible under multiple-line legislation.[26]

3. Increased capacity. It was felt that multiple-line underwriting would increase the direct and reinsurance capacity of the American market because fire insurers would be able to write casualty insurance and to reinsure casualty insurers and vice versa.[27]

Problems Created by Multiple-Line Insurance

Multiple-line insurance has not been introduced without problems.

[25] For other reasons there has been a trend in recent years toward increased fleet operations. Although the statistics for the industry as a whole indicate an increase in the number of companies in company groups, which may be attributable to several factors, several instances of simplification of corporate structure have been reported. See, for example, *1961 Annual Report*, Insurance Company of North America, Philadelphia, Pa., p. 2, and *1962 Annual Report*, Reliance Insurance Company, Philadelphia, Pa., p. 5. As implied in the 1962 Reliance Report, one method of taking full advantage of multiple-line underwriting powers is by acquisition of companies writing the kinds of business the parent company has had less experience writing. This partly explains the increase in the number of companies in groups. However, as the Reliance report indicated, subsequent consolidation of affiliate companies is often contemplated.

[26] Alfred M. Best, "Rating the Financial Structure of Insurance Companies," *loc. cit.*, pp. 82 and 85.

[27] John A. Diemand, "Developments in Comprehensive Property-Casualty Insurance (Multiple Line Underwriting)," *Journal of the American Association of University Teachers of Insurance*, Vol. 13, No. 1 (March, 1946), pp. 57–58.

When the wave of multiple-line legislation was at its height, there was an initial outburst of enthusiasm and a feeling that these changes would produce a panacea to cure the ills of the business. This has been followed by a reaction in some quarters that perhaps on the contrary just the opposite has occurred, that a Pandora's box has been opened.[28]

Multiple-line insurance problems have affected the insurance-buying public, regulatory authorities, companies, rating bureaus, agents, and brokers. In short, few of those associated with the insurance business have been unaffected. Most of the problems created by multiple-line legislation were foreseen before its passage. Many of the problems were cited in a criticism of multiple-line underwriting known as the Williams Report. The following is taken from this report:

Obviously, in the light of the development of the insurance business, the present conduct of that business and the theory and effect of state regulatory laws, embarkation upon multiple line underwriting would not only require the *broadening of corporate powers*, but a complete *revamping* of the *regulatory laws and rules and* the *practical conduct of the business*.

If all states broadened underwriting powers, would they continue to maintain delineated fields of regulatory purposes, rate and form super-vision, maintenance of data and the like, or would they revamp their respective regulations of all such matters and treat all existing fields as one?

Under existing state regulation—and predicated upon different perils, theories, *policy forms* and forms of coverage in the separate fields—the maintenance of experience data, rating methods [rating bureaus], *commissions* and many other factors [including rate regulatory laws] *vary* in those fields, and of course, the terms and provisions of coverage necessarily vary.

It is difficult to see how experience data could be intelligently main-tained on a basis of one form of all risk policy. In the first place, there would be no one such policy. In the second place, even if there could be such, it would involve many perils, hazards and combinations, with varying terms and provisions of liability. It is difficult to see how intelligent experience could be maintained on a conglomerate basis, and difficult to see simplicity in attempting to combine for each and every policy experience data geared to separate fields. It is not asserted that

---

[28] Thomas O. Carlson, "Multiple-Line Underwriting," address before the the Pacific Northwest Insurance Seminar, Seattle, Wash., March 26, 1952 (mimeo).

the difficulties in maintaining experience data are insurmountable, but it seems evident that problems will be more difficult to solve and that most likely, expense will be increased.[29]

For the purposes of this study, multiple-line *rating* problems can be divided into three groups:

1. Legal Problems. In 1951, Alfred J. Bohlinger, then Superintendent of Insurance of the State of New York, discussed the legal problems (legislative, administrative, and judicial) that still persist in some states concerning the applicability of monoline rating laws to multiple-line policies.

Multiple-line legislation is fairly limited in its language. For the most part, such legislation is confined to amendments of those provisions of insurance laws and codes which state what types of insurance may be written by what types of companies and what is required in the way of capital and surplus.

Legal difficulty arises from the fact that these amendments have been applied to insurance codes which in most states were drawn with the rigid division in mind to which I have referred earlier. For instance, many states have a separate fire and inland marine rate regulatory act. In such states there is no rate regulatory act which is specifically labeled as applying to rates on policies containing fire, inland marine and casualty perils.[30]

2. Jurisdictional Problems. After the passage of multiple-line legislation, no rating bureau was equipped legally, or with the necessary personnel, to function effectively in the multiple-line field. This presented the alternatives of creating a truly multiple-line rating bureau or coordinating the activities of a diversity of existing traditionally monoline rating bureaus. Additional complications arose regarding the role of independent insurers in the rating of multiple-line policies.

3. Actuarial Problems. Somewhat akin to the problem of who will rate multiple-line policies is the problem of how to rate

[29] "Summary of: Proposals for Multiple-Line Underwriting, Problems Involved and Conclusion," a statement authorized and approved by Insurance Executives Association and Association of Casualty and Surety Executives, June 3, 1944. Italics added.

[30] Alfred J. Bohlinger, "The Prospect for Multiple-Peril Underwriting," address before the New York Chapter of the National Insurance Buyers Association, Inc., New York, May 24, 1951 (mimeo).

these policies. Generally, the proponents of the cooperative approach among existing bureaus favored a divisible-premium rating method, while the proponents of a single multiple-line bureau favored an indivisible-premium rating method.

An understanding of multiple-line insurance necessitates consideration not only of its benefits, but also of its problems. The primary purpose of this volume is to study the problems involved in rating personal multiple-line insurance policies, mainly the homeowners policies. This requires a knowledge of basic rating principles and methods and a re-examination of the foundations of rate regulation, rating bureaus, and rate-filing procedures. The next four chapters are designed to provide this background. It should be noted that the study concentrates on the rating practices of bureaus rather than independent insurers. This was done to keep the scope of the study within reasonable bounds and with the thought that no great harm would be done since the bureau methods closely parallel those used by the major independents as the two groups react, one to the other.

CHAPTER II

Fundamentals of Insurance Rating

Rating is a name often given, in the business of insurance, to the entire process by which the prices of insurance contracts are determined. Multiple-line rating is complicated, and has been from its inception, by differences among the methods used in rating the various kinds of insurance which are integrated into multiple-line insurance policies. This chapter and the next are designed to present concepts which are common to all insurance rating. The varying applications of these concepts to three important multiple-line forerunners, which became major components of the homeowners policies, are discussed in more detail in Chapter VI. These three chapters provide a basis for analyzing the rating problems of homeowners insurance.

DEFINITION AND NATURE OF INSURANCE RATES

Generic Definition

An insurance rate "is the unit price of a particular contract of insurance, for a particular person and/or financial interest, against specified loss, during a specified period."[1] Except when loss

---

[1] Albert H. Mowbray and Ralph H. Blanchard, *Insurance* (5th ed.; New York: McGraw-Hill Book Co., Inc., 1961), p. 371.

and/or expense constants, premium modification plans (i.e., quantity discounts), minimum premiums, or precomputed and tabulated premiums are involved, the product of the rate and the number of exposure or insurance-coverage units determines the total price, or premium, for a contract of insurance. Exposure or insurance-coverage units are intended to be quantitative measures of the amount of insurance protection purchased, in the same manner that feet, pounds, and hours are used to measure quantities of other types of purchases. In the original pricing of homeowners policies, premiums were precomputed and tabulated by amounts of insurance purchasable on the dwelling building; however, exposure units were used in the computations.

Although the pricing process in insurance is called rating, the premium is likely to be at least as significant a price, to both the insured and the insurer, as the rate. For example, the fire coinsurance rate on a property is lower than the noncoinsurance rate. However, the resulting premiums are usually larger for a comparable policy with a coinsurance clause, because of the provisions of the clause which encourage purchase of insurance equal to a larger percentage of insurable value than would otherwise be purchased.

Legal Definition

In the New York Insurance Law, rates are defined, as the context may require, as "either the consideration to be paid or charged for insurance contracts . . . or the elements and factors forming the basis for the determination or application of the same, or both."[2] Thus in New York it appears that the components of a rate *and* the rules for its use must meet the standards of the law; i.e., the entire ratemaking process is subject to regulation.[3]

General Features of Rates

The general nature of insurance rates is better understood after the definition and nature of insurance itself are first understood.

---

[2] New York Insurance Law, Art. VIII, Sec. 180, Subsec. 2.

[3] J. J. Magrath, "New York Insurance Rating Law and Rating Organizations," *Examination of Insurance Companies* (Albany: New York Insurance Department, 1955), Vol. 5, p. 266.

"Insurance is a formal social device for the substitution of certainty for uncertainty"[4] whereby "average is substituted for actual loss."[5] According to Alfred Manes, "the essence of insurance lies in the elimination of the uncertain risk of loss for the individual through the combination of a large number of similarly exposed individuals who each contribute to a common fund premium payments sufficient to make good the loss caused any one individual."[6] In other words, insurance may be explained best perhaps by the cliché "the losses of the few are paid by the premium contributions of the many." Rates and premiums are more than prices; they are the heart of every insurance transaction, because it is through them that certainty is substituted for uncertainty and funds are accumulated to pay losses. They determine the relatively small but certain cost which is substituted for the uncertainty of having either significant or insignificant but uninsured loss.

Effect of Classification. Although insurance involves averaging, all insureds having protection against a particular peril should not, and do not, contribute through payment of premiums equally to the fund out of which losses are paid. The amount an insured should contribute to the fund relates to anticipated losses and expenses. However, it is not possible to know exactly what an individual insured's exposures will cost the fund. The determination of the expected cost involves classifying the exposures of the individual insured on the basis of easily identifiable characteristics that are believed to have an important effect upon insurance costs, and then assuming that the average insurance-cost experience of the group per exposure unit will be indicative of the individual insured's insurance cost. Of course, for a new kind of insurance the ratemaker will have to resort to other methods. Existing experience may be modified in some way to make it more indicative of what may be expected under the new coverage.

The rate and premium charged an insured depends upon the system of classification. Insureds in each classification generally

---

[4] C. A. Kulp, *Casualty Insurance* (rev. ed.; New York: Ronald Press Co., 1942), p. 10.

[5] *Ibid.*, p. 11.

[6] Alfred Manes, "Insurance Principles and History," *Encyclopedia of the Social Sciences* (New York: Macmillan Co., 1935), Vol. 8, p. 95.

pay the same rate, but their premiums vary because of variation in their exposure or insurance-coverage units. For each insured peril there are a multitude of characteristics which could be considered as bases for classification. In the establishment of a classification system, rating personnel attempt to include a sufficient number of characteristics in the plan to make each classification reasonably homogeneous, and at the same time they attempt to limit the number of classifications so that each contains a sufficiently large number of insureds to allow the development of credible classified experience statistics.

Territorial classifications are used in many lines of insurance. These classifications, for convenience of definition and determination, usually follow political subdivisions. Territorial classifications are as small as a city or county and as large as a state or country. For example, in lines of insurance protecting against the perils of burglary and theft, there may be a considerable variation in hazard between urban and rural areas, and therefore territorial classifications for such insurance usually are determined by the extent of urbanization.

An example of a rate varying with the basis of classification involves an insured situated on the border line of a territorial classification. A change in the border line could significantly change the rate of such an insured. This may occur, for example, when a state is subdivided into two territories, one encompassing the urban area and the other the remainder of the state. In a situation where the urban area may logically be either a city or the county in which the city is contained and with which it is almost coincident, the rate of an insured located outside the city but inside the county will depend upon whether the territorial classification is the city or the county. There are usually good reasons for either the city or the county to be the urban territorial classification, and therefore the decision is ultimately resolved by the exercise of informed underwriting judgment. It seems illogical to suggest that the inherent loss potential of an insured will change simply because territorial boundaries are redetermined, yet the applicable insurance rate may appropriately change because there is a change in territorial classification. Examples of a similar nature can be cited for other bases of classification.

As hazard conditions significantly change, so do territorial classifications. It often happens that as suburbia extends outward from the city limits into the country, the urban territorial classification changes. In other cases, especially when the insured population increases sufficiently in an area to achieve a degree of credibility, territories are subdivided in order to reflect more closely the hazard differences among areas. Reviewing, redefining, and refining rating classifications is a continuing process. Since reliable insurance-cost predictions cannot be made for most individual insureds, the essence of insurance rating is the grouping of insureds and the averaging of losses through rating classifications. There is no one proper rate, per se, for an individual insured or exposure. In other words, a proper rate for an individual insured is not entirely a function of intrinsic characteristics of the insured.

Other Factors Affecting Rates. A rate is intended to cover all of the costs of providing insurance protection. These costs may be broadly divided into losses, expenses (including legal fees), and profits. The magnitude of these costs depends upon and varies appreciably with contractual factors such as the amount of insurance carried in relation to maximum potential loss, whether the peril is insured separately or combined with other coverages, whether the coverage is primary or excess when other insurance exists, and elements of insurer operation such as underwriting practices, marketing system, and claims philosophy. In these situations, just as with the example of the territorial classification, it may be entirely proper for an insured to be subject to a variation in rate even though his *inherent* hazard does not vary. The contractual differences do constitute variation in hazard *presented to the insurer* and hence the difference in rate.

THE OBJECTIVES OF INSURANCE RATING METHODS

Before specific rating methods are considered, the objectives common to all insurance rating first should be reviewed. With these objectives in mind, the reasons for different approaches among and within the major lines of insurance are more easily understood.

Legal Objectives

Because insurance rates are subject to state regulation, at least three major rating objectives have been formalized in most of the state rating laws. These *objectives* are the same as the *results* obtained, in the theoretical economic model of pure competition, where prices are set equal to marginal costs.[7] In the long run, competitive *type* prices are neither excessive, inadequate, nor unfairly discriminatory. These beneficial results are stated in one form or another as the three major objectives in most state insurance rating laws. Competitive *type* prices are not excessive because the price of any good is limited to the marginal cost of producing the good. They are not inadequate (i.e., they are adequate) because, in the long run, the price of a good is equal to the average cost of producing it, where average cost is defined to include a reasonable profit. Competitive *type* prices are not *unfairly* discriminatory (i.e., they are equitable) because the price of a product is equal to the marginal cost of producing the product.

The standard of adequacy assumes that rates are supposed to cover losses and expenses, and provide a reasonable margin for profit and contingencies. The standard concerned with possible excessiveness is reflected in the magnitude of the profit factor and the allowance for expenses. The standard of equity is reflected in the establishment of rating classification systems in which the insureds in each class are reasonably similar (homogeneous). Each class makes premium contributions to the fund, on the average, in proportion to the expected losses and expenses attributable to the class. However, these objectives (actually standards) are undefined in most laws (and possibly this is as it should be) and

---

[7] H. Wayne Snider, "Inland Marine Rating and Rate Regulation," *The Journal of Insurance*, Vol. 30, No. 1 (March, 1963), p. 77. Marginal cost is the increase in total cost accompanying an incremental increase in the output or production of a commodity or service.

are subjective in nature, and therefore differences of opinion frequently arise between the rating and regulatory bodies. This problem is discussed further in later chapters.

Not all rating laws specifically state that rates are to be reasonable. However, this must be an implied objective of all rate regulation; otherwise, the objective of nonexcessiveness would be practically meaningless. A sizable portion of total insurance costs consists of operating expenses. Reasonableness requires that these expenses be legitimate, i.e., "companies cannot make clearly unnecessary expenditures and pass these on to the customers in the form of rates."[8] Furthermore, even legitimate expenses must be allocated in a reasonable manner to prevent excessive or inadequate rates among classifications of insureds.

Other Objectives

Corollary and secondary objectives of insurance rating methods are the same as those in other pricing considerations and include stability, responsiveness, simplicity, consistency, reasonableness, understandability, economy of operation, and resistance to manipulation by insureds to the disadvantage of the insurers. Incentive for loss prevention is another objective common to many rating systems. While often thought unique to insurance, prevention may be viewed as a particular form of cost control, an activity common to most businesses. The foregoing objectives are in keeping with the general goals of rate regulation.

In order to compete with lower priced competitors, insurers may simply lower their own rates. However, this may be contrary to the rating laws. To survive, an insurer must sell its products, and to grow, its sales must increase. Therefore, if a pricing method results in a stagnation or decrease of sales because prices are too high, the method may be abandoned temporarily for competitive reasons. This may result, at one extreme, in insolvency, or at the other extreme, in increased efficiency, which may enable the

---

[8] Roy C. McCullough, "Insurance Rates in the Courts," *The Insurance Law Journal*, No. 461 (June, 1961), p. 409.

insurer to return to its original pricing method and still remain competitive.

Interrelationships among Objectives

The three major objectives specified in the rating laws, as well as the corollary and secondary objectives, are interrelated in a way analogous to the relationships among the variables in the basic equation of thermodynamics:

$$\frac{PV}{T} = K$$

Pressure (P) times volume (V) divided by temperature (T) equals a constant (K). A final determination of one variable or objective cannot be made without a simultaneous determination of the others.

While the legal and practical business objectives are not necessarily at variance with each other, ratemaking involves a process of continual compromise between opposing and somewhat contradictory forces. At the outset there must be a compromise between the extent that the objectives are achieved and the cost of achievement, i.e., complete attainment of all objectives is bounded by economy of operation. Compromise requires the maintenance of a delicate balance between adequacy and non-excessiveness, stability and responsiveness, and other opposing goals. For example, it is desirable that the rating process be responsive to permanent and significant changes in loss experience to prevent rates from becoming either excessive or inadequate, but it also is desirable that the rating process be stable to prevent the adverse public reactions which would result from frequent rate changes and the expenses associated therewith. Currently responsiveness seems to be the greater problem. Attempts to increase responsiveness include the use of trend, projection, and weighting factors and shortened experience-review and contract periods, as well as more up-to-date time references. These factors are discussed more fully below.

The Importance of Judgment

While a minimum of information is needed to solve properly a rating problem, or the previously mentioned thermodynamic equation, there is no unique solution to a rating problem such as there is to a problem involving the thermodynamic equation. "It is the ... actuary's task ... to develop rates ... which fall within a 'zone of reasonableness' ... [and] will stand the test of probing criticism satisfying jointly the criteria."[9]

The primary reason for the lack of singularity in the solution of rating problems and the need for an acceptable zone of reasonableness in satisfying the objectives is the fact that judgment is fundamental to the rating process and intelligent judgment varies among individuals. Judgment is involved in virtually every step of the rating process, whether it be establishing classifications, devising statistical plans, selecting experience periods, constructing credibility tables, interpreting statistical data, or any other step. Furthermore, the legal rating objectives, "even considered jointly, are comparatively subjective in character, not being determinable in unassailably objective terms."[10]

There can be no assurance that actuarially proper rate adjustments, even with provision for trend, will produce rates which, in retrospect, were entirely satisfactory. "Indeed, a trend well developed in past experience might reverse itself completely so that the factor developed from the trend would help produce an inaccurate result."[11] However, a priori good judgment may dictate the use of an appropriate trend factor, and it must be remembered that a rate filing must be evaluated prospectively, not retrospectively.

Rating classifications which lack a sufficient number of insureds to generate credible experience are frequently established in order

---

[9] Thomas O. Carlson, "Rate Regulation and the Casualty Actuary," *Proceedings of Casualty Actuarial Society*, Vol. 38, Part 1, No. 69 (May, 1951), p. 16.

[10] *Ibid.*

[11] McCullough, *op. cit.*, p. 419.

to provide an incentive for loss prevention and to preserve loss prevention and safety engineering standards. In these situations it is necessary to use large doses of informed underwriting judgment in order to achieve a proper balance among the various rating objectives and to maintain proper rate relativities among rating classifications.

With the foregoing complications in mind, it can be seen that the work of the insurance ratemaker is difficult and complex. He must determine rates for future application, having as a guide the dubious experience of the past, which meet the legal objectives of the rating laws, as judged by the state insurance commissioner, and the practical business objectives of insurers, as judged by their officers. The importance of judgment in fulfilling these objectives cannot be overemphasized.

Persons engaged in multiple-line rating (increasingly these are actuaries qualified by professional examinations) should have good underwriting judgment based upon knowledge of and experience in the insurance industry, and also a good understanding of mathematical and business statistics, economics, law (especially the regulatory framework in which insurance operates), and several other subjects which may be found by examining the current *Syllabus of Study* for the examinations of the Casualty Actuarial Society.

Achievement of Objectives: A Function of Classification

An initial task required of any rating system is the classification of insureds. Although insurance is based upon the principles of pooling risks and sharing costs through the application of the law of large numbers, a simple averaging of all insurance costs among all insureds, as was discussed previously, is neither desirable nor practical.[12] Some insureds will have consistently greater or smaller losses and more or fewer expenses per unit of exposure or insurance than the average. Insureds with more hazardous and

---

[12] For an example of the undesirable consequences of simple averaging, see Dan M. McGill, *Life Insurance* (rev. ed.; Homewood, Ill.: Richard D. Irwin, Inc., 1967), pp. 27–29.

costly exposures should be charged proportionately higher rates. Fair discrimination (equity) requires a grouping of insureds on the basis of proven experience or "characteristics, common possession of which is supposed to produce approximately the same expected losses and expenses."[13] Thus it is necessary to allocate losses and expenses properly among groups of insureds.

It is not desirable to have either complete averaging or no averaging. Without averaging, each insured would pay his own costs. This is contrary to the basic insurance principle that losses be shared; without a sharing of losses there is no reduction in uncertainty, and thus no insurance. Second, without averaging there would be no stability in such a system, because rates would fluctuate violently from year to year. Finally, no averaging would lead to socialization of insurance, because the rates for those suffering loss would be unreasonable. Although equitable rates are desirable and achievable, it must be remembered that there are obstacles in their pursuit. The achievement of rate equity is essentially a matter of grouping or classification and it must be considered from this viewpoint.

Classification Limitations. A large group of insureds of the same quality (homogeneous) is desired so that credibility may be given to the experience of the group. The adequacy, reasonableness, and equity of a rating structure must be judged in light of the credibility which may be given to the experience data developed by the rating structure. If rates were made solely on the basis of statistical experience for a group which lacked a reasonable amount of credibility, rate changes would be subject to extreme chance variation, and successive changes would likely be in opposite directions. "The finer we classify our data the nearer we approach homogeneity, but the smaller the amount of data in each group: What we gain in homogeneity we lose in credibility of our loss experience."[14] Therefore, extreme refinement which results in

---

[13] C. Arthur Williams, *Price Discrimination in Property and Liability Insurance* (University of Minnesota Studies in Economics and Business, No. 19 [Minneapolis: University of Minnesota Press, 1959]), p. 19.

[14] L. H. Longley-Cook, "Notes on Some Actuarial Problems of Property Insurance," *Fire, Insurance Rate Making and Kindred Problems* (New York: Casualty Actuarial Society, 1960), p. 89.

rating classifications with negligible volumes of experience may result in inadequate, excessive, or unequitable rates if the rates are based largely on the experience of the classifications. Because of the desirability of having mass in rating classifications, it is unlikely that rating classifications will be completely homogeneous. On the other hand, it is always possible to regroup classifications in order to base the rate level for the combined classifications as a whole on credible data and to base the refined classification relativities largely upon engineering or other informed underwriting considerations.

Class versus Individual-Risk Rating. Most insurance authors make a distinction between class and so-called individual-risk rating in order to illustrate that more equity is obtained with individual-risk rating. The difference, if any, between the two is a matter of degree rather than kind. According to Kulp:

Individual risk rating ... systems ... measure hazard difference in individual risks within a classification and on this basis modify the classification or manual rate. .... In principle, if the number of risks given a rate variation is *relatively* large and if hazard differences among risks charged the same revised rate are *relatively* small, the new rate would appear to be on a new classification or subclassification. If the number of risks given a rate variation is *relatively* small and if hazard differences among members allowed a rate variation are *relatively* large, the rate would appear to be one on an individual risk.[15]

The arbitrariness of the division between class and individual-risk rating is illustrated by the difficulty of answering the following questions: At what level of subdivision does a rate become an individual-risk rate rather than a class rate? How many insureds are required to constitute a class for the establishment of an average? How many factors must be considered to make the result an individual-risk rate rather than a subclass rate? How many insureds within the original class may be eligible for rate modification without destroying the notion of uniqueness implied in the term *individual*-risk rating?

It should be remembered that both class and individual-risk rating are methods of modifying average rates for a large group

---

[15] C. A. Kulp, *Casualty Insurance* (3rd ed.; New York: Ronald Press Co., 1956), pp. 487–488. Italics added.

of insureds in a manner that is intended to produce the same aggregate premium that would result without modification. Actuaries refer to this as a *balanced* plan. Class rates result from a modification of the overall average rate for a kind of insurance, while individual-risk rates result from additional modifications of the hierarchy of class rates, i.e., individual-risk rating involves the creation of subclasses. The types of insurance with which this study is primarily concerned are considered to be class rated. The expense of inspecting each insured for individual rating in the personal lines of insurance would exceed the possible advantage that might result in terms of equity. Class rates are published in rate manuals which are used by insurance agents, who apply the rates when they write such insurance. Class rates also are referred to as manual and tariff rates; tariff also is used to refer to bureau-promulgated rates.

Objectives May Be Achieved at Various Levels

Because of the superficial distinction between class and individual-risk rating, it seems appropriate to limit the evaluation of the achievement of rating objectives to two primary levels: first, at the largest territorial classification level, such as a state (as opposed to the various rating territories within the state), and second, at the other rating classifications within the largest territorial classification. These include smaller territorial classifications and classifications based upon factors other than territory, or in combination with territorial factors. While it is desirable to achieve the basic rating objectives at the various subclassification levels, fortunately it is easier and more important that they be achieved at the largest territorial level. It is easier because the objectives need be achieved for only one relatively large group of insureds rather than several relatively small groups. It is more important because fulfillment of the basic function of insurance requires that rates be adequate in the aggregate, not for each subclassification. In the actual operation of an insurance company it is not anticipated that each classification will achieve the ideal of being self-supporting in a given year. The fulfillment of an insurer's basic function does not require that its rates be adequate by type of insurance or by state, but only in the aggregate, for all of its business.

Also, while some expenses can be associated directly with individual insureds, other expenses must be assigned on an indirect and somewhat arbitrary basis. Furthermore, as previously mentioned, rating is fundamentally a problem of grouping. Therefore, ultimately losses and expenses must be apportioned among groups of insureds rather than among individual insureds because of the averaging process. The larger the size of a group, the more likely the apportionment will be correct (at least for the group, but not necessarily for the individual insured). Although loss and expense statistics provide an indication as to whether or not the rate for a particular class is appropriate, they cannot prove that one classification *system* is necessarily superior to another. There are innumerable ways of logically classifying insureds and allocating costs. Although statistical studies can provide information which may improve both the classification system and the allocation of losses and expenses, judgment must be the final arbiter as to the extent to which rating objectives are achieved.

Objectives Achieved in a Time Framework

It cannot be expected that each of the objectives of insurance rating will be achieved on a year-by-year basis. It is hoped that they will be achieved on the average, over a reasonable number of years. In fire insurance, five or six years have been considered reasonable time periods on which to base rates, whereas in coverages providing protection against windstorms, as many as fifteen years may be considered reasonable. Thus, insurance averaging is done over time, as well as geographically and among classifications, and the amount of time required for effective averaging is a function of the peril being insured against.

THE LAW OF LARGE NUMBERS

Because of the fortuitous nature of insurance losses, insurance ratemakers have the formidable task of reducing the uncertainty involved in the prediction of future loss costs to a manageable level.   If there were no means whereby insurers could predict future losses with reasonable accuracy, insurance would be a form of gambling in which insureds bet that losses will occur while insurers bet that they will not.

The key that enables ratemakers to predict future losses *with a reasonable degree of confidence* is found in the law of large numbers, more commonly called the law of averages.   The importance given to the law in the field of insurance is illustrated by its embodiment in definitions of insurance.   For example, Riegel and Miller define insurance as "the application of the statistical law of large numbers to the economic problem of risk."[16]

Verbal Interpretation

A mathematical statement of the law of large numbers is complex.[17]   One verbal interpretation of its meaning says that "by choosing the sample size n sufficiently large, the *probability* that the value of the sample mean differs from the population mean by at most c can be made as close to 1 as we like.[18]

Longley-Cook and Pruitt have illustrated the law of large numbers, with reference to the probability of an apple falling upward, as follows:

> The pull of gravity is one of those facts we feel pretty sure about . . . it has happened every observed time so far as we know, and there have been many observed times.   Expressed statistically we might say that in any observed sample, S, of n free and detached apples, [there is a probability, which can be very small if n is sufficiently large, that] the percentage observed to fall upward will not deviate by more than k from the percentage that would be observed to fall upward if we had observed the behavior of all free and detached apples. . . . We would also say that k varies inversely with n, or, the greater the number of observations the

[16] Robert Riegel and Jerome S. Miller, *Insurance Principles and Practices* (4th ed.: Englewood Cliffs, N.J.: Prentice-Hall, Inc., 1959), p. 26.

[17] See, for example, William Feller, *An Introduction to Probability Theory and its Applications* (New York: John Wiley & Sons, Inc., 1957), Vol. 1, passim.

[18] Samuel Goldberg, *Probability: An Introduction* (Englewood Cliffs, N.J.: Prentice-Hall, Inc., 1960), p. 226.   Italics added.

smaller the [probability of] variation of the sample from the behavior of the whole population of apples.[19]

Hypothetical Example

Insurance loss behavior is not nearly so consistent as the direction of falling apples; at least, the natural laws governing insurance losses, if they do exist, have defied neat expression such as that for the force of gravity. Thus, based on the law of large numbers, an actuary might say that with his company's present book of homeowners business (say 7,000 policies), an average loss per policy of $50 is expected next year and the probability that the actual average loss will be greater than $55 is 1 percent. On the other hand, because of the law of large numbers, with a much larger book of business (say 106,000 policies) an average loss per policy of $50 is expected and the probability that the actual average loss will exceed $51.25 is 1 percent.

Because of the larger number of policies upon which to base his prediction, the actuary could say with the same degree of confidence, i.e., with a 99 percent chance of being correct, that the actual average loss is not expected to exceed $51.25 rather than $55. The actuary also could say that the chance that the actual average loss will exceed $55 would be reduced from 1 percent to less than 1 percent when the number of policyholders increased from 7,000 to 106,000.

However, it must be remembered that regardless of the number of policies, *actual* average loss may vary, possibly substantially, in either direction, from *expected* average loss, but the *probability* of wide variation is reduced as the number of policies is increased. Thus as the number of policies increases, the effect on loss prediction may be shown by answering either of two questions: What is the probability that the actual average loss will exceed the expected average loss by at least a certain amount as the number of policies is increased? What is the minimum actual

---

[19] L. H. Longley-Cook and Dudley M. Pruitt, "Law of Large Numbers," in H. Wayne Snider (ed.), *Readings in Property and Casualty Insurance* (Homewood, Ill.: Richard D. Irwin, Inc., 1959), p. 298.

average loss, greater than the expected average loss, which has a certain percent chance of occurring?

Thus, in the hypothetical example, when the number of policies increased to 106,000, there was only a 1 percent probability of the actual average loss exceeding $51.25 and there was a 5 percent probability that the actual loss would exceed $50.95. It is more likely that the actual average loss will exceed $50.95 than $51.25 when the expected loss is $50. However, as the number of policies increases, the probability that the actual loss will exceed either $50.95 or $51.25 decreases.

TABLE 7

HYPOTHETICAL ILLUSTRATION OF LAW OF LARGE NUMBERS
WITH EXPECTED AVERAGE LOSS OF $50.00

| Number of Policies | Probability of Actual Average Loss Exceeding Indicated Amounts | | |
	1%	5%	10%
7,000............	$55.00	$53.75	$53.15
12,000............	53.75	52.85	52.40
27,000............	52.50	51.90	51.60
106,000............	51.25	50.95	50.80

Without denying the importance of the law of large numbers, the limitations of any mathematical predictive probability model, which the law is, must be kept in mind to place the actuarial aspect of rating in proper perspective. As far as insurance is concerned, the law of large numbers may be thought of as the theoretical concept which provides a foundation for insurance cost (loss) accounting and thereby helps to separate insurance rating from mere speculation.

Credibility Theory[20]

An important application of the law of large numbers involves the notion of actuarial credibility. To say that a certain body of

---

[20] The material in this section is based largely upon the author's interpretation of L. H. Longley-Cook's *An Introduction to Credibility Theory* (New York: Casualty Actuarial Society, 1962). See also David B. Houston, "Risk, Insurance, and Sampling," *The Journal of Risk and Insurance*, Vol. 31, No. 4 (December, 1964), pp. 511–38.

data lacks credibility implies a belief that the data do not reflect the true loss probability. This belief is founded upon prior knowledge of the hazard and a feeling that a certain minimum of data, based upon the law of large numbers, is needed to confirm a change in underlying loss probability. "Classified underwriting experience, to be reliable, must have a sufficient spread as to the number of risks, territory and period of time to avoid violent fluctuations in results."[21]

The credibility to be attached to a given amount of data is not an inherent quantity; among other things, it depends upon the use being made of the data, the person evaluating the data, and the criteria assumed. Credibility theory involves the selection of credibility measures, such as the number of losses, expected dollars of losses, or premium volume, and the establishment of criteria for full and partial credibility.

Arbitrariness of Credibility Values. The assignment of quantitative credibility values to a range of probabilities is an "arbitrary" process. For example, one person may assign a value of 100 percent credibility to data for which the probability of the actual result varying from the expected result by more than a certain amount is 5 percent, while another person desiring more certainty for the assignment of 100 percent credibility may require that the probability of the actual result varying from the expected result by more than the same amount be only 2 percent. For any individual, however, consistency requires that the smaller the probability of chance variation, the greater the credibility to be given the data. The volume of data required to set the limits of 0 and 100 percent credibility is mainly a matter of personal judgment. "We can position these fiducial limits to reflect whatever degree of confidence a person may be in need of. The ideas are the same, and so too the theory and the development—only the figures will change."[22]

[21] National Board of Fire Underwriters, *Standard Classification of Occupancy Hazards* (3rd ed., rev.; New York, 1958); see "Statement of Principles" contained therein.

[22] Robert L. Hurley, "A Credibility Framework for Gauging Fire Classification Experience," *Fire Insurance Rate Making and Kindred Problems* (New York: Casualty Actuarial Society, 1960), p. 124.

Factors Affecting Credibility. If the data are not selected randomly and if the data are not homogeneous, a larger amount of experience data per se will not necessarily increase the credibility to be assigned the data. Therefore, while the combining of data "over broader territories by groups of states and nationally and also by groupings of similar classes of risks"[23] is said to increase credibility, the increase in credibility applies to the use made of the *aggregate* loss experience only, and not necessarily to the use made of the various subdivisions of the data. Furthermore, "a combination of the experience of differently operated companies will not produce greater credibility for establishing the overall rate level. However, it may well produce greater credibility for establishing rate differentials for classification sub-groups."[24]

Credibility Applications. "While the word credibility was originally introduced to indicate the credence that the actuary believes should be attached to a particular body of experience for rate making purposes, the use of the term has been extended to many rate making techniques associated with this general idea."[25] Different formulas and standards are used to establish the credibility which applies to rate revisions, rate relativities among classifications, experience rating, and merit rating.

In rate revisions, primary interest is in the amount of credibility to be given the indications of the recent experience data relative to the existing rates, which are based upon older experience data. "The credibility weighting process is utilized to provide the necessary balance between stability and responsiveness in the rate structure, and at the same time to provide the necessary link between statistical information and prior information while insuring utter consistency in the treatment of various bodies of statistics."[26] If a body of experience is considered large enough to have 100 percent credibility, rates will generally be changed

[23] National Board of Fire Underwriters, *op. cit.*

[24] Longley-Cook, *op. cit.*, p. 9.

[25] *Ibid.*, p. 5.

[26] Thomas O. Carlson, "Observations on Casualty Insurance Rate-Making Theory in the United States," *Proceedings of the Casualty Actuarial Society*, Vol. LI (1964), pp. 283–85.

according to the experience indication. However, if the experience data indicate a 20 percent increase in rates, for example, but the data have only enough volume to be considered 50 percent credible, most likely only a 10 percent increase would be sought. In essence, this results in a weighted average of the existing and the indicated rates. If the existing rate were $1, the indicated rate $1.20, and the credibility 50 percent, the existing and indicated rates each would be weighted 50 percent. The new rate would be $.50 (50 percent times $1) plus $.60 (50 percent times $1.20), or $1.10; i. e., the result would be a 10 percent increase.

While the volume of data under consideration may be fully credible for determining the overall statewide rate level or aggregate premiums for a kind of insurance, few of the subclasses provide sufficient data to give 100 percent credibility to the experience of subclassifications. Furthermore, there are patterns of association between subclasses, i.e., rate relativities, which are thought desirable, and these relationships are therefore often maintained even though the experience data may indicate different relationships. Therefore, "we must use credibility techniques and judgment to maintain a stable rate structure"[27] with proper rate relativities.

In experience rating "the weight to be given the experience of the individual risk as against the manual rate is (under most plans) governed by credibility standards based in the main on the size of the rated risk, expressed either in terms of premium, units of exposure or expected losses."[28]

In merit rating, credibility techniques enter to determine whether the experience of an individual exposure unit such as a home or a car is significant as a basis of *classification* of the risk. "There is no experience rating formula at work in . . . merit rating plans,"[29] nor is there a credibility factor in the experience-rating sense.

---

[27] Longley-Cook, *op. cit.*, p. 17.

[28] Roy C. McCullough, "Insurance Rates in the Courts," *The Insurance Law Journal*, No. 461 (June, 1961), p. 423.

[29] LeRoy J. Simon, "Merit Rating Myths and Mysteries," *Automobile Insurance Rate Making* (New York: Casualty Actuarial Society, 1961), p. 182.

In the rating of personal multiple-line insurance, credibility techniques were used to combine the experience developed under the multiple-line policies with that reflected in the rates of the component coverages.   Experience rating is not used in the personal lines of insurance.   Although merit rating is used in the personal multiple-line field by some independent insurers, it is not discussed any further because it has not been used to any great extent by the bureau insurers.

CHAPTER **III**

Fundamentals of Insurance Rating (Continued)

CONSIDERATIONS IN RATE-LEVEL REVISIONS

Underwriting Units

There are two groups of underwriting units commonly used to measure past experience for rate-level revision analysis. These are the so-called written-paid and earned-incurred units. Written-paid refers to written premiums or exposures and to paid losses, while earned-incurred refers to earned premiums or exposures and to incurred losses. Paid losses include all loss payments made during a period, regardless of when the losses occurred. Incurred losses include the value, at some point after the experience period elapses, of all losses which occurred during the experience period. Written premiums include the total of all premiums for coverages becoming effective during the experience period, while earned premiums include only the portions of written premiums on all coverages in force during the experience period that the coverage afforded during the experience period bears to the total period of coverage under such policies. Other things being equal, earned-incurred is generally considered a more accurate measure of underwriting experience. However, when loss adjustments involve very little delay and premium writings—and therefore premium earnings—are relatively stable, the written-paid ratio may be of practical value because of its timeliness.

Time References

The major time references are known as calendar year, accident year, and policy year. It is desirable that the time reference include premiums or exposures which are compatible with the losses of the time period. The basic idea is to compare the premiums or exposures and losses generated out of the use of a given set of rates to determine if the losses are in proper relation to premiums or exposures. More than one time reference may be used to test rates. The experience period used as a basis for testing may encompass several years, e.g., for fire insurance a 5-calendar-year period has been used, while for windstorm a period of 15 calendar years has been used.

The expense allowance used in the calculation of the permissible loss ratio (see below) may be based upon a different period of years than the one used in determining the experience-review loss ratio. In the interest of stability a longer period usually is used to calculate the review loss ratio because there is much greater variation in loss experience than in expense experience. The most recent year for which expense data are available may be sufficient for the determination of the permissible loss ratio.

Policy Year. The ideal time reference for having compatible premiums or exposures and loss data is the policy year. Policy-year loss ratios compare earned premiums with incurred losses for all policies written to become effective within a given consecutive twelve-month period.[1] Each transaction related to the group of policies is associated with the protection period involved. The policy year runs for two calendar years, commencing with the first day of the policy year and terminating at the expiration date of the policies which may be written on the last day of the first

---

[1] Paul Benbrook, "The advantages of Calendar-Accident Year Experience and the Need for Appropriate Trend and Projection Factors in the Determination of Automobile Liability Rates," *Automobile Insurance Rate Making* (New York: Casualty Actuarial Society, 1961), p. 59.

calendar year. For example, for the policy year 1968, the inception dates of the first and last policies to be assigned to it would be January 1, 1968 and December 31, 1968, respectively. Their termination dates would be December 31, 1968 and January 1, 1969, respectively.

Policy-year incurred losses equal the sum of all loss payments and all unpaid loss liabilities on policies having an inception date within the first calendar year of the policy year. Policy-year earned premiums equal the sum of all premiums applicable to the same set of policies. At the end of the policy year all of the premiums applicable to the policies are earned because all of the protection contemplated by the policies has been provided. Therefore, with this time reference there is complete compatibility of data, because both the numerator and the denominator of any ratios based upon these data arise from the same set of policies. The main disadvantage of this time reference is the time required for the maturation of the loss experience to ultimate values when liability coverage is involved. Not only does it take two years for all losses to occur, but it may take many additional months thereafter before such losses are settled completely.

Calendar Year. A less accurate though more practicable reference is the calendar year, in which all premiums earned during a calendar year, regardless of the inception date of the policies in force during the year, are compared with all losses incurred during the year.[2] Earned premiums may be calculated by a formula. They equal premiums written during the year plus the unearned premium liability at the start of the year minus the unearned premium liability at the end of the year.

Calendar-year incurred losses also are determined by a formula. They equal losses paid during a year plus the liability for unpaid losses at the end of the year minus the liability for unpaid losses at the start of the year.[3] By this method, incurred losses may be

---

[2] Frank Harwayne, "Workmen's Compensation Insurance Rates," *Examination of Insurance Companies* (Albany: New York Insurance Department, 1955), Vol. 5, p. 12.

[3] G. E. Michelbacher, *Multiple-Line Insurance* (New York: McGraw-Hill Book Co., Inc., 1957), p. 398.

negative because of changes in reserve valuation and differences between the actual and estimated value of the losses.[4] When the year of experience ends on other than December 31, this type of time reference is known as a fiscal year.

Accident Year. Somewhere between the foregoing time references, in comparability and practicability, is the accident year, which is similar to the calendar year in the method used to calculate earned premiums. However, accident-year incurred losses equal the sum of all losses actually occurring during the fiscal year as valued on a certain date subsequent to the end of the year. Therefore, if a loss occurs during the year under the accident-year method, incurred losses are positive.

Adjustments to Experience-Review-Period Data

The objective of the rate-review process is to determine the rates to be charged in the future, based upon past experience, which will meet the standards of the rating law. However, it is necessary to adjust the past experience so that it will reflect as accurately as possible either current conditions or, preferably, the conditions which can reasonably be expected to prevail during the period the rates will be in effect.

Rate-Level Changes. Rate levels may have been adjusted during the experience-review period; therefore, in order to review the experience at the current rate level, it is necessary to adjust actual earned premiums so that the premiums which would have been earned at the current rate level may be determined. Since the purpose of the rate-review process is the determination of a rate structure which will provide the "permissible" ratio of losses incurred to premiums earned, it is desirable to extend the proposed rate structure at the current exposure distribution in order to determine expected premiums earned. Ideally, the exposure distribution that will prevail when the proposed rates will be in effect should be used, as should the loss distribution which is most likely to prevail with such an exposure distribution. Currently

---

[4] Benbrook, *op. cit.*

neither the loss-ratio nor the pure-premium methods provide for such an adjustment of the loss experience. Both methods may provide for adjustments in the experience-review-period earned premiums to reflect differences between review-period and current rate levels; however, the pure-premium method is superior in regard to adjusting for changes in exposure distributions, because exposure data are collected under this method.

Loss-Development Factors. In some lines of insurance, such as liability, it is necessary to use loss experience in rate-level-revision analysis, which includes estimated liabilities for incurred but unpaid losses, because the amount payable as a result of a loss in the experience-review period may depend upon litigation or other time-consuming factors. Past experience indicates that the ultimate cost of a group of claims usually differs from the estimated cost, evaluated at certain periodic intervals after the claims have been reported. Therefore, loss-development factors, based upon past experience, are applied to the experience-loss data to reflect as closely as possible their ultimate cost.

Changes in the Value of Money. Actual adjusted (for development) incurred losses should also be adjusted to reflect the current value of money or, preferably, the cost conditions that may reasonably be expected to prevail during the period for which the rates are to apply.

For many years there has been an inflationary trend in our economy, and it is now generally accepted practice in some lines of insurance to make some adjustments in the loss data used in both the loss-ratio and pure-premium methods to reflect this trend. The adjustments are made by the use of trend factors, which evaluate the loss data for each year of the experience-review period in terms of the value of the dollar at some point in time subsequent to the experience-review period, or at least at the end of such period. If the loss data are evaluated only up to the end of the experience period, the adjustment factors are referred to as limited-trend factors. If the loss data are evaluated up to the effective date of the rate revision, the adjustment factors simply are referred to as trend factors.

If the evaluation date is some time after the effective date of the rate revision, usually the middle of the period during which the rates are expected to be in effect, the adjustment factors are referred to as projection factors. Trend and projection factors may be based either upon various indices, such as the Consumers' Price Index (CPI), which reflect the ultimate costs for the type of insurance for which they are used, or upon ratios of actual average claim costs.

Weightings. Another refinement commonly used in both the loss-ratio and pure-premium methods involves the weighting of the various years in the experience period to give greater weight to the more current years' experience in determining the proposed rate revision. Instead of calculating the experience-review-period loss ratio, for example, by dividing the total adjusted losses incurred by the total adjusted premiums earned, it is current practice in the homeowners and other lines to calculate a loss ratio separately for each year of the experience review period and take a weighted average of the loss ratios. The weights given the more recent years' loss ratios are larger than those given the loss ratios of earlier years.

Limitations of Formula Rate Revisions

Although formulas are used in both the loss-ratio and pure-premium methods of revising rate levels, it should be emphasized that the formula indications may not be followed strictly. There are too many factors to be considered in pricing to make rates automatically by use of a formula. Neither method makes any provision for the effect of rate changes on the amounts of insurance purchased. Theoretically, a pricing formula should include provision for *all* price-determining factors. Practically, this is an impossibility. Formulas cannot be expected to show accurately what will happen in the future.

Minimum and Maximum Rate Changes. The Fire Insurance Research and Actuarial Association (formerly Inter-Regional Insurance Conference), a qualified advisory organization for rating bureaus, recommends that no overall fire rate-level adjustment be made if the indicated profit during the review period is within 2 percentage points of the profit allowance in the rating formula.[5]   It is common to limit indicated changes to a maximum, such as 25 percent,[6] although much larger increases have occurred on some occasions.

Coverage Changes.   There are other ways of correcting for a divergence of actual and expected underwriting results without changing existing rates per se.   The broadening of policy coverage without increasing the rate effects a rate reduction for the original policy and it may benefit the insured more than an actual rate reduction.   Conversely, the scope of coverage may be reduced in lieu of increasing rates to levels that might be considered exorbitant.   The effect of coverage modifications on underwriting results cannot be calculated by a formula.   While some statistics may be available to help evaluate the effect of coverage changes, in the final analysis it is necessary to use underwriting judgment in estimating the probable effect of coverage modifications.

Exposure Units

In both the loss-ratio and pure-premium methods of revising rate levels, a consideration of fundamental importance in the determination of overall premium income and its proper allocation among classifications is the standard of quantitative measurement for which the price (rate) of an insurance contract is quoted.   This standard is called the exposure or insurance-coverage unit.   The unit varies widely among kinds of insurance.

Ideally, exposure units should be purely *quantitative* measures of expected losses.[7]   If the number of exposure units were doubled, the expected amount of losses should double.   Rates should be

---

[5] Inter-Regional Insurance Conference, "Basic Principles—Rate Level Adjustments," *Fire Insurance Rate Making and Kindred Problems* (New York: Casualty Actuarial Society, 1960), p. 155.

[6] Harold Sohmer, "Fire and Allied Lines Insurance Rates," *Examination of Insurance Companies* (Albany: New York Insurance Department, 1955), Vol. 5, p. 169.

[7] Kulp, *op. cit.* (3rd ed.), p. 460.

qualitative measures of hazard. Rates applied to identical exposure units for the same kind of insurance should reflect hazard differences between one insured's exposures and another's.

A rate should measure the loss potential of an insured's exposures, i.e., it should measure those features, internal and external, which contribute to loss frequency and/or severity.[8] However, it does not follow that as the rate increases, the insurability of the risk decreases. If rates are true measures of loss potential, an insured with a high rate is not necessarily less desirable than one with a low rate. Desirability is a function of profitability, which depends upon the magnitude of loss and expense *ratios*, not absolute loss and expense.

Imperfect Standard of Measurement. Ideally, an increase in the number of exposure or insurance-coverage units should not affect the loss-frequency *rate* (total number of loss occurrences divided by total number of exposure units) or the loss-severity *rate* (total dollars of insured losses incurred divided by total number of loss occurrences) because the increase in the total number of losses and the dollar amount of loss arising therefrom should be proportionate to the increase in exposure units. However, using the definitions of frequency and severity just presented, one would find in several lines of insurance that this is not the case. Consider fire insurance on a given number of dwellings, where the quantitative unit of measure is $100 of insurance purchased. An increase in the number of exposure units (an increase in the amount of insurance purchased, assuming less than coverage to value in the first instance, and most property is underinsured) would in the long run result in a lower frequency and a higher severity rate than otherwise would occur. This would result because most losses are partial losses. An increase in the ratio of the amount of insurance purchased to the total insurable value would not in itself cause an increase in the number of losses, but it could cause an increase in the insured losses incurred because some losses that previously were larger than the amount of insurance purchased on a particular dwelling, and

---

[8] Paul Dorweiler, "Notes on Exposures and Premium Bases," *Automobile Insurance Rate Making* (New York: Casualty Actuarial Society, 1961), p. 34.

therefore not completely covered by insurance, would be covered to a larger extent because of the increase in the number of insurance-coverage units purchased.

The relation between loss ratios and the proportion of insurable value actually insured is recognized in fire insurance by the application of coinsurance credits when insureds agree to maintain a specified relation between insurance purchased and insurable value (if they do not carry the agreed-upon percentage, their losses will not be paid in full). In virtually all states except New York, however, dwelling fire insurance is *not* written subject to coinsurance provisions. In the dwelling fire field the relatively recent introduction of loss and/or expense constants in the determination of premiums has resulted in a graded rate system, i.e., as the amount of insurance purchased increases (other things being equal), the total cost *per unit* of exposure decreases. In effect the amount of insurance purchased becomes a basis of classification.

The less than proportionate increase in losses mentioned above is not the only factor which suggests that either the exposed insurable value or the amount of insurance purchased be used as a basis of classification for rating purposes. It is well recognized that some expenses are relatively constant per policy, regardless of the size of risk as reflected by the number of exposure units. In fact, some expenses which are usually expressed as a fixed percentage of the premium, such as commissions, are willingly reduced on large risks in recognition of the economic redundancy of a constant percentage charge on such risks. Relatively little attention had been given to this subject in fire rating before the introduction of expense constants, although multiple-location and large deductible rating plans did, and still do, recognize expense variation directly or indirectly.

It is extremely difficult to find exposure units that vary directly with expected insurance loss and expense costs because of the multitude of diverse factors that affect losses and the practical requirements that exposure units be easily determinable, acceptable to insureds, not manipulatable, and preferably already in use for other than insurance purposes.[9]   However, the weakness also lies with the classification systems, because they fail to group insureds in a manner that is sufficiently homogeneous for the loss and expense costs per unit of exposure to be virtually the same for all insureds within a classification.

Variety in Use.   Different exposure or insurance-coverage units have been used in the rating of the individual coverages which have been integrated into homeowners policies.   Fire, extended-coverage, and personal-property floater insurance used $100 of insurance purchased as the quantitative measure, while personal theft used $1,000 of insurance purchased.   Furthermore, the amount of theft insurance purchased was used as a basis of classification because as the amount of insurance purchased increased by certain discrete amounts, the rate decreased.   For comprehensive personal liability insurance, most likely because of the minimum basic amount of insurance required (originally a basic limit of $10,000), one policy for one year was used as the quantitative unit of exposure.   Limits above the basic amount—excess limits—were available at less than proportionate increases in rates, so that in essence the amount of insurance purchased also was used as a basis of classification.   In the interests of economy and simplicity it was thought desirable to find a single exposure unit that would be suitable for the entire homeowners policy.   This is one of the problems of homeowners rating that will be considered in a later chapter.

Statistical Plans

In order for the experience of insurers to be pooled for rating purposes in a meaningful manner, the insurance commissioners have promulgated statistical plans by which insurers record and report to qualified statistical agencies loss, expense, premium, and exposure data in a uniform manner.   In most lines of insurance the statistical agency also acts as the rating bureau, although in some

---

[9] *Ibid.*, p. 36.

lines the two functions are performed by different organizations. In either event, the statistical agency is responsible for compiling the reported experience according to the statistical plans in classification detail.   Insurer personnel apply the appropriate statistical codes to the information contained in applications and loss reports so that they may comply with the requests made in the so-called statistical calls.

METHODS OF RATE-LEVEL REVISION

The computation of the overall percentage increase or decrease in manual premium level is called the determination of the rate level.[10]   This is the first major step in the rating process.   The second is the distribution of the overall (usually statewide) change by classification.   The second step is usually accomplished by first distributing the change over the territories, if any, and then over the classifications within each territory.   The two most common methods of revising rate levels are the loss-ratio and pure-premium methods.   They were often referred to in the past as judgment and statistical methods, respectively.   However, as stated by Carlson:

In the final analysis it must be re-emphasized that the determination of rates is not an automatic process but that *judgement enters* that determination at *every step* of the way, whether the rates be established on the basis of a formula or whether they be established as a direct result of judgment consideration.[11]

This is especially true at the classification levels.

Equivalence of Methods

Houston has shown that the loss-ratio and pure-premium methods will yield the same results if the same basic loss, expense,

[10] R. M. Marshall, *Workmen's Compensation Insurance Rate Making* (New York: Casualty Actuarial Society, 1961), p. 1.

[11] Carlson, "Rate Regulation and the Casualty Actuary," *loc. cit.*, pp. 41–42.   Italics added.

exposure, and premium data are used in each,[12] and a correction for any premium off balance is made in the pure-premium method. Although the two methods are mathematically equivalent, there usually is a difference in the nature of the insurance being rated and the data available for study in the two methods. Also, with the loss-ratio method it is necessary to know the rate level which was in effect when the premiums of the experience-review period were written as well as the existing rate level. With the pure-premium method, only the existing rate level must be known.

The data normally available for the types of insurance in which the pure-premium method is used often differ in at least five important ways from the data normally available for those types of insurance in which the loss-ratio method is used. Generally in the pure-premium method, as used in some casualty coverages and as opposed to the loss-ratio method used in fire insurance, frequency of loss occurrence is greater; the number of risks exposed to loss in each classification is larger; the possibility of catastrophic losses is less; the exposure or insurance-coverage unit is a more accurate measure of the potential loss; and the risks within each classification are thought to be more homogeneous.[13]

The fact that the pure-premium approach is sometimes referred to as a statistical method and the loss-ratio method is thought of as a judgment method is not due to the differences between the mathematical formulas or mechanics involved. The reason is that the amount of emphasis on judgment is normally, of necessity, greater when the loss-ratio method is used because of the nature of the data involved. However, "the history even of casualty liability ratemaking ... includes many an evidence that the pure premium rate-maker uses judgment, sometimes in large doses."[14]

---

[12] David B. Houston, "The Equivalence of the Pure Premium and the Loss Ratio Methods of Ratemaking," *Review of Insurance Studies*, Vol. III, No. 2 (Summer, 1956), pp. 72–75. Privately printed by a group of graduate students at the University of Pennsylvania.

[13] M. H. McConnell, "A Casualty Man Looks at Fire Insurance Rate Making," and L. H. Longley-Cook, "Notes on Some Actuarial Problems of Property Insurance," in Casualty Actuarial Society, *Fire Insurance Rate Making and Kindred Problems* (New York, 1960), pp. 36–37 and p. 89, respectively.

[14] Kulp, *op. cit.*, p. 462.

This is so because "no system of gathering past experience can produce a reasonable rate level unless it is adjusted to reflect current costs and to provide for a reasonable prediction of the losses that may be expected during the period that the rates are to apply."[15]   These adjustments must of necessity involve the use of judgment.

The division between loss-ratio and pure-premium methods is further clouded by the fact that an initial step in most pure-premium methods is the testing of the rate level by a loss-ratio technique.[16]   While the difference between the two basic methods are more apparent than real, it is still worthwhile to describe briefly each method, because each is commonly thought to be unique.   Besides the brief description given of each method at the end of this chapter, there are detailed illustrations of the application of each method in later chapters.

More points of similarity than difference exist among the two methods.   Both have common objectives and use several identical procedures.   Each is based upon the assumption that experience of the past is the best guide to the future.   The assumption also is made, wittingly or not, that changes in rates will not produce changes in either the amount of insurance purchased or the number of losses incurred.   This tenuous assumption implies a perfectly inelastic demand for insurance, i.e., the amount of insurance purchased will be constant regardless of the price charged after the revision.

The following descriptions of the two basic methods of adjusting rate levels give only their bare essentials.   In practice there are variations of each method and many refinements are often applied. The methods are discussed further in Chapter V.

The Loss-Ratio Method

This method involves a comparison of the ratio of actual (or adjusted actual) insurer underwriting loss outgo to premium

---

[15] Benbrook, *op. cit.*, p. 59.

[16] Thomas O. Carlson, "Trends in Casualty Insurance Rate Making," *The Journal of Insurance*, Vol. 30, No. 1 (March, 1963), p. 20.

income, with an expected or permissible ratio. For testing rates, use is made of a permissible loss ratio, also called balance-point and expected loss ratio, which is determined as follows: The rate or premium is divided into 100 percentage points. The difference between 100 and the sum of what are considered reasonable allowances, expressed as percentages for profit, contingencies, and expenses is the permissible loss ratio.

The profit and contingency allowances have been subjects of great debate. Although there have been attempts toward uniform allowances in this regard through the NAIC, there is some variation by line and by state. In fire and homeowners insurance, allowances of 5 and 1 percent for profit and contingencies (catastrophes), respectively, are most common. Premiums are equivalent to sales, and there is considerable doubt as to the propriety of regulating the profit on sales. Profit on the investment in a business would be more appropriate. Also the notion of a contingency allowance seems ludicrous when there is no provision for accumulating the allowance for the occurrence of the contingencies. Federal income-tax laws do not make allowances for reserving against such contingencies by insurers.

The expense allowance, in some lines, is based upon actual ratios of expenses to premiums on a nationwide basis. There is disagreement as to whether the expense ratios should be calculated by dividing the incurred expenses by written or by earned premiums. In some lines of insurance a hybrid approach is used in which commissions and taxes, for example, are divided by written premiums while the other expenses are divided by earned premiums. In some existing lines of insurance and for new kinds of insurance, the expense allowances are not based directly upon past expense ratios. Instead they are based primarily upon judgment and are termed "budgeted" expense allowances. Such allowances have been justified on the grounds that the use of actual expenses would encourage excessiveness because increases in expenses eventually would be accommodated in the rating formula.

The adjusted actual loss ratio (adjusted or modified losses incurred divided by premiums earned at current rate levels) is compared with the permissible loss ratio in the following manner to determine the percent of indicated change in the rate level:

$$\text{Indicated change} = \left(\frac{A - E}{E}\right) \times 100 = \left(\frac{A}{E} - 1\right) \times 100$$

where A and E are the adjusted actual and the permissible loss ratios, respectively.

In the application of the loss-ratio method, it is assumed that expenses vary directly with the gross premium. This assumption is generally true for items such as commissions and premium taxes, because they are usually expressed as a fixed percentage of the gross premium. However, when there are large changes in the average-size premium per policy, such as may occur because of the integration of several coverages into a single multiple-line policy, some adjustment in the commission expense percentage is appropriate and likely to be made.

In its simplest form, the essence of the loss-ratio method is the determination of the rates that should have been charged during the experience-review period so that the actual loss ratio would have equaled the permissible loss ratio. Then it is assumed that the rates so determined, if used in the future, will produce an actual loss ratio equal to the permissible loss ratio. This will be true if the conditions of the experience period continue to prevail during the period in which the new rates are to apply. Because this is unlikely, as was mentioned previously, certain refinements take into consideration the fact that the *same physical losses* which occurred during the experience-review period would *not* involve the same total *dollar* cost if they occurred at some other time. These refinements involve the use of trend and projection factors.

The Pure-Premium Method

Even in the pure-premium method, it is customary to compare in some way either the actual and expected loss ratios, or pure premiums, or both. The expected loss per unit of exposure is called the present, or underlying, pure premium. The latter term is derived from the fact that the present pure premium underlies the current gross rate, i.e., the present gross rate was constructed from the present pure premium by "loading" it for expenses.

The present pure premium divided by the present gross rate is equivalent to the expected loss ratio. In other words, the expected pure premium and the permissible loss ratio represent the portion of the current gross rate contemplated for the payment of losses. In some lines loss-adjustment expenses are included with losses and the expected ratio is called a permissible loss and loss-adjustment expense ratio. Loss-adjustment expenses are divided into so-called allocated and unallocated categories. The allocated category includes those loss-adjustment expenses which can be directly attributed to a particular loss, such as certain litigation expenses, while the unallocated category includes the remaining loss adjustment expenses which cannot be charged to a specific loss such as the salary of the home-office claims supervisor, for example.

The pure-premium method is frequently used when the exposure unit is other than a dollar unit of insurance. Such exposure units include one policy for one year and measures such as feet, square feet, and admissions, for example. An initial step in this method is to determine the average loss per unit of exposure, which is called the pure premium. The pure premium is equal to the quotient resulting from dividing total losses incurred (sometimes loss-adjustment expenses are included here) by total exposure units earned. An amount is added to the premium to cover expenses, including profit. The resulting figure is the gross rate. However, the amount added for expenses is usually expressed as a percentage of the gross rate. This percentage figure is equivalent to the expense ratio of the loss-ratio method. The determination of gross rate involves the use of the following formula:

$$\text{G.R.} = \text{P.P.} + (\text{E.R.})\,(\text{G.R.})$$
$$\text{G.R.} - (\text{E.R.})\,(\text{G.R.}) = \text{P.P.}$$
$$\text{G.R.}\,(1 - \text{E.R.}) = \text{P.P.}$$
$$\text{G.R.} = \frac{\text{P.P.}}{(1 - \text{E.R.})}$$
$$\text{G.R.} = \frac{\text{P.P.}}{\text{L.R.}}$$

where G.R. = Gross rate
P.P. = Pure premium
E.R. = Expense and profit ratio
L.R. = Permissible loss ratio

In other words, the gross rate is equal to the pure premium divided by the permissible loss ratio.

The pure premium is an average amount of loss per exposure unit. It is therefore more technically a rate rather than a premium. However, pure premium is a generally accepted term. Mathematically, the pure premium is equal to the product of the average amount of loss per loss occurrence (severity rate) times the average number of loss occurrences per exposure unit (frequency rate). It is useful to express the pure premium as the product of the severity and frequency rates in order to help determine the causes of changes in the pure premium and, if necessary, to help determine what remedial action might be taken to improve the loss ratio in lieu of changing the rates. Such action might result in the introduction or increased use of deductibles.

CHAPTER **IV**

Fundamentals
and Development
of Rate Regulation

Multiple-line legislation was passed, for the most part, without changing the remainder of the existing insurance laws that had been drafted on the basis of the monoline concept. Several problems encountered in the rating of homeowners policies were directly related to the application of monoline rating laws to multiple-line policies.

THE NATURE OF INSURANCE REGULATION

The objectives of regulation are usually expressed in vague generalities, such as "to promote the general welfare," "to protect the public interest," and "to implement public policy." Professor Glendon Schubert devoted an entire book to the subject of the public interest and concluded "that there is no public interest theory worthy of the name and that the concept itself is significant primarily as a datum of politics. ... It may ... be nothing more than a label attached indiscriminately to a miscellany of particular compromises of the moment."[1]

---

[1] Glendon Schubert, *The Public Interest* (Glencoe, Ill.: Free Press of Glencoe, Ill., 1960), p. 223.

Professor Spencer Kimball refers to the objectives of regulation in terms of an "intellectual construct called a 'social goal,' " which he defines "as a kind of vector sum of the goals of those persons in society whose purposes have any impact upon the legal machinery."[2] This vector sum is probably truly representative as far as what Kimball calls "external goals" are concerned, i.e., for those goals reflecting the larger purposes of society as exemplified in "our political structure and attitudes . . . our economic and social policies, and our . . . basic moral values."[3] Unfortunately, however, in regard to "internal goals," i.e., those goals which relate directly to the internal working of the insurance business, there is not equality of representation by the various segments comprising the public interest. Social goals, therefore, may be improperly weighted in favor of the more articulate and vociferous constituents.

The objectives of insurance regulation are usually defined in vague generalities, partly because of the difficulty of defining precisely the more specific objectives and partly because the specific objectives are continually changing and many are in conflict with each other. The goals in vogue at any particular time reflect a temporary balance of constituent goals. For example, as the subsequent sketch of the development of rate regulation will reveal, there is a fundamental conflict among the external goals inherent in a (faltering) laissez-faire policy and the internal goals which require for their fulfillment various degrees of legal control. Kimball points out that compromising this conflict has resulted in uneven regulation of various aspects of the business.[4] Rating has been subjected to very close control. In general, however, there has been a continued reluctance to regulate the components of the rate specifically, especially commissions.

---

[2] Spencer L. Kimball, "The Goals of Insurance Law: Means vs. Ends," *The Journal of Insurance*, Vol. 29, No. 1 (March, 1962), pp. 19–20. In this reference Kimball also notes that: "In a sense it is a misnomer to speak of the 'goals' of insurance law, for goals or purposes are psychological phenomena existing for individuals but hard to attribute to society as a whole."

[3] *Ibid.*, p. 22.

[4] Spencer L. Kimball, *Insurance and Public Policy* (Madison: University of Wisconsin Press, 1960), p. 310.

There is a need for a theory of insurance regulation which not only clarifies the objectives of insurance regulation, but also establishes a hierarchical relationship among the objectives and distinguishes means and ends.[5] Such a theory would have facilitated the development of multiple-line insurance.

Solvency is the most important goal of all insurance law and regulation, though it is not always given effect by individual courts or insurance commissioners. ... The question ... is, how far to press the demands of solidity in the face of the other values or goals that sometimes conflict with it, thus complicating the problem.[6]

Preoccupation with Rate Regulation

In the name of solvency, there has been a preoccupation with rate regulation. Those favoring greater reliance upon competition as a regulator of rates (for objectives other than solvency, e.g., reasonableness) believe rate regulation is an area where means and ends are at times confused. Although solvency may be the paramount objective of regulation, more effective and direct methods which cure causes, not symptoms, are required, in order to achieve the objective. These methods include more probing and timely examinations of insurers and the enactment of more stringent and meaningful regulations for capital, surplus, and the evaluation of liabilities.[7] Furthermore, while solvency may be the

---

[5] Spencer L. Kimball, *Problems in Regulation of Insurance*, transcript of a panel discussion during the 55th Annual Meeting of the National Association of Attorneys General (Chicago: The Council of State Governments, July 10, 1961), pp. 16–17.

[6] Spencer L. Kimball, "The Goals of Insurance Law: Means vs. Ends,' *loc. cit.*, p. 21. Kimball believes solvency is of primary concern, "because without it the institution doesn't do the job that it should do at all. It doesn't insure." (*Problems in Regulation of Insurance*, p. 18.) However, others have suggested that it is possible to insure the risk of insurer insolvency. See Richard M. Heins, "Liquidations of Insurance Companies," in Charles C. Center and Richard M. Heins (eds.), *Insurance and Government* (New York: McGraw-Hill Book Co., Inc., 1962), pp. 237–68.

[7] "Almost no statutes and little regulatory activity seek to compel a capital and surplus fund which bear a realistic relationship to the scale of the operation" (Spencer L. Kimball and William Conklin, *The Montana Insurance Commissioner* [Ann Arbor: University of Michigan Law School, 1960]), p. 23.

paramount internal objective of rate regulation, it may not in all
cases outrank the sum total of all other objectives, which for want
of a better expression may be properly termed "protection of the
public interest." For example, it is generally thought desirable
to have rather "free" entry into a business by new firms. In this
regard, very substantial minimum capital and surplus requirements, though fostering solvency, might unduly hinder entry into
the business of insurance.

According to James B. Donovan, "no matter how regulatory
statutes may satisfy legalistic concepts, they are only in the public
interest if the industry subject to them is enabled to serve the
needs of the buying public on a sound and reasonable basis."[8]
Rate-regulatory statutes may be an example where ends have
been confused with means. Furthermore, insurer solvency cannot
be guaranteed through rate regulation. Unfortunately, in the
name of rate regulation there have been times when insurers
have been prevented from serving the needs of the public on a
sound basis.

Rates are based upon broad averages. The underwriting
results of individual insurers may vary considerably from the
average upon which rates are based simply because of chance
fluctuation. The law of large numbers illustrates not only why
most insurers are unable to make rates based solely upon their
own experience, but also why rate regulation is insufficient in and
of itself to prevent insolvency due to adverse loss experience, such
as that resulting from a conflagration or a hurricane.

Problem of Interpretation

The objectives of insurance regulation are, theoretically at
least, reflected in the various insurance laws. However, there
is always the practical problem of interpretation, which is often
complicated by a lack of legislative history which would reveal
legislative intent. Insurance statutes may be ambiguous; some
are even contradictory. A former insurance commissioner

---

[8] James B. Donovan, "Rate Regulation Revisited," in Center and Heins
(eds.), *op. cit.*, p. 291.

observed that in 20 years the 1939 New York Insurance Law was amended 100 times, and every time it was amended there was difficulty determining what the amendments meant.[9]   Therefore, "there is always a battle to control the government agency because if you get Commissioners of one point of view their decisions will tend to reflect that view and if you get Commissioners of another point of view their decisions will read accordingly."[10]

The degree to which legislative objectives are implemented depends upon several factors.[11]   Although judicial interpretations rendered in cases involving legislation determine to an extent the limits within which such acts are effective, the actual administration of the acts is usually paramount because in most instances the courts will not reverse administrative decisions unless a matter of law is involved.   This is so even if there is specific evidence for a reversal.[12]

DEVELOPMENT OF RATE REGULATION UP TO 1909

The early period of insurance history in the United States contained very little rate-regulatory activity.   However, certain attitudes and events which developed in the early period of insurance history in this country played a significant role in shaping the development of rate regulation.   The prevailing public attitude toward business during the formative years of insurance was laissez-faire.   This attitude continues to have an impact upon rate regulation.   Originally, fire insurance was the predominant type of property insurance written; other kinds of property and

---

[9] Statement of Alfred J. Bohlinger, quoted in *Hearings on the Insurance Industry* (report of the Subcommittee on Antitrust and Monopoly, Committee on the Judiciary, U.S. Senate, 85th and 86th Congress, 1958–60), p. 1792. These hearings will be cited hereafter as *Hearings*.

[10] Senator Joseph C. O'Mahoney, *Competition vs. Collectivism*, address before Sixth Annual Meeting of the National Association of Independent Insurers, Chicago, November 2, 1950 (pamphlet), p. 8.

[11] For a discussion of some of these factors see J. Edward Hedges and Clyde V. McMasters, *The Effects of Public Law Fifteen on the Local Insurance Agent* (Bureau of Business Research, Study No. 34 [Bloomington: University of Indiana, 1952]), p. 60.

[12] See testimony of Abraham Kaplan quoted in *Hearings*, p. 1456.

liability insurance did not come into their own until well after the turn of the century. Therefore, most of the articulated attitudes toward rate regulation in the late 1800's and early 1900's were concerned with fire rating practices. These attitudes have had a continuing influence not only in the regulation of fire insurance rates, but in the regulation of other property and liability insurance rates as well.

Insurance is subject to three levels of regulation: industry (self-regulation), state, and federal. However, the regulation of insurance rates is an activity in which the federal government has not participated directly.

Self-Regulation

Self-regulation was originally the paramount form of rate regulation, and it continues to be a dominant factor in determining governmental regulatory policy.

Insurance men quite early developed a sophisticated theory: if insurance was to provide its intended protection, rates must be fixed and adequate, and prevention of rate competition was a necessity of sound cooperation of the business and should be sanctioned by forfeiture of corporate charters.[13]

Early industry efforts toward self-regulation of insurance rates and agents' commission rates resulted in the creation of the progenitors of rating bureaus. Therefore, self-regulation of insurance rates will be examined more closely in the next chapter, which deals with the development of rating bureaus. However, it is appropriate to mention here that industry regulation is difficult to maintain without the sanction and enforcement powers of some level of government. Through the years the industry has therefore turned to government for aid in preventing rate competition. The sincerity of the industry's beliefs and the continual pleas for uniform rates by a large segment of the industry in the not too distant past have made an impact upon the theory that is generally acknowledged to underlie rate regulation.

---

[13] Kimball, *Insurance and Public Policy*, pp. 95–96.

State Regulation

The landmark case which fostered the pattern for *state* regulation of the insurance business was *Paul v. Virginia*.[14]   In this case the U.S. Supreme Court held that insurance was not commerce in the constitutional sense, and, therefore, the states had the right to continue to regulate the insurance business.   Although the industry presently is rather solidly opposed to federal regulation, it is interesting to note that the industry had hoped that the *Paul* case would oust jurisdiction over insurance regulation from the states and move it to the federal government.

Compartmentalization.   Twenty years prior to the *Paul* decision, New York had enacted its first insurance law, which ultimately, because of the Appleton Rule, compartmentalized the insurance business in the United States.   Although this law did not directly pertain to rate regulation, it did establish the principle of separate regulatory provisions for the various kinds of insurance. This principle was subsequently applied to rate regulation and became the source of several multiple-line rating problems because it fostered separate and different treatment of rating matters for the various kinds of insurance.   The compartmentalization of the insurance business continued to have a restraining influence on the development of multiple-line insurance even after the passage of multiple-line legislation.

Anticompact Legislation.   The theory behind the laissez-faire attitude, which was very strong in the early 1800's, was that competition would be a sufficient regulator to protect the public interest.[15]   Gradually the laissez-faire policy toward business was modified.   In the third quarter of the 19th century, the federal government passed two famous laws, the Interstate Commerce Act of 1887 and the Sherman Antitrust Act of 1890, in reflection of the changing public attitude toward "big business."   This new antitrust attitude was supported by the theory that government regulation was necessary to suppress trusts and to enforce the

---

[14] 8 Wall (U.S.) 168 (1869).

[15] Raymond T. Bye and William W. Hewett, *The Economic Process* (New York: Appleton-Century-Crofts, Inc., 1952), p. 189.

maintenance of competition.[16] The force of competition alone was not considered sufficient to protect the public adequately against the exploitation of excessive and discriminatory prices.

Before and after the passage of the Sherman Act, a number of states also adopted various kinds of antitrust legislation. Such legislative acts relating to the business of fire insurance were known as anticompact statutes. In 1885 Ohio became the first state to pass an anticompact law.[17] Between 1885 and 1912, 22 other states also passed laws forbidding insurance rate-fixing combinations.[18]

Application of the antitrust principle to insurance rating was thought by many to be inconsistent with the basic principle of insurance and insurance rating. A. F. Dean attributed the passage of anticompact laws to a misunderstanding of fire insurance.

> Popular beliefs ... are stubborn things, and no array of facts presented by fire underwriters or by state officials themselves seems to have had the slighest effect in convincing the public that fire insurance is not a trust or that it is not reaping fabulous profits. It is this belief that is responsible for the existence in many states of laws prohibiting the companies from acting jointly in the measurement of fire hazard and from the publication of common rates as a basis of information for all companies.[19]

The objective of the anticompact laws was to keep rates as low as possible through enforced competition. The laws failed in this regard because they were easily evaded by the use of Fire Insurance Advisory Bureau rates.[20] There was also dissatisfaction with the anticompact approach because of alleged discriminatory practices attributed to enforced competition and the resulting lack of uniform rates (among and within insurers) for the same class

[16] *Ibid.*, p. 190.

[17] Harry Chase Brearley, *The History of the National Board of Fire Underwriters* (New York: F. A. Stokes Co., 1916), pp. 76–77.

[18] Statement of Julius S. Wikler, counsel, and Donald Knowlton, chairman, Committee on Preservation of State Regulation, National Association of Insurance Commissioners, "State Regulation of Insurance," quoted in *Hearings*, p. 4867.

[19] A. F. Dean, "State Regulation of Fire Insurance," in W. R. Townley (ed.), *The Philosophy of Fire Insurance* (3 vols.; Chicago: Edward B. Hatch, 1925), Vol. I, p. 10.

[20] C. A. Kulp, *Casualty Insurance* (rev. ed.; New York: Ronald Press Co., 1942), p. 623.

of insureds.   This contributed to the demise of anticompact legislation.

It is likely that the great San Francisco conflagration of 1906 made the public more sympathetic toward insurer pleas for scientific rating, which was said to be possible only through concerted action.   Also there was economic justification (expense savings) for the application of rating schedules by a bureau. According to Mr. Dean, "the cordial approval of rating schedules by the commissions of several important states was probably the cause of the Anti-Discriminatory Laws which began to supplant Anti-Compact Legislation."[21]

Antidiscrimination Legislation.   As their name implies, the primary objective of antidiscrimination statutes was to prevent *unfair* discrimination among insureds within the same rating classification.   These statutes also failed to be effective regulatory devices because "it is not possible to know whether risks are of the same class until general criteria of classification are set up; if there is no standardization and control of these criteria and of their application the statute becomes meaningless."[22]   Most states apparently believed that achievement of the objective of preventing unfair discrimination required at a minimum the sanctioning of rating bureaus.   Other states went so far as to compel insurers to form and affiliate with rating bureaus.

Rating Laws.   The regulation of rating bureaus was the primary objective of the various rating laws enacted after 1908. The laws contained other provisions besides the antidiscrimination standard.   These provisions included the requirement that rating classifications, rating rules, and the overall rate level be filed with regulatory officials to determine whether they should be approved as meeting the additional standards of adequacy and non-excessiveness.

The findings of several insurance legislative investigating committees in the early 1900's provided impetus for the recognition and regulation of rating bureaus.   A Pennsylvania commission found, for instance, from the testimony adduced before it that combinations of insurance companies, or their representatives or

---

[21] Dean, *op. cit.*, Vol. II, p. 250.
[22] Kulp, *loc. cit.*

their agents, are in accordance with a wise public policy, necessary to the solvency of the insurance companies and are beneficial to the public.

Reporting upon concerted rating as performed by rating bureaus, a Missouri commission stated that "the economic forces supporting this practice cannot be restrained and that in the making, or rather estimating rates, joint and cooperative action must be recognized in such cases as the companies see fit to adopt it, subject, of course, to proper limitations and official supervision."[23]

The first state to pass rate-regulatory legislation more highly developed than that embodied in anticompact and antidiscrimination laws was Kansas, in 1909.[24] The Kansas statute required the filing of fire insurance rates with the insurance commissioner and authorized the commissioner to hold up rate changes and to order rate revisions in order to prevent the use of excessive or inadequate rates. The statute was upheld as not being in violation of either the due-process or the equal-protection clauses of the Federal Constitution.[25] New York, however, "appears to have been the first state to permit (fire) insurance companies to combine in bureaus for rate-making."[26] This approach was adopted almost universally by the other states.

DEVELOPMENT OF RATE REGULATION AFTER 1909

The Merritt Report[27]

The legislation leading to the New York rate-regulatory laws of 1911 was based upon the so-called Merritt Committee Report.

---

[23] Bearley, *op. cit.*, pp. 129–30.

[24] Clarence W. Hobbs, "State Regulation of Insurance Rates," *Proceedings of the Casualty Actuarial Society*, Vol. XI, No. 24 (June, 1925), p. 221.

[25] *German Alliance Insurance Company v. Lewis*, 233 U.S. 389, 58L. Ed. 1011, 345, Ct. 612 (1914).

[26] Kulp, *op. cit.*, p. 624.

[27] The material in this section is based upon: State of New York, *Report of the Joint Committee of the Senate and Assembly of the State of New York Appointed to Investigate Corrupt Practices in Connection with Legislation, and the Affairs of Insurance Companies, Other than Those Doing a Life Insurance Business*, Assembly Document No. 30, 134th Session (1911). The report is quoted in *Hearings*, pp. 2791–882.

This was one of the most influential of all the reports of insurance legislative investigating committees issued in the early 1900's. In the wake of the Armstrong Investigation into the practices of life insurers, the Merritt Committee was appointed in New York in 1910 to investigate the practices of nonlife insurers. The committee was named after its chairman, Senator Merritt.

The committee's report noted that the fundamental problem of fire insurance was rating and that the important questions relating to this problem were economic rather than legal in nature. The committee reiterated the fact that in the long run insurers can pay out only what they collect, yet this fact, it was felt, was commonly lost sight of by the public. The central problem was said to be the necessity of charging in advance for something that may or may not happen.

Because of the infinite complexity of the existing and arising hazards affecting fire loss, and the possibility of large conflagrations, which were too infrequent to allow the working of the law of averages, the committee thought it impossible for rates to be made properly on the basis of a single insurer's experience. Therefore, and also because of expense savings which would result from elimination of the duplication of rating efforts by several insurers, combination was considered desirable. Hence, the committee was in favor of allowing insurers to form rating bureaus.

Competition was denounced because it was said to result in rate wars where prices were cut below the actual cost of the indemnity provided. Furthermore, the committee concluded that in open competition rates were not adjusted to the hazards found in individual risks, but were determined largely by the strength of the insured's bargaining power. This resulted in unfair discrimination. The committee conjectured that because the costs of insurance are not definitely known at the time the price is set, there is no restraining influence, such as exists in other industries, to prevent rate wars. Insurance costs do "not stare the underwriter in the face in the same way that the buying price of sugar confronts the grocer." The corporate form of organization was also said to encourage irresponsibility in price making.

The committee did not favor rates made by state agencies, because there would be a tendency to make rates purely on the basis of an individual state's experience. This would break down a fundamental principle of insurance, because one state was considered insufficient to stand the shock of a large conflagration such as the San Francisco fire.

The committee also considered the extent of profits in the insurance business and decided that the insurers had not been making excessive profits. The question was whether expenses had been excessive. The insurers had an interest in preventing excessive profits because excessive profits would attract new competition into the business, if there was an awareness that such profits existed.

The committee also noted that excessive rates would be discouraged not only by the fear of attracting new competitors, but also by the strong competition that already existed in most parts of the country from nonboard and mutual companies. The committee also recommended greater reliance upon the use of statistics in rating, and noted that the insurers had failed to cooperate in collecting common loss experience. Therefore, it was recommended that steps be taken to enable the states to obtain the desired statistical information.

Early Rate Laws

The 1911 New York rating law permitted insurers to affiliate with rating bureaus and to adhere to the rates established and filed by such organizations. The state superintendent of insurance was authorized to supervise and inspect the various rating organizations. However, the superintendent was not authorized to order changes in rates unless he found them to be unfairly discriminatory.[28]

Although the legislative trend was toward permitting cooperation and collaboration in rating, the rating laws undertook to regulate such activities in order to prevent the possibility of abuses. In consideration of the right to combine, rating bureaus

---

[28] Joseph F. Collins, "Rate Regulation in Fire and Casualty Insurance," *Examination of Insurance Companies* (New York: New York Insurance Department, 1955), Vol. 5, p. xviii.

were charged by many states with the responsibility of making adequate but nonexcessive rates.[29]   In 1914 a committee of the National Convention of Insurance Commissioners (NCIC; now the National Association of Insurance Commissioners, NAIC) recommended passage of legislation that would bring the rating process under social control and provide for public representatives to review rates.[30]   By 1915 a dozen states were regulating the rating process.[31]

The Lockwood Report[32]

In 1921, a commission known as the Lockwood Committee was appointed in New York to investigate the effect of insurance rates on the cost of providing housing facilities in New York City. This committee felt that legitimate cooperation had been abused and had resulted in the establishment of uniform but excessive rates.[33] Both competition and regulation were deemed absolutely essential to protect the public.[34]   Therefore, in 1922 several changes were made in the New York rating laws as recommended by the Lockwood Committee. Rating organizations were required to furnish their services to any insurer licensed in New York that applied for services. Provision also was made for bureau members or subscribers, subject to the approval of the superintendent, to file uniform percentage deviations from the rates of the rating organizations. Insurers were required to file annually premium and loss experience in accordance with classifications approved by the superintendent. The most drastic change in the law was the provision authorizing the superintendent to order changes in rates which he found excessive or inadequate after due notice

---

[29] However, to this day in the large majority of states these terms are undefined in the statutes.

[30] *Proceedings of the National Convention of Insurance Commissioners,* 1914, p. 19.

[31] *Ibid.,* 1915, p. 11.

[32] State of New York, *Intermediate Report of the Joint Legislative Committee on Housing,* Legislative Document No. 60 (1922), pp. 198–243.

[33] *Ibid.,* p. 199.

[34] *Ibid.,* p. 201.

and hearing. Provision was also made for judicial review of the superintendent's findings.[35]

The addition of the requirements of nonexcessive and adequate rates to that of no unfair discrimination, and the provision for filing rates and subjecting them to administrative review, made the 1922 New York law very complete. In fact, it was essentially the same as the present New York rating law.

Industry Agreements Affecting Insurance Rates and Rating

After the 1922 amendments to the New York insurance rating law, there was little further development in the sophistication of statutory requirements pertaining to rate regulation. However, in the period between 1922 and 1944 certain agreements among insurers influenced the development of rating and its regulation. One group of agreements related to expenses and resulted in the Acquisition Cost Conferences. The other agreements related to *continuing and strengthening* the *separation* of underwriting powers. These latter agreements culminated in the 1933 Nationwide Marine Definition, which fostered a continuation of the differences in rating practices among the various kinds of insurance and prevented integration of coverages into single contracts.

The Acquisition Cost Conferences. Control of the cost of business production has been achieved essentially through self-regulation. However, voluntary efforts, such as agreements to limit commission rates, are always at a handicap because all insurers may not choose to conform. In the early 1920's the New York superintendent of insurance gave the industry a choice between having either more effective self-regulation or state regulation of expenses, especially commission rates. The insurers preferred more effective self-regulation and therefore formed the Conference on Acquisition and Field Supervision Costs for Casualty Insurance in 1922. Subsequently, conferences were formed for other kinds of insurance.

---

[35] Collins, *op. cit.*, p. xix.

Although commission regulation per se was not provided for in the New York law,[36] several New York insurance superintendents were instrumental in the formation of the cost conferences.[37] The primary purpose of these conferences was to keep production costs within reasonable bounds by limiting both the commission percentage payable to agents and the number of agents each insurer could appoint.

The significance of these conferences, as far as this study is concerned, lies in their recognition of the importance of acquisition costs in the rating structure and the possible need for cost regulation to prevent excessive rates. This is illustrated by the fact that in 1932 Superintendent Van Schaick required insurers doing business in New York to file their cost rules with the intention of considering an overpayment of commissions the same as an illegal rate reduction.[38] The cost conferences and the action of Superintendent Van Schaick point up the futility of rate regulation, as presently practiced. Effective rate regulation by the state conceivably requires regulation of all the components of the rate. For example, if under given conditions a rate is deemed adequate, it may become inadequate should commissions or some other item of expense be increased. This would indicate the need for a limitation of expenses, at least in their aggregate. Regulation of the components would restrict management's prerogatives and therefore discussion of this problem is usually avoided. However, failure to discuss the fundamental issue of expense regulation makes effective rate regulation difficult, if not impossible.

After the *SEUA* decision, the acquisition cost conferences were abandoned because of their antitrust implications. Apparently no efforts were made to legalize the conferences through legislative provision, as was done for rating bureaus. Evidently it was felt that the components of the rate could be kept within reasonable

---

[36] State of New York, *78th Annual Report of the Superintendent of Insurance*, 1937, Part I, p. 50.

[37] Francis R. Stoddard, *The History of Acquisition Costs in New York* (pamphlet, n. d.).

[38] *Ibid.*, p. 28.

bounds by limiting the aggregate rate itself. Although New York, for a short time, had a statute known as the Barrett-Russo Law, which required specific consideration of commissions by the superintendent when evaluating rates, the practice in New York and most other states is to view the rate as a budgetable aggregate. Therefore, the entire rate can be divided by insurers as they see fit. On the other hand, if solvency is the basic objective of rate regulation, it seems that each factor within the rate must be regulated to a certain extent. Otherwise, rates which are approved under one set of expense provisions can become inadequate because of an increase in one expense component without a corresponding decrease in another. Perhaps for this reason Professor Kulp stated that "it seems inevitable ... that in the not so long run casualty acquisition cost regulation ... will be taken over by the state, perhaps at the consent of the companies."[39]

The Nationwide Marine Definition.   Events occurring in the 1920's regarding the coverages which inland marine insurers could underwrite temporarily checked the multiple-line trend. These events prevented the development by inland marine underwriters of what are considered today as multiple-line coverages and tended to preclude inland marine concepts from dominating the multiple-line trend when it resumed.

The flow of new types of insurance coverages in the 1920's to marine insurers was primarily due to the fact that the marine insurers "were not hampered by legal restrictions as to rates and forms of policies."[40]   Controversy arose among casualty, fire, and marine insurers as to the scope of their respective coverages. Many insurers were thought to be exceeding their charter and/or statutory powers by writing certain coverages under an inland marine label.

Several organizations were formed which sought to define lines of demarcation among the kinds of coverages which could be written by the different types of insurers. These organizations included the Interstate Underwriters' Board representing the fire

---

[39] Kulp, *op. cit.*, p. 604.

[40] Earle Appleman, *Inland Marine Insurance* (New York: McGraw-Hill Book Co., Inc., 1934), p. 9.

companies, the Casualty Committee, the Marine Casualty Committee, and the Inland Marine Underwriters' Association.

The first agreement covering limitation of coverages was known as the Casualty-Marine-Merchandise Agreement. It was entered into by casualty and marine underwriters, effective July 1, 1930.[41] Joint committees representing each segment of the industry persistently tried to reach agreement as to the scope of their operations, without lasting success. Without the force of law, such agreements were next to impossible to maintain. Superintendent Van Schaick was instrumental in obtaining industry agreement to and enforcement of solutions to the questions regarding limitation of underwriting powers. After holding several hearings with industry representatives, the superintendent issued a ruling on September 30, 1932, based upon recommendations made by an industry committee, defining the business which marine companies would be allowed to write. The superintendent stated:

> The purpose and scope of this ruling is to clarify, in respect to the kinds of insurance ... the meaning and application of ... the insurance law with particular reference to the question of overlapping powers of various kinds of insurers and also with regard to certain insurance coverages as to which there has been misapprehension or dispute among fire, marine and casualty insurers.[42]

The original Nationwide Marine Definition, which was based largely upon Superintendent Van Schaick's ruling, was adopted by the National Association of Insurance Commissioners (NAIC) in June, 1933. The resolution adopting the Nationwide Definition also approved in principle a plan of administration for carrying out the definition and created a commissioners' committee in connection therewith.[43] Subsequently, many states adopted the definition by statute or by administrative ruling.

---

[41] William H. Rodda, *Inland Marine and Transportation Insurance* (2nd ed; Englewood Cliffs, N.J.: Prentice-Hall, Inc., 1958), p. 44.

[42] From statement of Harold L. Wayne, general manager, Inland Marine Underwriters Association and Inland Marine Insurance Bureau, quoted in *Hearings*, p. 2634.

[43] *Ibid.*

The definition was revised several times by many of the states which adopted it. Twenty years after its original adoption, the NAIC undertook a study which led to a complete revision of the definition and the methods of administration.

In a 1952 report to the NAIC, the Joint Committee on Interpretation noted that as long as the established classes of insurance were to exist and the statutes continued to subject different classes of insurance to different kinds and/or degrees of regulation definitions of those classes would serve a useful purpose.[44]

The joint committee recommended amendment of the definition in light of the passage of multiple-line laws and the numerous state amendments to the definition. The committee felt that the need for a definition was as great in 1952 as it was in 1933, perhaps more so, because of the enactment or amendment of rating laws which did not apply uniformly to all types of insurance.[45]

In June, 1963, the NAIC approved a new definition and adopted a proposal for the appointment of an industry committee for recommending interpretations of the definition.[46]

The stated purpose of the 1953 definition reads as follows:

> To describe the kinds of risks and coverages which may be classified or identified under State Insurance Laws as Marine, Inland Marine or Transportation Insurance, but does not include all of the kinds of risks and coverages which may be written, classified or identified under Marine, Inland Marine or Transportation insuring powers, nor shall it be construed to mean that the kinds of risks and coverages are solely Marine, Inland Marine or Transportation insurance in all instances.[47]

The definition also prescribed that it "shall not be construed to restrict or limit in any way the exercise of any insuring powers granted under charters and license whether used separately, in combination or otherwise."[48]

The 1953 definition has not been an impediment to the development of multiple-line insurance. However, the arbitrary

---

[44] *Ibid.*, p. 2637.

[45] *Ibid.* For example, only certain types of inland marine coverages are subjected to rate *filing* requirements.

[46] *Ibid.*, p. 2639.

[47] *Ibid.*, p. 2640.

[48] *Ibid.*

classification of insurance coverages among the various kinds of insurance continues. In this regard, a New York Insurance Department official stated:

> Although many forms of inland marine policies provide similar coverages on an "all-risk" basis, the preponderance of opinion is against the idea of amending the Nationwide Marine Definition in this state to include all types of dealers. I agree with the general opinion that these new types of policies should be classified under the Multiple Line or Multiple Peril category.
>
> This general category is more logically descriptive and also affords a more favorable situation for the future development of broader forms of policies.[49]

South-Eastern Underwriters Association (SEUA) Case

On June 5, 1944, the Supreme Court of the United States, in *United States v. South-Eastern Underwriters Association, et al.*,[50] overruled the *Paul* decision by a four-to-three decision. The court ruled that insurance was commerce, and therefore its interstate aspects were subject to congressional control and all federal statutes regulating interstate commerce were applicable to the insurance industry.

The indictment alleged a conspiracy to fix and maintain arbitrary, noncompetitive rates and to monopolize trade and commerce in violation of the Sherman Antitrust Act. A demurrer to the indictment had been sustained in August, 1943. However, on appeal the United States Supreme Court overruled the district court, sustaining the indictment on the ground that the defendants were engaged in interstate commerce and therefore were subject to the Sherman Act. The court distinguished the line of cases starting with *Paul v. Virginia* from the *SEUA* case in that these earlier cases involved the validity of state statutes. The *SEUA* case was the first one to present squarely the question of whether

[49] From Arthur F. Lamanda, "Opinion and Decision in the Matter of Independent Rate Filings for Commercial Property Coverages by the North America Companies and the American Casualty Company," New York Insurance Department (August 6, 1958), quoted in *Hearings*, p. 2101.

[50] 322 U.S. 533; 64 S. Ct.; 88L. Ed. 1440. This case is quoted in *Hearings*, pp. 4380–404.

the commerce clause grants to Congress the power to regulate insurance when conducted across state lines.

The *SEUA* decision jeopardized state regulation of the insurance business. The future of concerted rating was of paramount concern to the fire and casualty industry because the Sherman Antitrust Act, which forbids price fixing, became applicable to the business of insurance.

The McCarran-Ferguson Act—Public Law 15[51]

After the *SEUA* decision it was obvious that the insurance business needed time to adjust to its newly acquired status under federal laws. The NAIC and representatives of the insurance industry coordinated their efforts and prevailed upon Congress to pass legislation which would preserve state regulation and provide some type of exemption from the federal laws so that concerted rating could continue. A special NAIC Committee on Federal Legislation held hearings over a period of several months. As a result of these hearings the committee prepared and submitted a proposed bill to Congress which, in somewhat altered form, became the McCarran-Ferguson Act, commonly referred to as Public Law 15. The act declared that continued regulation of insurance by the states was in the public interest and that future silence on the part of Congress was not to be construed to impose any barrier to regulation by the states.

The act created a moratorium until January 1, 1948 (later extended to June 30, 1948), with respect to the application of the Sherman, Clayton, Federal Trade Commission, and Robinson-Patman Antidiscrimination Acts. However, during the moratorium period, as well as thereafter, the Sherman Act was to remain applicable to acts of boycott, coercion, and intimidation. After the end of the moratorium period, the Sherman, Clayton, and Federal Trade Commission Acts would be applicable to the business of insurance "to the extent that such business is not regulated by State Law."[52] The moratorium was to serve a dual

---

[51] 15 U.S.C. 1011–1015 (1945).

[52] *Ibid.*

purpose: (1) to afford the several states sufficient time to pass laws which would adequately regulate the insurance business and (2) to give the insurers sufficient time to change methods of operation which ran counter to applicable federal law and which would not receive legislative sanction and regulation by state laws.[53]

The All-Industry Bills

Public Law 15 required affirmative action by the states in order to oust the application of federal laws, which would otherwise be controlling, to insurer practices. The *SEUA* decision and Public Law 15 made it clear that concerted rating, if unregulated by the states, was in violation of the federal antitrust laws. Rate-regulatory legislation was the first matter to be considered. Even before the passage of Public Law 15, NAIC was studying the problem of adequate rate regulation.[54]

Although uniform legislation was not considered necessary to meet the challenge of Public Law 15, NAIC felt a responsibility to prepare and submit to its members suggested drafts of model fire and casualty rating bills, and as a consequence an All-Industry Committee (AIC) was formed to draft such model bills.[55] After careful study and consideration the All-Industry Committee[56] decided that:

> With respect to fire, inland marine, casualty and surety insurance, the *important objectives* of *safeguarding* insurance *company solvency and ensuring fair and equitable practices* in the public interest could most certainly be secured under a state regulatory system which permitted cooperative activity in rate making to be conducted under adequate and affirmative regulatory safeguards. It was recognized that such activities might, in the absence of state regulation, be violative of the Sherman Act and thus that state regulation of the sort which would make the Sherman Act inapplicable was essential. It was also believed that the *preservation*

---

[53] Such as the Acquisition Cost Conferences.

[54] *Proceedings of the National Association of Insurance Commissioners*, 1945, p. 155.

[55] *Ibid.*, 1946, p. 98.

[56] The AIC was organized in May, 1945, to aid NAIC in the formulation of legislation to strengthen state laws within the meaning of Public Law 15.

of competitive opportunity in the insurance business *was likewise essential and* that this objective *should* likewise *be secured, to as great an extent as was possible without defeating the paramount objectives.*

Our efforts and those of the National Association of Insurance Commissioners have been directed not only toward developing rate regulatory bills under which these objectives would be secured by attaining a proper balance among them. *Divergent and* sometimes *conflicting views had to be reconciled, not only among various branches of the industry but also among* insurance *commissioners and between* insurance *commissioners and the industry.*[57]

In 1947, the year following approval by NAIC of the AIC Bills, rate-regulatory laws were enacted or amended in 37 jurisdictions. Generally, these laws were patterned after the AIC Bills. The statutes usually attempted to achieve a balance between the stability associated with concerted rating and the competitive freedom associated with independent rating. These laws have tended to formalize the rating process. Their technical differences, as will become apparent in Chapter VII, tended to retard the development of multiple-line insurance. This occurred even though Section I of both AIC Bills, "Purpose of Act," reads as follows:

The stated purpose of this Act is to promote the public welfare by regulating insurance rates to the end that they shall not be excessive, inadequate or unfairly discriminatory, and to authorize and regulate cooperative action among insurers in rate making and in other matters within the scope of this Act. Nothing in this Act is intended (1) to prohibit or discourage reasonable competition, or (2) to prohibit or encourage except to the extent necessary to accomplish the aforementioned purpose, uniformity in insurance rates, rating systems, rating plans or practices. This Act shall be liberally interpreted to carry into effect the provisions of this Section.[58]

---

[57] Letter from the Secretary of the All-Industry Committee, Henry Wood, to Senator McCarran, September, 1946, as quoted in *Insurance as Interstate Commerce: The First Two Years* (New York: Lawyers Press, Inc., pamphlet). Italics added.

[58] Quoted in *Hearings*, p. 4552.

CHAPTER V

Development of Rating Bureaus and Kindred Organizations

Contrary to life and health insurer practice, many fire and casualty insurers are either members of or subscribers to licensed rating bureaus which make and file rates on behalf of their affiliated insurers. Fire and casualty insurers which do not delegate their ratemaking responsibilities to rating bureaus are known as independents. The existence of several rating bureaus, making rates for different coverages or perils included in multiple-line policies, compounded the problem of deciding who should rate multiple-line policies. There is no bureau which promulgates all of the rates which apply to all of the component coverages in a multiple-line policy when they are sold as separate policies. The difficulty of coordinating the efforts of the several bureaus not only prompted formation of multiple-line bureaus and advisory organizations, but also encouraged some insurers to become independent for rating multiple-line policies.

This chapter will trace briefly the historical development of the bureaus which rate the various kinds of insurance that have been integrated into multiple-line policies. This will help provide an insight into the reasons why there are differences in the ways the various bureaus operate and explain why bureau operations have changed through the years.

TYPES OF RATING AND KINDRED ORGANIZATIONS

There are numerous rating and kindred organizations through-out the country. Many of these organizations are remnants of the monoline era. Although multiple-line underwriting has provided increased motivation for consolidation of many industry organiza-tions, a multitude remains, largely due to forces of inertia which tend to preserve the status quo. Separate organizations exist for the various kinds of insurance and in some instances for sub-divisions within a particular kind of insurance. While some organizations are national in scope, regional, state, and local organizations also exist. Moreover, in some instances, partisan organizations, such as stock or mutual organizations, are main-tained for essentially the same functions.

Although rating bureaus are of main concern here, it should be realized that kindred organizations, especially major trade and advisory associations, often wield considerable influence on rating bureaus and the ratemaking process.[1] For instance, the Western Actuarial Bureau, a qualified regional advisory organization, listed over sixty rating, advisory, statistical, and technical organi-zations from which it received or to which it gave counsel on rating matters.[2]

Several of the important trade organizations have functioned as rating bureaus at various times in their history, and they continue to exert influence on ratemaking, especially on general policy decisions. Although rating bureaus and advisory organizations are regulated under rate-regulatory laws, trade organizations are not. The All-Industry Committee (AIC) model rating laws define an advisory organization as one "which assists insurers which make their own filings or rating organizations in rate-

---

[1] *The Insurance Industry: Insurance: Rates, Rating Organizations, and State Rate Regulation,* (Report No. 831, Subcommittee on Antitrust and Monopoly, Committee on the Judiciary, U.S. Senate, 87th Congress, 1st Session, 1961), pp. 21–28; 50–55; 59–66; 124–25. Cited hereafter as "1961 report."

[2] Illinois Insurance Department, *Report of Examination of Western Actuarial Bureau* (August 29, 1958), reproduced in *Hearings on the Insurance Industry* (report of the Subcommittee on Antitrust and Monopoly, Committee on the Judiciary, U.S. Senate, 85th and 86th Congress, 1958–60), p. 2483 ff. Cited hereafter as *Hearings.*

making, by the collection and furnishing of loss or expense statistics, or by the submission of recommendations, but which does not make filings."[3]   Whereas advisory organizations have formal recognition of their part in ratemaking, trade organizations are associated with ratemaking on an informal basis.

BUREAU ADMINISTRATION

It must be remembered that all of these organizations are organizations of insurers.   They are performing functions which the majority of insurers apparently feel can be done cooperatively more satisfactorily than individually.   Today most rating bureaus are unincorporated associations of private insurance companies supported by assessments based upon the premium writings of their members and subscribers.   With the exception of a few major mutual bureaus, most of the rating bureaus are operated by stock insurers.   In either case other types of insurers may subscribe for bureau services, usually at the same rates as member companies.   However, subscribers usually have little or no voice in the management operation of the bureau.

Although most of these organizations have staffs, policy decisions are made by committees composed largely of insurer officers.   The trade-organization committees are normally composed of senior company officers, while the bureau committees are generally composed of lesser officers.   The chief company executives advise their junior executives on the rating-bureau committees of the decisions made by the trade organizations regarding ratemaking policies.   It is quite natural that the junior executives will act accordingly.   The distinction between rating and kindred organizations is at times dubious, if not meaningless, at least as far as basic policy determination is concerned.   Furthermore, the same organization may act as a rating bureau for certain services or in some territories, and at the same time act as an advisory or trade organization for other services or in other territories.[4]

---

[3] Quoted in 1961 report, p. 21.

[4] Georgia Insurance Department, *et al.*, *Report of Examination of South-Eastern Underwriters Association* (December 31, 1957), pp. 13–14.

BUREAU PURPOSES AND FUNCTIONS

The purposes and functions of all the various rating bureaus are essentially the same. The following list of purposes is a composite adopted from the constitutions and articles of association of several prominent rating bureaus. Although the enumerated purposes of individual bureaus are not so exhaustive, most bureaus attempt to achieve essentially all of the following:

1. To prepare and administer statistical plans.
2. To collect, compile, and analyze the resulting statistical experience.
3. To formulate, file, promulgate, and adminster rates, rating schedules, and rating plans.
4. To make rating surveys and inspections.
5. To establish underwriting rules and prescribe standard terms or provisions for policy contracts and endorsements.
6. To act as agency for members and subscribers for filing special rates, rules, schedules, and forms.
7. To provide a forum for the discussion of rating and other matters relating thereto, and serve as a medium for exchange of information and cooperation among insurers, organizations and regulatory authorities.
8. To promote the public welfare through loss-prevention inspections and related activities.
9. To promote a high ethical standard in the conduct of the business of insurance and adherence to sound principles and correct practices.
10. To perform such other duties and functions as may be necessary or incidental to accomplish the foregoing in compliance with any applicable laws.

FIRE AND ALLIED LINES RATING BUREAUS

Cooperative ratemaking has had a long history in the United States. At least as early as 1819 local associations, such as the Salamander Society in New York, were formed to control rates and commissions.[5] These associations were mostly composed of agents

---

[5] E. R. Hardy, *The Making of the Fire Insurance Rate* (New York: Spectator Co., 1926), p. 43.

rather than companies or rate specialists.[6]   Most of the pre-1900 organizations were short lived.

Until 1810, few companies were in existence, and conditions seemed to have been fairly stable; but many new organizations appeared during the next twenty years, and the supply began to exceed the demand.   Eras of rate-cutting were succeeded by spasmodic attempts to get together; but bands would soon snap and the strife would be resumed. ... In 1821, New York City had a rate-agreement, but seventeen new companies were formed between 1823 and 1825, and the schedule was abandoned under pressure of the resulting competition. ... An association was formed in January, 1826, to make another effort to maintain rates.   In 1835, the New York conflagration ruined eighteen companies, and the survivors promptly raised premium rates to a profitable figure, whereupon there was another influx of new companies and another fight for business. The association was given up in 1843, and again rate-cutting was unrestrained.   Then came the conflagration of 1845 ... history repeated itself; once more many companies were forced to discontinue, once more rates were raised by the survivors and once more a number of new companies were organized to profit by the advanced rates.   Under the stimulus of the law of 1849, New York City produced no less than seventy new companies by the year 1865.[7]

The periods of high profits, and even those with illusionary profits, that existed between devasting conflagrations attracted new competition because insurers were relatively easy to form. This competition tended to dissolve existing cooperative rating agreements.   This situation prevailed for several years.   No formal rating schedule existed, and policy forms varied among insurers.[8]

The National Board of Fire Underwriters (NBFU)[9]

The National Board of Fire Underwriters was organized in 1866, when 75 insurers announced a common purpose in the following terms:

[6] Walter H. Bennett, *The History of the National Association of Insurance Agents* (Cincinnati: National Underwriter Co., 1954), p. 8.

[7] Harry Chase Brearley, *History of the National Board of Fire Underwriters* (New York: Frederick A. Stokes Co., 1916), pp. 9–10.

[8] Illinois Insurance Department, *Report of Examination of Western Underwriters Association* (May 15, 1958), p. 2.

[9] The material in this section is based primarily upon Brearley, *loc. cit.*

1. To *establish* and *maintain,* as far as practicable, a system of uniform rates of premium.
2. To *establish and maintain a uniform rate of compensation to agents and brokers.*
3. To repress incendiarism and arson by combining in suitable measures for the apprehension, conviction, and punishment of criminals engaged in this nefarious business.
4. To devise and give effect to measures for the protection of our common interests and the promotion of our general prosperity.[10]

By 1869 tariffs were prepared for 1,824 localities, a rating bureau was organized, and the United States was divided into 6 departments.

By the end of 1869, however, the National Board's influence upon local boards weakened; many insurers gave discretionary power to their agents to meet demands for cheaper insurance. In February, 1870, the National Board's executive committee authorized local boards to "modify, suspend, or declare advisory any or all rates fixed by them."[11] During 1876 and 1877, it was proposed that the board relinquish its ratemaking powers to the local boards and that it cut yearly expenses of operation from $113,000 to $15,000. Until this time, the National Board had been primarily concerned with rate control, which required a large organization. Only a fraction of such an organization could be continued on such a small budget.

There were several reasons why the National Board discontinued national rating. The main question was whether or not the board could maintain obligatory rates. It was feared that the nonboard element would take the entire business if board members could not compete ratewise. Some members had felt the disadvantages of restraint because other member companies frequently acted on their own judgment and disregarded pledges. This resulted in demoralization and loss of faith among members.

When the National Board was formed there was a complete lack of modern communication facilities. This must have contributed to the difficulty of centralized control and probably

---

[10] *Ibid.,* p. 13. Italics added.
[11] *Ibid.,* p. 26.

accounted for complaints of "unresponsiveness" by "the executive committee to the woes of the local agents."[12]   Other factors that led to the downfall of the National Board's authority were sectional jealousy, varying interests of members writing different kinds of business, and differences in building construction which affected rates and rating schedules.

Regional Organizations

The National Board abandoned its attempt to control rate-making in 1877.   Later, company organizations were established on a regional basis, starting around 1879, with the formation of the Western Union.   This was followed by formation of the Southeastern Tariff Association in 1882, the New England Insurance Exchange in 1883, the Pacific Insurance Union in 1884, and others at later dates.[13]   These organizations provided machinery for stabilizing rates and commissions.   Later the regional organizations established "independent raters," i.e., individuals who promulgated "advisory" rates.   This device was used to contravene the anticompact laws, which forbade combinations of *insurers* to fix or maintain rates.

Local Fire Rating Bureaus

Schedule rating, which became widespread after 1900, required physical inspection of risks and provided a strong argument for maintaining local rating bureaus.   Kimball believes that the fact that local bodies, and not industry-wide, nationally oriented trusts, did the price fixing may have had great significance for the legal validation of price fixing by the industry.[14]   Eventually the operations of the "independent raters" and the local boards of agents evolved into the state fire rating bureaus.   Aside from a few "specialty" mutual rating bureaus, some of which operate

---

[12] *Ibid.*, p. 53.

[13] *Ibid.*, p. 64.

[14] Spencer L. Kimball, *Insurance and Public Policy* (Madison: University of Wisconsin Press, 1960), p. 95.

nationally,[15] most fire rating bureaus continue to operate locally[16] and are supported by stock insurer members and nonstock insurer subscribers.

Allied Lines Rating Bureaus

When the NBFU was established, fire insurance was the only kind of insurance which was generally written by fire insurers. However, with the passage of time fire insurers became interested in other kinds of insurance, including lightning, windstorm, hail, explosion, riot, and others. These coverages became known as allied lines, and quite early separate organizations, called conferences or associations, were formed to rate several of these kinds of insurance.

Gradually the rating of several kinds of insurance was assumed by a single organization, although in some parts of the country the local fire bureau rated some of the other allied lines. For example, the Explosion Conference, which was organized in New York in June, 1917, eventually assumed the rating of riot and civil commotion, aircraft and vehicle property damage, earthquake, vandalism and malicious mischief, and the extended-coverage endorsement, as well as explosion and a few other kinds of insurance.[17]

By 1947 the Explosion Conference was being operated by the same management and office force as the Eastern Tornado Association and the Sprinkler Leakage Conference. In that year these organizations were consolidated into the Allied Lines Association (ALA).[18] A few years later the rating functions of the

---

[15] Such as the Factory Mutual Rating Bureau and the Mill and Elevator Rating Bureau. See Rhode Island Insurance Department, *Report on Examination of the Factory Mutual Rating Bureau* (December 31, 1961), p. 2, and Illinois Insurance Department, *Report of Convention Examination of Mill and Elevator Rating Bureau* (June 30, 1958), pp. 1–2.

[16] However, there also exist rating bureaus which operate in two to seven states, often under the name of the (state) inspection and/or rating bureau. See 1961 report, pp. 24–26.

[17] New York Insurance Department, *Report on Examination of the Explosion Conference* (September, 1945), passim.

[18] New York Insurance Department, *Report on Examination of the Allied Lines Association* (June 9, 1952), p. 2.

ALA were assumed by the local fire rating bureaus;[19] its advisory functions were assumed by the Inter-Regional Insurance Conference (IRIC) in 1954.[20]   In 1963, with the reorganization of IRIC into two new and separate organizations, these advisory functions were assumed by the Fire Insurance Research and Actuarial Association (FIRAA).

CASUALTY RATING BUREAUS

There are two major national casualty bureaus that rate multiple-line constituent coverages, the National Bureau of Casualty Underwriters (NBCU) and the Mutual Insurance Rating Bureau (MIRB), organized by stock and mutual insurers, respectively.

National Bureau of Casualty Underwriters (NBCU)[21]

Although of later origin than the fire rating bureaus, the NBCU has had a long evolutionary development, which in many respects was similar to that of the fire rating bureaus.   National Bureau progenitors date at least as far back as 1896 with the formation of the Bureau of Liability Insurance Statistics, also known as the Liability Conference.   This bureau compiled experience for employer's and public liability and workmen's collective coverages, and issued rates based upon the statistical compilations of the cooperating companies.

In 1911, in the interest of economy and efficiency, the member companies merged the bureau with and assumed the name of the Workmen's Compensation Service and Information Bureau, which had been formed the previous year by 20 stock companies.   The activities of this bureau during its early existence consisted chiefly of the classification of risks, the establishment of rates for em-

---

[19] *Ibid.*

[20] New York Insurance Department, *Report on Examination of Inter-Regional Insurance Conference* (May 1, 1962), p. 4.

[21] The material in this section is based primarily upon New York Insurance Department, *Report on Examination of the National Bureau of Casualty Underwriters* (April 15, 1954).

ployer's liability, public liability, and workmen's compensation insurance, and the regulation of agents' and brokers' commissions. In a short time the bureau became the official rating and statistical bureau for stock casualty companies.

In March, 1913, the name of the bureau was shortened to Workmen's Compensation Service Bureau, but the scope of its activities was extended to include public relations, inspection of risks, and assisting in the formation of reinsurance agreements among member companies. In March, 1916, the name of the bureau was changed to National Workmen's Compensation Service Bureau, "National" being added to give emphasis to the breadth of its scope. Provision was made for the formation of branch bureaus for administrative purposes, but determination of general principles and rates was retained in New York.

Between 1914 and 1922 the bureau acted as headquarters for central committees formed to guide the independent state workmen's compensation rating bureaus established during this period. The central committees developed into the National Council on Workmen's Compensation Insurance, which became an association of rating bureaus, and in 1922 the council became the National Council on Compensation Insurance. Workmen's compensation rating was moved from the bureau to the National Council. The bureau continued to rate automobile bodily-injury liability, property-damage liability, and collision coverage other than automobile. Rating associations also had been formed for some of the other kinds of casualty insurance. In 1918, in the interest of economy, the companies began planning to form a central organization which would supply technical service and clerical assistance to each of the rating bodies, and thereby avoid duplication of effort. The planning culminated in November, 1921, with the formation of the National Bureau of Casualty and Surety Underwriters.

In November, 1923, the bureau organized a burglary division and absorbed the Burglary Insurance Underwriters Association, which had been established in 1908. A boiler and machinery department was established in September, 1924. In June, 1930, the Boiler and Engineering Insurance Service Bureau, which had been organized originally in 1913 as the Steam Boiler and Fly-Wheel Service Bureau, was merged with the corresponding department of the National Bureau. A glass department was organized in October, 1925. After the formalities of organization of this department were completed in October, 1929, the members of the National Bureau which wrote plate-glass insurance became members of the glass department. The office of the late W. F. Moore, which previously had been rating plate-glass insurance for practically all companies writing this coverage, though never absorbed by the bureau, ceased its rating activities in 1934.

In 1936 the bureau transferred its claim and conservation work to the Association of Casualty and Surety Executives, which subsequently became the Association of Casualty and Surety Companies, which in January, 1961, was merged into the American Insurance Association. Prior to this transfer, the bureau's claim department concerned itself with the solution of problems created by dishonest, fraudulent, and unethical claims practices, and the conservation department was active in promoting accident prevention and safety education. These activities being of value to all stock companies, it was decided that their effectiveness would be increased if they were undertaken by the larger number of companies represented by the association. Inasmuch as the bureau never provided rates for surety coverages, its name was changed in 1947 to the National Bureau of Casualty Underwriters. The NBCU is a statistical agent and rates the comprehensive personal liability and residential theft coverages which were incorporated into the homeowners policies.

Mutual Insurance Rating Bureau (MIRB)[22]

The forerunners of MIRB date from the organization, in October, 1929, of the National Mutual Rating and Inspection Bureau, whose name was subsequently changed to New York Mutual Automobile Rating Bureau. Until December, 1932, the bureau

---

[22] The material in this section is based primarily upon New York Insurance Department, *Report on Examination of the Mutual Insurance Rating Bureau* (August 15, 1955).

rated only automobile liability insurance, but at that time it extended its scope to general liability coverages. In 1934 its name was changed to Mutual Casualty Insurance Rating Bureau. In December, 1939, the bureau extended its scope to include burglary and glass insurance. In 1949, in anticipation of further expansion due to multiple-line underwriting, its name was changed to the Mutual Insurance Rating Bureau. The bureau acts as statistical agent for mutual casualty companies.

INLAND MARINE RATING BUREAUS

There are two national inland marine rating bureaus, the Inland Marine Insurance Bureau (IMIB) and the Transportation Insurance Rating Bureau (TIRB), organized by stock and mutual insurers, respectively. These two bureaus are the most recently formed of those bureaus rating multiple-line components. The impetus for their organization stemmed from the *SEUA* decision.

Inland Marine Insurance Bureau (IMIB)

The immediate progenitor of IMIB was the Inland Marine Underwriters Association (IMUA), which was formed in January, 1931, as a voluntary industry organization of stock insurers for the self-regulation of the inland marine business. However, prior to the formation of IMUA "there was some voluntary and self-imposed restraint introduced through the operation of the several so-called 'conferences,' such as the Jewelers Block Conference, the Personal Effects Conference and others."[23] The lack of success of these conferences and the encroachment of inland marine insurers into areas considered the domain of fire and casualty insurers led to the adoption of the Nationwide Marine Definition and the formation of IMUA.

Those earlier developments threatened to cause all inland marine insurance to be placed under an intolerable yoke of regulation through rate filing requirements.

---

[23] "Inland Marine Insurance and the IMUA," *Hearings*, pp. 2670–71.

It should require little imagination to see that considerable violence might result, competitively and financially, to branches of the business required to comply with strict rate regulatory laws should another branch of the industry enjoying freedom from such regulation use its freedom as a device to invade a regulated field.[24]

During several stages of its development IMUA was confronted with the difficult task of preserving its membership and its authority, as the following excerpt from minutes of a 1931 Executive Committee meeting illustrates.

We have reached a critical point in the life of the IMUA and while the questions to be decided may appear, on the surface, to be comparatively unimportant points concerning compensation to various types of agents, to those who look below the surface, the real question is whether the larger number of Fire companies now taking up the Inland Marine business and the older Marine offices which have written it for many years can function harmoniously in a single organization which can effectively preserve the balance between them, bring these and other important Inland Marine lines under a proper measure of control and enable all the companies interested to present a united front against the many opposing influences which seek to restrict the future development of the business. . . .

Members whose background is primarily the Fire business . . . are accustomed to operating in an organized way with standardized form, rates and underwriting and agency rules, although the observance of those rules has by no means always been on a 100 per cent basis. . . .

Companies or groups whose background is primarily Marine . . . have been accustomed to the utmost freedom of operation and to considering each proposition on its individual merits, whether the points to be considered were matters of forms of policy, rates, underwriting rules or agency arrangements.[25]

IMUA weathered a stormy existence, but the *SEUA* decision threatened to sound its death knell. After the *SEUA* decision, the inland marine branch of the industry was confronted with a choice between two alternatives.

Until that time one of our most important tasks had been resistance of efforts to subject inland marine insurance to rate regulation requiring rate filings. We were successful in convincing State insurance depart-

---

[24] *Ibid.*, p. 2671.
[25] *Ibid.*, pp. 2678–79.

ments and State legislatures that such regulatory laws would not be in the best interests of either the public or the companies and, in spite of all that has since transpired, we need offer no apologies for that viewpoint.

The S.E.U.A. decision, however, made it imperative that the industry either discontinue all of its acts in concert and co-operation which were forbidden as a result of the decision or, as an alternative, seek legislation which would give to the companies the legal backing envisaged in Public Law 15, as adopted by the Congress following the Court's decision.[26]

The inland marine insurers concluded that concerted rating, which had long been an IMUA function, was in the best interests of public and companies, and therefore they would pursue legislative backing "just so long as the necessary State regulation did not force into the strait-jacket of rate filings that large and important segment of the business which required complete freedom of action."[27]

In the light of developments following the *SEUA* decision, IMUA decided to divest itself of rate and commission controls and to operate, as it does today, as a trade association. Hence IMIB was formed in June, 1945, to function as a national inland marine rating bureau, primarily for stock insurers. The IMIB is a statistical agent and rates the personal property floater which was incorporated into the homeowners policies.

Transportation Insurance Rating Bureau (TIRB)[28]

TIRB resulted from the merger of the Mutual Marine Conference, formed in 1936, and the Mutual Aircraft Conference, formed in 1941. To help meet the mandate of the McCarran Act it was decided that the rating functions of the Marine Conference should be set up on a more formal basis, and therefore both conferences obtained licenses as rating bureaus. The Marine Conference subsequently changed its name to the Transportation Insurance

---

[26] *Ibid.*, p. 2684.

[27] *Ibid.*

[28] The material in this section is based primarily upon Illinois Insurance Department, *Report of Convention Examination of Transportation Insurance Rating Bureau* (October 10, 1956).

Rating Bureau. In January, 1947, the Aircraft Conference was merged with TIRB. TIRB is licensed to rate inland marine, aircraft physical damage, and multiple-line insurance.

SUMMARY AND CONCLUSIONS

National Fire Rating Bureau

Of the three kinds of rating bureaus which rate multiple-line components—fire, casualty, and inland marine—only the fire bureaus operate on a local basis. However, almost a century ago fire rating was attempted on a national basis by NBFU. This effort failed for several reasons, not the least of which must have been the lack of modern communications. This tends to be borne out by the fact that the casualty and inland marine bureaus, and even some "specialty" fire bureaus, all of more recent origin than NBFU, have functioned satisfactorily on a national basis. Although there are good reasons why fire rating also should be centralized in a national bureau, and such a proposal has been made on several occasions, the opponents of this idea have prevailed.[29]

While the situation is difficult to evaluate, it seems logical to believe that the complex task of coordinating the operations of a multitude of fire rating bureaus with those of the casualty and inland marine bureaus tended to slow down the development of multiple-line coverages.

Bureau "Jurisdiction"

The previous discussion should make it apparent that the extent of any bureau's "jurisdiction" (scope of operation geographically and by types of insurance) is mainly a matter of accommodating its member and subscriber insurers. Legally any rating bureau may obtain license authority to rate any kind of

---

[29] See documents from the National Board of Fire Underwriters reproduced in *Hearings,* pp. 4108–16, and documents from American Insurance Association reproduced in *Hearings,* pp. 2960–99.

insurance for which it is properly qualified. The history of rating bureaus in this country is replete with examples of bureaus accommodating their affiliates by rating additional coverages.

From a legal viewpoint, the question of bureau "jurisdiction" does not involve pre-emption of an area of rating activity. However, as will be discussed more fully in later chapters, in many states an insurer is prohibited specifically or by implication from belonging to more than one bureau for the same kind of insurance.[30] Thus there were practical problems created by the multiplicity of bureaus. Several bureaus sought to extend their jurisdiction to include multiple-line insurance. The discord that resulted probably tended to delay actual development of multiple-line insurance.

---

[30] This prohibition arose to prevent unfair discrimination, which might result if an insurer had two sets of rates for the same class of insured.

CHAPTER VI

Rating of Multiple-Line Forerunners

Prior to the enactment of multiple-line legislation there had been a considerable amount of broadening and integrating of coverages within the fire, casualty, and inland marine lines of insurance. Three multiple-line forerunners that provided better insurance products and wider sales thereof, at generally lower prices, were the extended-coverage endorsement (ECE), comprehensive personal liability policy (CPL), and the personal-property floater policy (PPF). The stimuli that led to the development of these innovations were economic in nature and similar to those which led to the development of multiple-line insurance policies. The manner in which these coverages were designed and rated provided valuable precedent and experience for the development of multiple-line policies. These multiple-line forerunners attempted to provide, and to price, protection for a group of coverages as a whole rather than coverage by coverage. The general success of these coverages, and the fact that such broadening of coverage within a single policy for personal risks had seemed to reach a limit within the monoline legal framework, provided impetus for the passage of multiple-line legislation.

The package approach, which is widely used today, was one method of providing comprehensive coverage prior to enactment of multiple-line legislation. This method was used first to combine coverages which were classified under a single type of insuring power, such as fire or casualty. The extended-coverage endorsement and the comprehensive liability policies are of this type. There were also policies, such as the personal-property floater, which provided all-risk property-damage coverage. These were, in essence, multiple-line policies; however, they were arbitrarily classified under a single insuring power—that of inland marine insurance. This chapter is devoted to a study of these three important coverages.

THE EXTENDED-COVERAGE ENDORSEMENT (ECE)

Background

Although all the coverages provided by the ECE came within the charter powers of fire insurers, not all fire rating bureaus rated its component coverages. The nationally operating Explosion Conference, organized in June, 1917, rated the perils of explosion, riot, and civil commotion. The Eastern Tornado Insurance Association, organized in December, 1916, rated windstorm coverage in the eastern states. However, in the rest of the country, especially in the Middle West, where over half of the windstorm premium volume originated, the rating of windstorm insurance had been done by the fire rating bureaus for many years.[1]

The exact origin of the ECE is difficult to pinpoint. Certain of its coverages were combined at a very early date. Shortly after World War I a policy was issued which insured against riot, insurrection, civil commotion, and explosion at "a rate as low as had originally been charged for the natural gas explosion clause alone."[2] It was said that the integration of coverages in a single policy helped contribute to the low rate.[3]

Great impetus was provided for the development of broader coverages by favorable loss experience and a reduction in premium

---

[1] For example, provision was made for the writing of tornado insurance at least as early as 1910 in the *Advisory Rules* of the Illinois Inspection Bureau.

[2] John Eugene Pierce, *Development of Comprehensive Insurance for the Household* (Homewood, Ill.: Richard D. Irwin, Inc., 1958), p. 223.

[3] *Ibid.*

income resulting therefrom. In the 1920's "aggregate premiums on policies insuring against fire alone appeared to have reached something in the nature of a saturation point."[4] The prospect was for continual improvement in fire loss experience with concomitant rate reductions and loss of premium income. The problem of diminished fire premium volume with an attendant reduction in economic operating efficiency and an increase in expense ratios was of equal and similar consequence to agents and companies, so both searched for a premium stimulant. Because the public was not demanding rate reductions, it was possible to try to prevent the decline in premium volume by broadening coverages in lieu of reducing rates.

Several methods of accomplishing this objective were suggested and tried. At the time, at least three methods were considered, each at a different level of integration. Probably the least desirable of the three methods was employed in the "dwelling catastrophe cover supplemental contract," commonly called the supplemental contract, which was an immediate forerunner of the ECE. The shortcoming of this approach lay in its nature as a rider, or optional extra, a low level of integration. Less aggressive agents might not sell the rider because of the extra sales effort and operations involved; skeptical insureds might feel they were being sold a lot of unnecessary trimmings because the additional coverages were not integrated into a single policy with fire peril. However, because of its wide use the supplemental contract is discussed further below.

A more desirable method involved a two-item *policy*, with a separate rate for fire and lightning and a separate rate for the additional coverages. This method represented a higher level of integration than the supplemental contract because the additional coverages were printed in a single document with the fire policy. However, the insured still had to elect specifically the additional coverages and a separate rate was charged for the inclusion of the additional coverages. This method is currently being used in the "dwelling and contents" form; however, it apparently received

---

[4] *Ibid.*, p. 225.

little favor in the twenties and thirties, except in the Middle West, where there had been frequent windstorms. Because the windstorm hazard was well recognized by the insuring public and mortgage lending agencies, considerable use was made of a combination fire and tornado policy in this part of the country. However, the combined policy was written at the full fire and tornado rates; there was no rate reduction afforded on the tornado rate. A higher level of integration was also considered at that time in the form of the so-called comprehensive policy, a discussion of which follows.

The Comprehensive Policy

This policy, which represents the highest level of integration of the three methods being discussed, also apparently received little favor at the time it was proposed. However, it deserves detailed study because it foreshadowed the homeowners concept and certain of its principles were applied in the construction of the supplemental contract.

This policy was proposed in 1930 by an Ohio agent in a truly visionary analysis of the problem of falling premiums which was confronting companies and agents.[5] He proposed to supplant the standard fire policy with the comprehensive policy, which would be a single-amount contract. Each of the additional perils would be for the same amount as the fire coverage. The fire coverage would also be the basis of contribution for all items of coverage in the pro rata contribution clause. This meant that the insured would have to purchase the same amount of coverage against the additional perils as he purchased against fire or otherwise he would not be entirely indemnified for losses due to any of the additional perils.

The only way to get insurance to value on the additional coverages was to relate them to the fire coverage. By including all of the coverages in the policy at a single rate, it was thought

_____
[5] Clayton G. Hale, "A Comprehensive Policy," *The Spectator* (December 11, 1930), p. 28 ff.

that the policy would be considered "the standard proposition." With all of the coverages recited in the policy, the agents could use the policy just as it was printed and insureds were more likely to accept the policy without modification. To accommodate those insureds insisting upon fire and lightning only, the additional coverages could be endorsed out, but this would require specific election not to buy. It was suggested that the mechanics of endorsing out the additional coverages be cumbersome in order to influence agents to sell and insureds to buy the entire policy. Election not to buy would require use of a prominently labeled exclusion endorsement, which would be designed to place the insured on the defensive and make him begin to wonder if he ought not to have the "standard coverage." It was also felt that mortgagees could be taught to insist upon the comprehensive policy, which would cover many more perils for little more money. These merchandising devices were intended to secure insurance to value and reduce adverse selection.

The perils proposed for inclusion in the comprehensive policy were limited to those insured against by fire insurers because few fire companies had casualty charters and not all had casualty runningmates. The perils suggested were the same as those in the supplemental contract, discussed below. Earthquake was considered but thought of too little significance in Ohio, the home of the expositor of the comprehensive policy, to justify the probable increase in rate that earthquake coverage would require.

Ohio was suggested as an experimental state because Ohio business had been profitable, most fire insurers did business in the state, the state had no standard fire policy law, and the rates for the additional perils were practically uniform throughout the state. Thus it was thought that in Ohio the comprehensive policy would yield a broad company experience, give promise of profit, and lend itself to simple rating.

While the rate was the prerogative of the companies, the agent suggested a three-year loading of $.20 as compared with the then existing combined cost of the individual perils when written separately of $.875. The decrease in rate was justified on the basis of *"wide spread with fair insurance to value."*[6]   In any event, if the existing individual rates for the additional perils were continued, an insured desiring $10,000 fire and $5,000 windstorm coverage would find that it would cost almost as much as $10,000 protection against all of the perils when bought in the comprehensive policy.

The Supplemental Contract

Following preliminary introduction in Cook County, Illinois, the dwelling supplemental contract was adopted by several fire rating bureaus in the Middle West.   In the fall of 1930 the dwelling catastrophe cover supplemental contract was adopted by a number of fire rating bureaus throughout the country to cover dwelling property only against loss caused by explosion, riot, aircraft, motor vehicles, hail, or windstorm.   It did not cover smoke damage, which, however, could be covered under a separate smoke-damage contract.   The rates for this contract varied among rating territories, but generally they were considerably lower than the total charged for separate policies.[7]   The rates were the result of underwriting judgment and expense savings were cited as an important reason for the lower rates.[8]   In the Middle West rates were based on the windstorm rate, plus a nominal loading for the additional perils.   In other parts of the country the principal rate increment represented the manual rate of the highest rated additional peril, and again there was a nominal loading for the other perils provided by the contract.

In some parts of the country the name of the supplemental contract was changed in February, 1936, to "additional hazards supplemental contract."   The limitation to dwelling property was removed, and the Explosion Conference assumed the function of rating the contract, except that this function was retained by the

---

[6] *Ibid.* Italics added.

[7] G. Carter Johnson, "An Analysis of the Supplemental Contract," *The Insurance Post* (August, 1935).

[8] New York Insurance Department, *Report on Examination of the Explosion Conference* (June 1, 1933), pp. 6 and 13.

fire rating bureaus in the Middle West and in some other sections of the country.   Later that year an endorsement was adopted which provided for extending the coverage against loss or damage due to smoke at an additional charge.   A year later coverage by endorsement against vandalism and malicious mischief was made available at manual rates.

The Development of Endorsements

1937 Extended-Coverage Endorsement (ECE).   The additional hazards supplemental contract was superseded in December, 1937, by the ECE in an effort to secure countrywide uniformity.[9] Whereas previously the coverage against the additional hazards was provided by a separate *contract*, the ECE, as its name implies, extended the fire policy to insure against the perils listed in the endorsement as a single indivisible contract.   The ECE could be used to cover only the same interests, the same property, and the same amount as specified in the fire policy to which it had to be attached in order to be written.   This is still true today.

The 1937 ECE extended the fire policy to include direct loss by windstorm, hail, explosion, riot, riot attending a strike, civil commotion, aircraft, vehicles, and smoke.   However, the total dollar limit of liability, or face amount, of the policy was not increased, whether a given loss occurrence was caused by any or all of the insured hazards.   In other words, the policy was no longer just a fire policy, but one policy for the same amount applying to all the perils specified in the policy.   The ECE continues to operate in this fashion.

1939 and 1944 ECE.   There were general revisions of the endorsement in 1939 and in 1944, which included broadening of the explosion coverage and providing for smoke coverage in the

---

[9] New York Insurance Department, *Report on Examination of the Explosion Conference* (September 3, 1941), p. 15.

In Illinois, however, "Supplemental Contract" was used as a subtitle of the ECE "because of such sales value as has been built up in recent years." Illinois Inspection Bureau, *The Extended Coverage Endorsement (Supplemental Contract)* (February, 1938).

body of the endorsement without increase in rates.[10] The former action was not necessary in all states because the Middle West, for example, already had been providing smoke coverage in the ECE without a specific charge.[11]

Generally all dwellings not occupied by more than two families were charged the same rate in a given rating territory. In New York the 80 percent coinsurance dwelling rate was $.06. This was the same as the 50 percent coinsurance windstorm rate.[12] In Illinois, as an example of a state without coinsurance rate recognition in the dwelling class, the dwelling rate was $.18. This was an increase of $.02 over the then prevailing windstorm rate of $.16.[13] The principle of indivisibility was applied to the ECE rates.

Because of the indivisibility of rates, insureds were subtly discouraged from comparing the cost of the ECE with the cost of the individual components. This helped prevent insureds from exercising adverse selection against the companies. Adverse selection also was reduced by providing that the ECE could be canceled only by canceling the fire insurance as well.

The pro rata contribution clause made it impossible to under-insure the ECE perils without also being underinsured for fire, unless the insured purchased separate policies for the ECE perils at higher rates.

Interbureau Cooperation. The rating of the ECE illustrates the working of interbureau cooperation. The fire bureaus generally adopted and made identical filings of the rates, rules, and forms filed by the Explosion Conference, except in the Middle West, where the applicable windstorm rate continued to represent the principal component of the ECE rate, irrespective of rating formulas used in other parts of the country.[14] Furthermore, the supplemental contract had been developed previously through the

---

[10] Pierce, *op. cit.*, p. 231.

[11] Illinois Inspection Bureau, *Advisory Rule Book* (November 15, 1937), p. 18 d.

[12] New York Insurance Department, *Report on Examination of Explosion Conference* (September 1, 1945), p. 31.

[13] Illinois Inspection Bureau, *Advisory Rule Book* (November 15, 1937), p. 18 f.

[14] *Ibid.*

joint efforts of the Explosion Conference, the Eastern Tornado Insurance Association, and the Western Actuarial Bureau.[15]   The Explosion Conference also acted as statistical agent for explosion and allied lines, including the ECE.   In 1942 the ECE became a separate line of insurance in the annual statement.   By 1945 the premium volume on the ECE had become so sizable that the New York Insurance Department recommended that the statistical plan make provision for breaking down experience by broad occupancy and construction categories.

The Effect of Windstorm Catastrophes.   From 1937 until the late 1950's, ECE premium writings showed a continuous increase, which was especially pronounced following catastrophes such as the devastating eastern storms of 1938, 1944, and 1950.[16] However, prior to the offering of the ECE there was "a long and somewhat unsuccessful experience of the business in trying to sell the components as separate coverages."[17]   The tremendous increase in the sale of the ECE can be attributed both to its appealing rate and other advantages of packaging and to the stimulus provided by natural catastrophes.   In consequence "the companies gained a broad diversification of risk which ... permitted the original rate levels for extended coverage on dwellings to be substantially reduced over the years."[18]

This downward trend began to reverse itself in the early 1950's, and an almost continuous sequence of catastrophe losses since then have required both upward adjustments in rate levels and the use of windstorm and hail deductibles, which are either mandatory or waivable at substantial cost.   Catastrophes created rating problems because of the relatively high cost involved in covering numerous small claims and because of the need for providing a catastrophe factor in the ECE rating formula.

---

[15] New York Insurance Department, *Report on Examination of the Explosion Conference* (April 25, 1936), p. 10.

[16] The eventual leveling off and decrease in ECE premiums since the late 1950's was due to the writing of these coverages in multiple-line policies.

[17] H. C. Conick, "Multiple Line Insurance," address before the Southwest Chapter of the Society of Chartered Property and Casualty Underwriters at Dallas, Texas, November 3, 1950 (mimeo).

[18] *Ibid.*   In Illinois the ECE rate went from $.18 in 1937 to $.12 by 1957.

Deductibles in ECE. In July, 1949, the New York Insurance Department approved an ECE filing made by the Allied Lines Association providing for an optional $50 deductible applicable to losses by windstorm and hail.[19] Proposals for a mandatory deductible or a minimum additional premium for elimination of the deductible were not approved in New York because it was believed that full coverage should be available for those who desired it, at an appropriate rate. Subsequent experience indicated that the difference in rate at the time between full and deductible coverage was not sufficient to induce the *purchase* of deductible coverage on dwellings. Another problem with deductibles was, and is, inducing agents to *sell* them. Many agents dread having to tell an insured that a loss is not covered or will not be paid in full because of a deductible clause.

During 1951 the New York Fire Insurance Rating Organization (NYFIRO) filed an ECE rate revision, which was approved by the New York Insurance Department, that increased rates for full and deductible coverages on dwellings 100 and 60 percent, respectively. In this filing the differential between deductible and full-coverage rates on dwellings was increased from $.02 to $.06. This revision reflected the severe loss experience resulting from the catastrophic windstorm in the northeastern states in November, 1950. This storm climaxed a 10-year period, ending December 31, 1950, that developed a loss ratio of 106 percent in New York.[20]

ECE experience has clearly indicated the desirability of placing coverages which include the peril of windstorm on a deductible basis. The 1951 New York revision was designed to encourage the sale of deductible coverage. In approximately 30 states deductibles are now mandatory, and in most of the other states the forms are on a deductible basis with a provision for the "buy-back" of full coverage at a substantial premium. In Illinois, for

[19] New York Insurance Department, *Report on Examination of the Allied Lines Association* (June 9, 1952), p. 30.

[20] Documents from the New York Fire Insurance Rating Organization reproduced in *Hearings on the Insurance Industry* (report of the Subcommittee on Antitrust and Monopoly, Committee on the Judiciary, U.S. Senate, 85th and 86th Congress, 1958–60), p. 3298. Cited hereafter as *Hearings*.

example, the $50 deductible may be waived for an annual premium of $16.

A mandatory deductible as to windstorm and hail in the ECE is the ultimate objective. ... With an optional deductible, a "buy-back" at a realistic flat premium charge is preferable to a rate differential as an incentive toward the increased use of the deductible, particularly in the dwelling class. ... This has indeed been the recent experience in a Middle-western State as compared with the experience with the previous inadequate sale of deductible cover at a rate charge.[21]

A 1955 Eastern Underwriters Association (EUA) report covering 12 states showed that there were 98,770 claims totaling $10,931,742 resulting from a hurricane which occurred in 1944. Of these claims, approximately 56 percent were under $50 and accounted for 11 percent of total payments.[22] The report stated that a 1950 northeastern storm produced approximately 1.5 million claims amounting to $150 million. A review of nearly 500,000 of these claims showed 40 percent under $50. Furthermore, seasonal winds and thunderstorms result in thousands of small claims. In 1955 the EUA estimated that it costs a minimum of $10 per claim to adjust claims under $50. Processing costs in agency and company offices were not included in this estimated minimum. The report also revealed that a study of 846,641 claims totaling $32,794,817 which were reported by the Western Underwriters Association (WUA) companies for 1950 showed that some 606,680, or approximately 70 percent, were less than $50 each and represented approximately 28 percent of the total dollar amount paid for all the claims. Because of the difficulty in distinguishing between maintenance and proper insurance losses and the disproportionate cost of adjusting small losses, the EUA declared that the use of a mandatory deductible was essential to retaining a reasonable rate level for ECE.[23]

---

[21] Documents from the Inter-Regional Insurance Conference reproduced in *Hearings*, p. 2923.

[22] Eastern Underwriters Association, Public Relations Committee, *History and Development, Mandatory $50 Loss Deductible Clause, Windstorm and Hail Perils—Extended Coverage Endorsement* (July, 1955).

[23] *Ibid.*

Catastrophe Factor in ECE Rates. ECE rate-level revisions generally followed the same methods as those used for fire revisions, except that the period of review was usually longer, being 10 to 15 years. The overall underwriting experience for the ECE for the past 20 years has not been satisfactory. An acceptable solution to this problem requires a rate structure that is neither "inadequate ... redundant or ... wildly gyrating."[24] The general principles upon which ECE rate levels should be revised lie in the answers to four questions presented by a National Association of Insurance Commissioners (NAIC) subcommittee studying this problem. The questions concern (1) the definition of an ECE catastrophe, (2) the territorial basis for application of the definition, (3) the period of time over which catastrophe experience should be related to rates, and (4) the conversion of this experience into a percentage factor or element to be added to the normal ECE rate.[25]

An industry committee recommended answers to these questions along the following lines:[26]

1. Definition of Catastrophe. A catastrophe should be defined as any occurrence of ECE perils which results in aggregate losses in excess of whichever of the following amounts is the greater:

 (a) $1 million or

 (b) 50 percent of the earned ECE premium of the state at the current rate level as applied to the year of occurrence of the loss.

2. Territorial Basis. The catastrophe definition should be applied to each state individually. Each state can serve as a reasonable basis for application of an ECE rate-level review formula if the following three interrelated conditions are fulfilled:

 (a) castastrophe is appropriately defined,

 (b) a compatible catastrophe experience-review period of sufficient span of years is selected, and

 (c) a provision is provided for a minimum catastrophe factor in all states, whether or not the particular state has suffered a catastrophe loss.

The committee reasoned that a state constituted a practical geographical basis because it was consistent with the pattern of rate regulation in

---

[24] *Proceedings of the National Association of Insurance Commissioners, 1962,* Vol. II, p. 523.

[25] *Ibid.,* pp. 523–24.

[26] *Ibid.*

the United States, even though it was recognized that the major perils under ECE, wind and hail, transcend state lines.

3. Temporal Basis. The noncatastrophe losses should be reviewed over the latest available six-calendar-year experience period.[27] The catastrophe factor (except the minimum factor, for which provision is otherwise made) should be reviewed over not less than the latest available 15-calendar-year experience period.[28] Consideration should be given to as long a period as the developing experience may indicate.

4. Catastrophe Percentage Factor. The overall ECE rate level by state should reflect both the noncatastrophe and long-term catastrophe factors, each of which should be computed individually. The noncatastrophe portion should be reviewed annually. The catastrophe factor should be subject to modification only at long-term intervals. However, there should be a minimum catastrophe percentage factor (e.g., 1 percent) for any state, regardless of whether or not the particular state has suffered an ECE catastrophe.

General Principles—Extended-Coverage Rate-Level Adjustments.[29] The industry committee recommended the following general principles, based upon the foregoing answers, as a proposed guide in making overall ECE rate-level revisions. These principles were to be supplementary to the general principles established for property insurance rate-level revisions:

1. Extended-coverage rates shall contain a separate element (1 percent minimum) for catastrophe losses. This element shall be determined from all available pertinent data, including, if possible, the loss experience of not less than the most recent 15 years. It is contemplated that this separate catastrophe element shall be subject to revision, upward or downward, only at long-term intervals as the developing catastrophe experience may warrant.

2. A catastrophe is defined as any occurrence (under any one of the ECE perils) which results in an aggregate loss in excess of whichever of the following amounts is the greater: (a) $1 million or (b) 50 percent of the state ECE earned premiums in the year of occurrence.

3. Noncatastrophe ECE experience shall be defined as experience excluding the catastrophe element of the premiums and the portion of losses of any catastrophe within the state which is in excess of the aggre-

---

[27] The current procedure is to incorporate a 10-year experience-review period for noncatastrophe losses.

[28] For catastrophe experience, the bureaus currently employ all available experience, which at the present time extends over about 17 years.

[29] *Ibid.*, pp. 524–25.

gate loss amount used to define catastrophe. Noncatastrophe ECE experience shall be reviewed for the latest six-year period including that of the immediate past year, with earned premiums adjusted to reflect current tariff rate levels.

In September, 1962, the Inter-Regional Insurance Conference (IRIC) promulgated a "Recommended Procedure for Rating Bureau Review of the Overall ECE Rate Level by State." This constituted implementation of the foregoing report of the industry committee, which had been adopted by the NAIC subcommittee. The procedure was recommended as supplementary to "Basic Principles—Rate Level Adjustments" as revised in March, 1962.

The ECE General Principles were four in number, the first three being the same as those above in the industry-committee report. The fourth read as follows:

4. In reflection of the separate catastrophe element, the principle of a 5 percent underwriting profit factor, together with expenses, shall be maintained in review of both the catastrophe element and the noncatastrophe portion of the overall extended-coverage rate level.

Summary and Conclusions regarding the ECE. Experience with the ECE has revealed certain principles that are applicable to the development of multiple-line insurance policies. Integration and broadening of coverages, at a rate lower than the sum of the existing rates for the component coverages, is facilitated when favorable loss experience or other factors tend to reduce aggregate premium income, when competition becomes keen, when rating methods are similar, when legal sanction exists, and when development and rating are done by a single organization rather than by several cooperatively. The expense savings inherent in the elimination of several policies by a single policy also may be important in this regard.

It is possible to broaden coverage in lieu of simply reducing rates when the insuring public is not demanding rate reductions. The attractiveness of broadened but lower rated coverages leads to their widespread sale. The success of a new coverage depends upon wide advertising and promotion of an inseparable core of basic coverages tied to the peril of fire as being the standard coverage. The higher the level of integration, the more the coverages are treated as an inseparable core. Relating the package of coverages to the peril of fire also tends to decrease adverse selection as to peril and amount of coverage because the peril of fire is generally covered more universally and more adequately than other perils. The reduction in adverse selection tends to lower rates, which tends to increase the number and amounts (limits or dollars of coverage) of policies sold. Thus, although it was not mandatory for all fire policies to be written with the ECE, it was necessary for the insured to buy protection against all of the perils in the ECE at the ECE indivisible rate in order to receive the benefit of the low package rate.

The indivisible-premium approach is very important in this whole process because it has the psychological effect of promoting the package as an inseparable and standard core of coverages. An indivisible premium makes it difficult to compare the additional cost of purchasing coverages which might not be purchased as separate coverages. The expense savings inherent in the indivis-ible-premium approach, which tends to eliminate the use of endorsements, among other things, helps to offset the cost of purchasing the additional perils. The increase in protection resulting therefrom is beneficial for society as a whole.

Experience with the ECE has also demonstrated the need to incorporate deductibles and catastrophe factors into the rating formula for packages which include the peril of windstorm. This tends to keep rates (1) reasonable, by eliminating budgetably small so-called maintenance and nuisance claims; (2) stable, by budgeting for catastrophe losses; and (3) adequate, by anticipating catastrophe losses.

Because of monoline restrictions existing at the time of its development, the inclusion of perils in the ECE was limited to those which fire insurers were authorized to write. After the passage of multiple-line legislation another supplemental endorse-ment, known as the additional extended-coverage endorsement (AECE), was developed. The AECE, which is attachable to a fire policy if the ECE is also purchased, extends the fire policy to cover several additional specified perils, several of which were from the casualty line of insurance.

THE COMPREHENSIVE PERSONAL LIABILITY (CPL) POLICY

Coverages

The CPL policy was introduced by the National Bureau of Casualty Underwriters (NBCU) and the Mutual Insurance Rating Bureau (MIRB) in January, 1943.[30] This was the first time that personal liability coverages were standardized nationally. The CPL included, indivisibly, coverages which previously were available only by election or endorsement, and required payment of additional premiums.[31] All personal activities of insured persons were covered except business activities and a few other specified exclusions.[32] Because there was no need to elect coverages, and less than full coverage could be obtained only by purchase of a schedule policy at higher rates, there was incentive to purchase the complete protection provided in the CPL.[33] Provisions were incorporated into the policy for electing coverage for property-damage liability, premises medical payments, employer's liability, and employer's medical payments. This tended to encourage their purchase. All of the CPL coverages were not necessarily sought by all insureds. The desire to allow individual selection of coverages needed had been a principal force retarding integration of personal liability exposures.

However, the applicant would seldom purchase all the types of which he might have some need but would take only those covering hazards or activities out of which loss was most likely to occur. Hence, it seemed doubly desirable that the obtaining of strict equity through careful fitting of coverages should be sacrificed in the interest of completeness of protection and avoidance of the expense of special treatment. The fact that this method also served to avoid adverse selection enabled the policy to include coverages which were often but not always needed, with such a small extra premium that it was of little consequence whether or not they

---

[30] Pierce, *op. cit.*, p. 106.

[31] "New Standard Provisions for Personal Liability," *The Eastern Underwriter*, Vol. XLIV (January 8, 1943), pp. 28–29; E. W. Sawyer, *Comprehensive Liability Insurance* (New York: Underwriter Printing and Publishing Co., 1943), pp. 147–48.

[32] Pierce, *op. cit.*, p. 108.

[33] "New Standard Provisions for Personal Liability," *loc. cit.*

were sometimes superfluous. This procedure also had the advantage that if a further need should develop during the policy term it would already be provided for.[34]

In June, 1944, the policy was revised to essentially its present form. Bodily injury, property damage, and employer's liability were all included under the same insuring clause on a single-standard limit of $10,000 per occurrence. Property damage and coverage of occasional employees were included in the basic premium of $10, applicable countrywide.

Premiums[35]

The Original Premium. When the CPL was introduced in 1943 the premiums for standard limits were $10 and $2.50 for bodily injury and property damage, respectively. This represented "a substantial reduction in the rates previously charged for this insurance."[36] The coverage integrated in the CPL required relatively low pure premiums but entailed relatively high expense ratios. Therefore, expense provisions were an important matter to be considered when CPL was originally rated. The normal administration percentage provision for general liability insurance, when applied to the premiums of the component coverages and even to the ultimate CPL premium, would generally produce less than $1 for administration of low unit premium policies. To provide more realistically for administrative expenses, a constant of $2.50 was used for that item in building up the CPL premium.[37]

From information contained in the 1954 New York CPL filing, it is reasonable to assume that the 1944 premium for standard

---

[34] Pierce, *op. cit.*, p. 113.

[35] The price of the CPL policy is generally referred to as a premium because the number of units of coverage (thousands of dollars of coverage) has been standardized. The original standard limit was $10,000. However, excess limits were and are available. The increase in premium is less than proportional to the increase in dollars of coverage.

[36] "New Standard Provisions for Personal Liability," p. 34.

[37] The author was unable to locate the original or the 1944 CPL filing letters and supporting information. Such documents might not have existed since the filing was made prior to the *SEUA* decision and Public Law 15. However, information contained in the 1954 New York CPL filing revealed the use of the $2.50 administrative expense constant.

limits contemplated $3.55 for losses, $3.95 for expenses other than administrative, and $2.50 for administrative expenses. This meant that only 35.5 percent of the CPL premium was intended for losses. One can readily imagine the great reduction in expense loadings, percentagewise, that must have resulted from the combination and integration of the personal liability coverages into a single policy.

Premium Revisions. There were no changes in the $10 premium which was made effective in 1944 until December, 1953, when the premium was increased to $11 in Missouri. In February, 1954, the rate for New York was increased to $14. Upward premium revisions also have been made in other states. All of these revisions have been based on essentially the type of procedures used in the 1954 New York revision, which is described below.

The 1954 revision was based upon a review of the experience available for all CPL and farmers CPL codes, in classification and territorial detail, where available, for policy years 1946 to 1950, inclusive. Average paid-claim cost data showing the trend in loss costs since policy year 1950 were used to adjust basic-limits incurred losses to the level of July 1, 1953. Because exposures were reported only for a few of the more important classifications, the experience for all 15 classes under review was combined on a total-limits basis (which included data on medical payments) in order to calculate an overall loss ratio. Incompatible exposure units, such as area and residence, are also used in rating personal liability. Therefore, the only way the experience for all liability coverages can be combined in a meaningful manner is on a loss-ration basis.

The expense constant of $2.50, established in January, 1943, had long been regarded as inadequate, and provision was made in this revision for increasing the constant to $2.75. The 1954 filing letter stated that it was believed, even with the modest increase, that the companies would still be processing CPL policies at a loss, from an expense standpoint.

The filing also provided for consolidation of certain rating classifications. The three principal classifications accounted for over 91 percent of the premium volume of the 15 classes under review. It was therefore, necessary, after determining the new rate for the major class, to adjust the rates for the other classes *largely on the basis of judgment in order to maintain logical class relativities.* The major class, personal liability including initial residence premises, for example, should logically have a lower rate than personal liability including initial residence premises with incidental office, professional, private school, or studio occupancy. For other classes not having such a direct relation with the major classes, differentials were based upon differences in loss ratios or indicated pure premiums, as the case might be, which were derived for some classes from countrywide stock and mutual experience.

The use of the expense constant in calculating CPL rates results in a modified pure-premium formula as follows:

$$\text{Rate} = \frac{\text{Pure Premium} + \text{Administrative Expense Constant}}{\text{Permissible Loss and Administrative Expense Ratio}}$$

In the 1954 revision, the permissible loss and administrative expense ratio, including allocated loss-adjustment expenses, was 60.5 percent. This was based upon a 39.5 percent "other expense" ratio which was allocated as follows:

Production allowance.............................	25.0%
Tax allowance...................................	3.0
Profit allowance.................................	3.5
Unallocated loss-adjustment expense...............	8.0
	39.5%

The application of the pure-premium formula required calculation of the pure premium, from the following data, in the following manner:

1.	Number of earned exposure units.............	388,403.1
2.	Basic-limits incurred losses, including allocated loss-adjustment expense....................	$2,055,432
3.	Trend factor to adjust losses to July 1, 1953, level..	1.092
4.	Basic-limits losses on July 1, 1953, level (2) × (3)...................................	$2,244,532
5.	Pure premium (4) ÷ (1)....................	$5.78

Then, substituting in the formula, the indicated rate is determined as follows:

$$\text{Rate} = \frac{\$5.78 + \$2.75}{.605} = \$14.10$$

On the basis of the foregoing, the National Bureau of Casualty Underwriters (NBCU) proposed a rate of $14 for the major CPL class, which was accepted by the New York department.

It should be noted that the actual provision in the $14 rate for losses and loss-adjustment expenses was $5.78 + 8 percent of $14, or $6.90. This meant that slightly more than half of the rate was allocated to expenses and profit. However, the original and revision rating of the CPL illustrate the possibility of reducing expenses relatively as the total premium per policy is increased.

Conclusions regarding CPL

The important principles developed in the rating of the CPL which have application for multiple-line policies may be found in the following:

Insurance for the separate items of exposure had been available under individual policies, and I particularly wish to remind you that for each of these items the expense portion of the rate structure was far in excess of the pure premium portion. In effect, therefore, we brought together into one package, insurance for many exposures each of which required a very modest pure premium. ... We made the package inflexible so that the buyer was forced to purchase insurance for nonexistent exposures. He could not exclude items of exposure and thereby reduce the cost. There perhaps is not more than one risk in 1000 that actually presents all the exposures covered by the policy. Thus, almost every buyer of the comprehensive personal liability policy is paying in part for something that he doesn't need. Yet this has not been a sales deterrent and the reason is simple. The packaging process had greatly minimized the needed expense loading and any attempt to save pure premium by picking and choosing coverage to fit known exposures could only fail because such attempts would re-introduce expense loadings greater in amount that the pure premium that might be saved.[38]

---

[38] Louis R. Burbach, *Multiple Line Package Insurance,* address before the Mutual Insurance Advisory Association, New York, November 14, 1950 (pamphlet), pp. 5–6.

The CPL represented the culmination of a series of broadening and integrating developments in the field of personal liability insurance. Elimination of duplicated expenses which were relatively high in relation to losses provided impetus for development of this coverage and justified rates lower than the sum of existing rates for CPL component coverages. Practically all personal liability exposures were included, inseparably, in the CPL for an indivisible premium. This tended to reduce adverse selection, and the favorable loss experience which resulted for several years after the introduction of the CPL permitted broadening the coverage provided by the CPL policy.

THE PERSONAL-PROPERTY FLOATER (PPF)

The personal-property floater (PPF) is designed to provide all-risk (with specified exclusions) coverage on household furnishings and other personal property. Instead of specifying the perils which are covered, the PPF specifies those perils which are not covered. Because property is exposed to an innumerable number of perils, all-risk coverage is usually more complete than broad named-peril protection. Coverage is provided partly on a blanket basis and partly on a schedule basis. The more valuable items are covered on a schedule basis. This section is concerned with the rating and the development of the blanket coverage in the PPF. The specific rates applicable to the scheduled items, being for property of such a special nature, are not of interest here.

The development of the PPF represented a long period of evolution.[39] Typical of inland marine coverages, the PPF was tailored, and rated, by individual insurers to meet their own needs as to the proper writing of this coverage. Standardization of forms and rating methods for the immediate PPF predecessors was accomplished to a certain degree by company "conferences," such as the Tourist Floater Conference, which approved a standard personal-effects floater in January, 1927.[40]

---

[39] See Pierce, *op. cit.*, pp. 31–91.

[40] *Ibid.*, p. 41.

The decline in fire premiums in the period following 1927 "induced many fire insurance carriers to enter the inland marine business. The result was a continued period of intense competition which brought about several ... changes in floater coverages within a relatively few years."[41]   In 1931 the Inland Marine Underwriters Association (IMUA) adopted a new version of the personal-effects floater which was but two steps removed from the PPF.   The personal-effects floater could be transformed into a PPF by extending protection to the insured's residence and substituting "personal property" for "personal effects" in the insuring clause.

Although coverages equivalent to the PPF previously had been sold under various names, the coverages were not standardized by the IMUA as the PPF until October, 1931.   However, apparently insufficient attention was paid to the detail of the wording in this version of the policy, because coverage was provided for "a number of losses attributable to uninsurable causes."[42]   Many of the defects in the 1931 version were corrected in the 1932 version.

Nation-Wide Marine Definition

The 1933 Nation-Wide Marine Definition prohibited the coverage of property under conditions substantially equivalent to those of the personal-property floater, sometimes referred to as the householder's comprehensive, as marine and/or transportation insurance.[43]   Because the coverage could not be written as fire or casualty insurance, strict adherence to the definition would have eliminated the coverage from the market.   Not all states adopted the definition, however, and subsequently at least 16 states modified the definition to allow the writing of some form of the PPF.   For example, Florida, Mississippi, South Carolina, and Texas permitted the writing of the PPF if it excluded coverage for

---

[41] *Ibid.*, p. 43.

[42] *Ibid.*, p. 56.

[43] Earl Appleman, *Inland Marine Insurance* (New York: McGraw-Hill Book Co., Inc., 1934), p. 180.

fire and windstorm on the residence of the insured.[44]

A revised version of the PPF was adopted in April, 1936, by IMUA, effective in those states which permitted the PPF. Revisions were made also in 1938, 1942, and 1945. Several of the modifications in the 1945 revision "were obviously in answer to changes in the competing forms which it was intended to supplant in the individual case, if not in the aggregate."[45]

Loss Experience

The broadening of coverage in the 1940's created loss potential which was not reflected in the deceptively low loss experience at that time. Loss experience began to worsen as more insureds and agents became aware of the scope of the PPF coverages. Approval of the PPF for use in New York and several other eastern states, starting in 1944, also seemed to have an adverse effect upon experience. "The severe theft hazard of these areas and the insurance-wise, claim-conscious policyholders obtained by some metropolitan brokers contributed to the problem."[46] Because of the inflationary trend in the economy, the difficulty of maintaining adequate insurance to value, as contemplated by the rules and rating plan, was another factor tending to increase the loss ratio. Rather than try to correct this situation with a coinsurance clause, which might have introduced other problems, insurers required in 1949 that the breakdown of property items requiring evaluation in the declarations be increased from 9 to 15.

Rating

The rating system for the "blanket unscheduled portion of the PPF is based upon a mixture of fire and casualty insurance rating theory."[47] The applicable fire rate is used as a base, to which is

---

[44] A. Chalmers Charles, *Historical Background and Definition of Inland Marine Insurance* (New York: Insurance Institute of America, 1939), pp. 8–9.

[45] Pierce, *op. cit.*, p. 80.

[46] *Ibid.*

[47] William H. Rodda, *Inland Marine and Transportation Insurance* (2nd Ed.; Englewood Cliffs, N.J.: Prentice-Hall, Inc., 1958), p. 445.

added graduated loadings for the other coverages. In certain territories, where the windstorm hazard is high, an additional loading is added to reflect this hazard.

The Marine Office of America (MOA) used the following formula in 1941 to compute PPF rates:

PPF rate = A, basic fire rate, plus B, tornado rate (loading where required), plus C, PPF loading-charge rate.

"From the outset, PPF loadings have been on a territorial basis originally influenced to some extent by the early burglary territories."[48] Furthermore, following casualty practice, the loadings were on a graduated basis. For example, the 1941 MOA loadings varied according to territory and policy size in the following manner:

First $5,000	Next $5,000	Next $10,000	Next $30,000	Excess of $50,000
$.95–1.15	$.65–.75	$.25–.30	$.10–.10	$.10–.10

The fire rate was not graduated because it was felt that a total fire loss was a possibility in almost any residence.[49] The PPF loadings, which are the charges made for the coverages other than fire in the PPF, are graduated. This is because for most of these coverages "there is not the same chance of a total loss under the larger policies."[50] It might seem more logical to build the PPF rate using both fire and ECE rates as a base upon which to add a loading for the other hazards, but this was not done because the PPF rating system was formulated before the ECE had been developed.[51] "A judgment factor was included in the loading to take care of windstorm (the principal extended-coverage hazard) except in those states where the hazard of windstorm was considered to be high."[52] In such states a separate windstorm loading

---

[48] Letter to the author from Robert B. Taylor, assistant to the general manager, IMIB, August 20, 1963.

[49] Rodda, *op. cit.*, p. 445. The present use of "loss constants" in many states, however, is tantamount to the use of a graded rate.

[50] *Ibid.*

[51] *Ibid.*, p. 446.

[52] *Ibid.*

was required. Subsequently, with the development of the ECE, provision was made to charge a loading (where required) for windstorm and hail equal to the contents ECE rate or the contents 80 percent coinsurance windstorm rate, whichever was less.[53]

Deductibles. Originally, the PPF provided full coverage, i.e., no deductibles were used. However, in 1944, when inland marine insurers were authorized to write the PPF in New York, optional deductibles of either $15 or $25 were provided, at 20 percent and 30 percent rate reductions, respectively. Later when $50 deductible coverage on contents in the open became optional under windstorm and hail insurance and the ECE at reduced rates, it became necessary, if such deductible rates were used as a PPF loading, to make the PPF subject to a deductible with respect to windstorm and hail. Because of the extremely poor loss experience under full coverage, a $50 deductible clause was introduced in April, 1951, at a 50 percent reduction in *rate* for the blanket coverage, subject to a minimum reduction of $20 and a maximum of $50.[54] "Due to severe loss ratios and the difficult market situation,"[55] in April, 1951, a rate revision, estimated as a 25 percent increase, also was made for the New York City counties by increasing loadings and minimum premiums.[56]

Rate Revision Formula. In February, 1953, IMIB adopted a rate level revision formula which used actual losses and expenses incurred and provided 6 percent for profit and contingencies as related to earned premiums.[57]

The general procedure provided for annual review of the experience of the latest preceding five years available, adjusted for interim rate revisions. Incurred losses and earned premiums would be determined from the IMIB statistical reports. Incurred expenses would be determined from the Insurance Expense Exhibit.

---

[53] Inland Marine Insurance Bureau, *Forms-Rules-Rates, PPF,* reprinted July, 1950.

[54] New York Insurance Department, *Report on Examination of the Inland Marine Insurance Bureau* (September 1, 1961), p. 112.

[55] *Ibid.* (March 1, 1955), p. 75.

[56] *Ibid.* (September 1, 1961), p. 112.

[57] *Ibid.,* (March 1, 1955), pp. 85–6.

In adopting the formula the bureau stated:

It is essential in rate making and in the adjustment of rate levels that due consideration be given to certain fundamental factors to avoid frequent rate changes which produce little in the way of savings to the Assured or increased revenue to the companies, as well as curtailment of available market by reason of rates considered inadequate for the risks assumed, regardless of statistical indications.[58]

Therefore, the formula indication would be limited by the following factors:

1. Limitation of any single indicated increase or decrease not to exceed 25 percent to avoid reversal of trends in future reviews.
2. A reasonable latitude, which will vary by class, within which no change will be made, so as to avoid inconsequential changes which are costly, impractical, and serve little, if any, useful purpose.
3. Trend, if a major change from the norm is indicated.
4. Credibility of the figures under review, considering among other things, the premium volume of the class and nature of the risks involved from the standpoint of loss frequency and susceptibility.[59]

Trend in Loadings. Since 1953 IMIB has made a number of countrywide rate revisions, generally following the 1953 formula. In accordance with experience indications over a period of five years, PPF loadings have been increased and decreased, depending upon the rating territory. However, the general trend has been an increase in loadings coupled with increased deductible requirements. In April, 1963, loadings varied according to territory and policy size in the following manner:[60]

First $5,000	Next $5,000	Next $10,000	Next $30,000	Excess of $50,000
$.90–3.00	$.50–1.50	$.18–.70	$.07–.23	$.07–.22

New York City Rating Problems. New York City has presented especially difficult rating problems because of the poor loss experience and the strict regulatory atmosphere there.

[58] *Ibid.*, p. 86.
[59] *Ibid.*, p. 87.
[60] Compare with 1941 loadings, p. 120.

In 1956 IMIB submitted a filing applicable to New York City which proposed:

1. A mandatory $100 deductible with a 45 percent credit of not less than $20 nor more than $50, the deductible to apply to *all perils except fire and lightning.*

2. An annual minimum premium of $120 for coverage of unscheduled property.

3. That unscheduled property be made subject to 80 percent *coinsurance* for each loss on the entire policy and for each item.[61]

The New York Insurance Department accepted the filing subject to the following modifications:

1. The maximum premium credit for the $100 deductible be increased to $52.50.

2. The annual minimum premium be reduced from $120 to $100.

3. Certain proposed loadings for Bronx County be reduced.[62]

The filing met considerable resistance from New York City producers. This led to a number of conferences among the department, the bureau, and producers' organizations. Subsequently the bureau filed amendments which became effective retroactively to the original filing date of September 1, 1956:

1. Amendment 1 eliminated the 80 percent coinsurance requirement.

2. Amendment 2 permitted increase of liability for each item in the declaration from (a) to (o) to 125 percent of the estimated values subject to an increase in premium of 15 percent.

3. Amendment 3 increased the maximum credit for the $100 deductible to $60.[63]

A special filing applicable to New York City was made March 19, 1957, following a number of conferences among the department, producers' organizations, and IMIB, which proposed the following revisions:

---

[61] New York Insurance Department, *Report on Examination of the Inland Marine Insurance Bureau* (September 1, 1961), p. 115.

[62] *Ibid.*

[63] *Ibid.*, p. 116.

1. Provision for mandatory deductible but allowing option of $50 or
   $100. Credits for the $50 deductible to be 30 percent, subject to
   a minimum credit of $15 and a maximum of $40. Credits for
   $100 deductible to remain at 45 percent, subject to a minimum
   credit of $20 and a maximum of $60.
2. Elimination of the coinsurance clause.
3. The limits of liability set forth for separate items (a) to (o) to be
   subject to an extension with respect to property acquired subsequent to policy inception not to exceed 10 percent of the blanket
   portion (3a of the policy) or $2,500, whichever is less.[64]

Two days later the New York Insurance Department accepted
the filing with the understanding that policies issued under the
filing of September 1, 1956, would be construed as covering in
accordance with the revised rules regarding coinsurance and limits
of liability. Another 1957 filing eliminated the $15 deductible in
certain New York counties.

In a filing in January, 1959, further retrenchment included
elimination of the $25 deductible and exclusion of losses caused by
pets, flood, and accumulation of exterior surface and subsurface
water.[65] However, certain liberalizations of coverage were
included with this filing to correspond with similar coverage in the
homeowners policies.

Conclusions regarding PPF

The rating of the PPF has illustrated certain negative features
to be avoided in rating multiple-line policies. Probably the most
significant features relate to the necessity for a deductible provision in the writing of broad property damage coverage and
the need for some control over insurance to value when rates
contemplate a high percentage of value insured. The rating of the
PPF could be simplified, it seems, by the use of premium tables,
such as those used in pricing homeowners, which are explained
later. At least two insurance departments have questioned the
propriety of continuing to use fire rates as a base for inland marine

---

[64] *Ibid.*, pp. 117–18.
[65] *Ibid.*, p. 119.

rating.[66] The experience under the PPF illustrates the importance of using accurate losses-incurred premiums-earned data. "It is probable that the early favorable experience was partly illusory. The insurance companies were writing a larger and larger volume of the personal property floater each year, and the experience was calculated as a ratio of losses paid to premiums written."[67]

---

[66] *Ibid.*, pp. 154–55, and Illinois Insurance Department, *Report on Examination of the Transportation Insurance Rating Bureau* (June 30, 1954), p. 18.

[67] Rodda, *op. cit.*, p. 449.

CHAPTER VII

Multiple-Line Rate Regulation

Certain legislative, administrative, and judicial events structured the legal framework in which multiple-line insurance coverages are devised and rated. This chapter considers the effect of these events on the development of multiple-line insurance.

NAIC DIEMAND COMMITTEE REPORT

Consideration had been given to the desirability of multiple-line legislation for many years prior to its eventual enactment. The final impetus for its enactment stemmed from a report of the Multiple-Line Underwriting Committee, generally known as the Diemand Committee, that was presented to the Subcommittee on Laws and Legislation of NAIC in June, 1944. As previously mentioned, the report recommended that all states permit fire, marine, casualty, and surety companies to write the following:

1. Insurance or reinsurance, other than life insurance or annuities, on risks *outside* of the United States, provided each maintains a minimum policyholders' surplus of $1.5 million.

2. Any and all kinds of reinsurance, other than life insurance and annuities, provided each maintains a minimum policyholders' surplus of $1.5 million.

3. Insurance against any and all of the causes of damage to automobiles or against liability arising out of ownership, use, and maintenance of automobiles.

4. Insurance against any and all of the hazards of loss from damage to aircraft and against liability arising out of ownership, maintenance, and use of aircraft.

5. The personal-property floater on an all-risk basis.

IMPLEMENTING LEGISLATION

New York and other important states enacted all five of the foregoing recommendations during 1946 and 1947. However, the foregoing committee recommendations provided for only partial multiple-line underwriting and fell far short of allowing full multiple-line undeiwriting. In 1949 New York amended its law to allow fire and marine insurers to write all kinds of casualty and surety coverages, and, conversely, to allow casualty and surety companies to write all kinds of fire and marine coverages. Similar action was taken in the other states, and by 1955 full multiple-line underwriting was authorized in all states.

However, legislation relating to multiple-line underwriting was very limited in its scope since it was confined to permitting expansion of charter powers. This was done by amending both the provisions of insurance laws relating to the kinds of insurance which may be written by various types of insurers and those specifying the minimum capital and surplus required in order to write the various kinds of insurance. The rate regulatory laws were not amended.

Regulatory problems arose from the fact that multiple-line legislation simply amended segments of insurance laws which generally were based on the monoline concept. Since multiple-line legislation did not change the existing monoline *rate-regulatory statutes*, most states continued to have different rate-regulatory laws for fire and inland marine insurances on the one hand and casualty and surety insurances on the other. These laws generally were patterned after the AIC Model Bills.[1] In such states no rate-regulatory law was labeled as being applicable to policies containing fire, inland marine, and casualty coverages. Differences between the two model bills led to problems in developing multiple-line insurance, although it was clear that the legislators foresaw the use of multiple-line insuring powers to provide multiple-line policies.

The statutory provisions of the two model bills were different in certain respects. This created uncertainty as to how multiple-line policies should be treated for rate-regulatory purposes. It was necessary to decide whether multiple-line filings needed to meet the requirements of one or the other or both laws.

The differences between the two bills were largely procedural, involving such matters as the type of deviations allowed. The basic requirements and objectives of the two were fundamentally the same. However, the existing differences presented an opportunity for those opposed to multiple-line underwriting, those desiring a slower pace of development, and those disfavoring independent filings to raise questions concerning the applicability of the monoline rate laws to multiple-line policies and the propriety of independent multiple-line filings. "It was a relatively simple matter to change the laws of the states to permit multiple-line underwriting. It is considerably more difficult to change the philosophy of the insurance business from one of compartmental insurance to one of multiple-line underwriting."[2]

It must be remembered that multiple-line underwriting descended upon the business after many years of separation of lines. During that period dissimilar principles and practices became firmly established. It appears that much of the controversy regarding multiple-line regulation was merely a front to preserve the status quo.

---

[1] See AIC Bills reproduced in *Hearings on the Insurance Industry*, (report of the Subcommittee on Antitrust and Monopoly, Committee on the Judiciary, U.S. Senate, 85th and 86th Congress, 1958–60), pp. 4992–5021. Cited hereafter as *Hearings*.

[2] William D. Winter, "The Multiple-Line Concept," *Examination of Insurance Companies* (New York: New York Insurance Department, 1953), Vol. 1, p. 540.

It is apparent that the legislators were aware that the ultimate benefits of multiple-line underwriting lie in the development of multiple-line policies. This is the assumption most insurance commissioners seemed to have made, possibly following the lead of at least two New York superintendents who took this view.[3] Furthermore, it was assumed that the legislators deemed the existing rate-regulatory machinery adequate and flexible enough to permit the rating of multiple-line policies without undue obstruction, or the legislators would have amended the rating laws as well. A New York superintendent stated:

When they enacted the multiple-line laws the Legislatures ... did not require that the entire Insurance Law of each state be overhauled and reworded. To me this is a recognition that these Legislatures felt that existing regulatory machinery would suffice to permit ... writing of multiple-peril policies.[4]

Therefore, administrators in New York and the majority of other states proceeded on the premise that restrictive interpretations of insurance laws would *not* be in the public interest, and therefore they gave liberal interpretations to the rating laws in order to facilitate the development of multiple-line underwriting.

NATIONAL ASSOCIATION OF INSURANCE COMMISSIONERS (NAIC) COMMITTEE ON CLASSIFICATION OF INSURANCE

Between 1944 and 1949, various subcommittees appointed by NAIC considered formulation of "a plan to create standard definitions or classifications of fire, marine, and casualty insurance or combinations thereof."[5] In May, 1949, NAIC appointed a special committee on classification of fire, marine, and casualty insurance to continue consideration of such a plan. The purposes of the plan were:

---

[3] See Robert E. Dineen, "The Battle of the Bureaus," address before the New York State Association of Agents, Inc., Syracuse, May 9, 1950 (mimeo), and Alfred J. Bohlinger, "The Prospect for Multiple-Peril Underwriting," address before the New York Chapter of the National Insurance Buyers Association, Inc., New York, May 24, 1951 (mimeo).

[4] Bohlinger, *op. cit.*

[5] *Proceedings of the NAIC*, 1949, p. 465.

1. To afford assistance to supervisory authorities in interpreting regulatory statutes.

2. To place kinds of insurance in broad categories to aid in ratemaking and administration of rate-regulatory laws.

3. To fix the scope of rate-regulatory laws as to the kinds of insurance included thereunder.

4. To avoid unnecessary overlapping in the scope of rating and statistical bureau activities.

5. To point the way to solving problems arising when different tax rates or laws apply to different kinds of insurance.[6]

The special committee submitted a proposed plan at the December, 1949, meeting of NAIC and stated that the plan "would be helpful . . . particularly in view of recent statutory enactments with reference to rate regulation and underwriting powers."[7] The committee created by the proposed plan was to have the power to recommend "definitions, classifications and interpretations thereof, respecting Fire, Marine, Inland Marine, Casualty and Surety insurance or combinations thereof, and allocations to a class or classes of any type or kind of risk."[8]

The NAIC Committee on the Definition and Interpretation of Underwriting Powers, which received the report of the industry special committee, thought the proposed plan represented "a forward step in a voluntary program of industry to assist in an orderly transition to the exercise of full multiple line powers."[9] It offered a voluntary basis for achieving reasonable uniformity. The NAIC committee believed that the plan, if properly administered, would aid, not retard, the development of multiple-line underwriting, and, it therefore recommended adoption of the plan.[10] The plan was adopted at the June, 1950, meeting.

The Committee on Classification, which was established under the classification plan, made its first report at the December, 1950,

---

[6] *Ibid.*

[7] *Ibid.*, 1950, p. 104.

[8] *Ibid.*, p. 105.

[9] *Ibid.*, p. 375.

[10] *Ibid.*

meeting. This report noted that attempts by insurers to exercise multiple-line powers led to a multiplicity of problems and therefore an aim of the Plan was "to bring about reasonable uniformity among the states and rating organizations in dealing with these problems."[11]   On the occasion of its second report to NAIC, the special committee acknowledged receipt of a request, and establishment of a subcommittee, to classify the so-called manufacturers output policy (MOP).[12]   However, no report by the special committee on the classification of the MOP ever appeared in the proceedings of NAIC.

The special committee and the plan under which it was created have been largely ineffective. The special committee noted in its report to the winter, 1953, meeting of NAIC that "accomplishment of the objective of the Plan, it seems ... is being deterred because opinion on so-called miscellaneous business is at variance within the Industry and among the States."[13]   The primary purpose of the committee was subsequently changed and the accomplishments of the special committee have been limited to recommending amendments to the Nation-Wide Marine Definition.

NAIC M-1 COMMITTEE

Concern and diversity of opinion regarding the multiplicity of problems arising out of the exercise of multiple-line underwriting problems reached an apex during the so-called M-1 controversy. In 1956 a committee was appointed by the chairman of the NAIC Rates and Rating Organizations Committee to be "a Subcommittee to Study the Statistical, Rating and Filing Problems Resulting from Multiple-Line Contracts." This committee was known as the M-1 Committee. An industry committee was also appointed to cooperate with the subcommittee.

---

[11] *Ibid.*, 1951, p. 142.

[12] *Ibid.*, pp. 344–58.

[13] *Ibid.*, 1954, Vol. I, p. 100.

Subcommittee Proposals

The subcommittee reported to the December, 1956, meeting of NAIC and recommended that multiple-line package policy experience be coded in a manner which would permit statistics for the package to be compiled as a whole and separately for fire, extended coverage, and all other perils—the three major components of the early commercial packages. Cause-of-loss codes were suggested so loss statistics could be compiled for the principal perils included in the all-other portion, such as theft, water damage, sprinkler leakage, and transportation.[14] The subcommittee asked that it be continued in order to receive any related problems which the states might submit to NAIC in connection with multiple-line statistical, rating, and filing problems. A proposed agenda of future activities included consideration of the following questions raised by Commissioner Taylor of Oregon at the May, 1956, meeting of the Rates and Rating Organizations Committee:[15]

1. What statistical plans should be followed?
2. What would be the effect of withdrawing premiums from established classes and placing them under the heading of multiple lines?
3. Should multiple-line premiums be divided by formula and reassigned to specific classes to support the named-peril rates, or should they be allowed to be just a bulk rate and stand on their own feet?
4. In multiple-line rating what formula, if any, should be applied to existing named-peril rates, or should any consideration be given named-peril rates in promulgating multiple-line rates?
5. What type of statistics should be required to support multiple-line rates pending the accumulation of statistics specifically applying to multiple-line rating?
6. What provisions, if any, should be made for multiple-line rating and stamping bureaus?
7. What tax allocation should be made of multiple-line premiums for the support of fire-marshal departments and others depending on special levies against insurance premiums?

---

[14] *Ibid.*, 1957, Vol. I, p. 125.
[15] *Ibid.*, 1958, Vol. I, pp. 215–16.

8. Should the standard fire insurance policy be the basic form or should multiple-line underwriting be exempt from the use of the fire policy?

9. How far should multiple-line underwriting be permitted in the various classes of insurance? Shall we attempt to include disability and life insurance under these powers for companies chartered to write such classes?

10. In multiple-line underwriting, where there is a conflict of statutes dealing with the classes to be combined, which section shall apply, or shall a separate statute be provided to deal with multiple-line underwriting and rates?

On the basis of these questions, the subcommittee proposed that:

1. The subcommittee study multiple-line filing procedures with the end in view of securing uniformity with respect to such procedures among the several states. In connection with such study the subcommittee would consider:

    a. Recommending rules having criteria against which a multiple-line filing could be measured to determine whether it was an independent filing or a deviation from a bureau filing.

    b. Examining the practicability of the so-called hand-in-hand filings by the various rating organizations with respect to multiple-line packages and recommending appropriate changes.

    c. Examining the problem of restrictive licenses of rating and advisory organizations in regard to the propriety of such organizations' making multiple-line filings.

2. The subcommittee study the question of whether the rating laws ought to be amended to define multiple-line filings and to standardize the procedures for handling such filings.

The M-1 Report

At the June, 1958, NAIC meeting the commissioner's subcommittee submitted its so-called M-1 Report,[16] but because various industry representatives requested that an all-industry committee be formed to work out divergent views within the industry with respect to the report, the subcommittee recom-

---

[16] *Ibid.*, Vol. II, pp. 404–408.

mended that final action on the report be deferred until NAIC's December, 1958, meeting.

The M-1 Report was divided into the following six sections: (1) Situation, (2) Problems, (3) Recommendations, (4) Results Expected, (5) Communications, and (6) Details. These six sections are discussed in the following paragraphs.

The background leading up to the necessity for this report was presented in the "Situation" section. The following factors were mentioned: (1) multiple-line legislation in most instances did not encompass changes in the rating laws; (2) "multiple line" was not defined; (3) existing statutory definitions did not adequately define "kind" or "class" of insurance to include multiple-line contracts; and (4) there were no formalized filing procedures for multiple-line contracts.

These factors led to a multiplicity of filing procedures and an increase in partial subscribership, both of which presented difficult administrative situations.

The "Problems" section of the report raised the broad question of whether hand-in-hand filings, which tend to force some companies into affiliation with bureaus, were contrary to the intent of Public Law 15. Twelve specific questions were enumerated. These only partially illustrated the problems created by multiple-line insurance. These questions concerned the distinction between independent and deviation filings and their scope, the propriety of partial subscribership, and its effect upon the income of bureaus and their ability to make rates. Questions also were raised about the practicability of the hand-in-hand filing procedure, multiple-line bureau license requirements, the extent to which bureaus must actually *make* the rates they file, the criteria for distinguishing between "divisible" and "indivisible" packages, and whether the distinction was pertinent to filing procedures. Finally there was a question concerning the desirability of packages standing alone for statistical and rating purposes.

The "Recommendations" section was divided into two parts; the first part included 10 specific recommendations intended for immediate adoption and the second part involved a suggestion for a complete review of existing rate-regulatory legislation. If revision were deemed necessary and advisable it was felt that a model bill encompassing such revisions should be developed. The specific recommendations were essentially as follows:

1. Multiple-line package should be defined as "an integrated package of coverages which includes two or more of the following kinds of insurance, using their customary trade-usage definitions: (1) fire and allied lines, (2) casualty, (3) surety, and (4) inland marine."

2. Packages including fire and allied lines and/or inland marine coverages should be filed under the Fire Rating Law.

3. *Any* bureau or independent insurer wishing to file a specific multiple-line package should assume full responsibility for the filing of the complete package. (Any number of bureaus could file the same package, but companies could have only one filing made in their behalf for each package.)

4. Any such single filer shall file and support the rates, rules, forms, and statistical plan for the complete package. Qualified and competent advice may be obtained from existing advisory and statistical organizations.

5. Companies should be allowed to file independently or affiliate with a single bureau for a specific package and either follow the bureau filing or obtain permission to deviate therefrom. Companies affiliated with bureaus may withdraw from the bureau *for specific packages* and file them independently.

6. Only the deviator and the single bureau involved shall be entitled to be heard on deviations.

7. Deviations as to rules and forms as well as rates should be permitted on the entire package as per recommendation number 2 of the report.

8. Partial subscribership should be permitted without regard for subscribership status on other kinds or classes.

9. Each bureau must obtain new authorization from each of its companies to indicate clearly what kinds, classes, and packages it is authorized to file on behalf of the companies.

10. "Independent filings" of substantially the same coverage as that already *filed for the "independent filer"* by a bureau shall be considered as deviations.

The "Results Expected" from the adoption of the foregoing recommendations were clearer understanding, reasonable uniformity, simplification of filing procedures, reduction of expenses, and establishment of a sound and reasonable, yet not unnecessarily rigid, basis for future development.

The "Communications" section of the report provided that if the recommendations in Section III of the report were adopted by NAIC they should be transmitted to each state insurance department, insurance company, rating bureau, and advisory organization by letter from the president of NAIC.

The "Details" section contained general statements of fact in support of the recommendations made in Section III. The final comment and observation made in this section was that "All Multiple Line packages should be considered as separate and complete entities as insurance instruments and should be so treated in all matters involving rating techniques, filing procedures, statistical reporting and statutory proceedings."[17]

Effects of the M-1 Report

The AIC could not agree upon a unified position regarding the M-1 Report. Five separate expressions of industry opinion were submitted to the December, 1958, meeting of NAIC. Generally speaking two divergent views were taken: one expressed approval of the M-1 Report while the other expressed disapproval and offered alternative recommendations. The M-1 subcommittee meeting was marked by spirited debate between the two factions. Those opposed to the M-1 Report were concerned with preserving the bureau system and proceeding with the development of multiple-line insurance on a slow and cautious basis.

After these discussions, the proposed M-1 subcommittee report was not adopted by NAIC. It was decided that study of the problem would continue with a view toward taking definitive action at the June, 1959, meeting. However, the divergence of opinion continued. Comment was made concerning the fact that the laws of the several states were not identical and the matters in question were then under administrative and judicial consideration. Therefore, in lieu of the proposed M-1 Report,

---

[17] *Ibid.*, p. 408.

the subcommittee recommended "a statement of principle," which read as follows:

It is recommended that the National Association of Insurance Commissioners reaffirm that it is in favor of *vigorous lawful competition* as to rules, rates, and forms, subject to regulation by the States in the public interest, and that it supports the principle that, where compatible with applicable law, affiliation with a rating organization should not affect the freedom of an insurer to file independently any multiple line package.[18]

Upon final determination of the pertinent cases under judicial review, the subcommittee would report its analysis of their import and effect. As of Winter, 1959 a final determination of the cases had not been reached. The subcommittee requested that it be discharged and that the Subcommittee to Review Fire and Casualty Rating Laws undertake its work. This is often the "traditional procedure" of NAIC when widespread agreement cannot be reached on a particular subject.

Although the M-1 Report itself was not adopted by NAIC, its net effect was favorable to the development of multiple-line insurance for at least two reasons. First, the fact that an NAIC subcommittee, rather than an industry committee, originally made favorable recommendations must have had a salutary effect. Second, in lieu of adopting the report, it was recommended that NAIC reaffirm (1) that it favored *vigorous lawful competition* and (2) that it supported partial subscribership. Acceptance of these recommendations was crucial to the unrestricted development of multiple-line insurance because in one sense the essence of multiple-line insurance was competition, and partial subscribership provided an important method of implementing competitive innovations concerning price and product.

The Subcommittee to Review Fire and Casualty Rating Laws

This subcommittee was created at the June, 1959, meeting of NAIC and was subsequently chaired by Joseph Gerber, commissioner of Illinois. The Gerber Committee held numerous meetings; however, like other committees dealing with multiple-

---

[18] *Ibid.*, 1959, Vol. II, p. 542. Italics added.

line rating problems, it did little more with the subject than
provide a forum for discussion. Therefore, the resolution of
multiple-line rating problems was not made collectively by
NAIC, but rather rested with individual insurance commissioners,
the courts, and the marketplace.

IMPORTANT ADMINISTRATIVE AND JUDICIAL DECISIONS

Relatively few important administrative and judicial decisions
have been made in connection with multiple-line rating. Those
that were made, however, were of great significance. The earliest
multiple-line administrative decisions were made by the New York
Insurance Department, shortly after the passage of full multiple-
line legislation. These were never brought up for judicial review,
probably because those opposed to independent and rapid development of multiple-line policies had not as yet marshaled their forces
for concerted legal opposition. Then, too, while the opposition
viewed with alarm the administrative decisions allowing independent filing of the manufacturers output policy (MOP) and approving
other early multiple-line coverages, the feeling (or hope) was
expressed that the decisions would not be considered as firm
precedents but rather as justified prods for concerted action by the
industry to develop multiple-line insurance. While adverse
administrative decisions would surely have slowed down the
development of multiple-line policies, it is more than likely that
the legislatures would have removed the artificial barriers created
by such decisions through passage of additional amendments to
the insurance laws.

In mid-twentieth century ... it was abundantly clear that any form
of the business that ministered to legitimate economic or personal needs
would receive legal approval, *even if that required the modification of
opposing legal rules.* Legal dogma gave way before the insistent demands
of a security-conscious society as commercial insurance adapted itself to
meet the needs of business and as the legislature used insurance to solve
the social problems of an increasingly complex and interdependent social
order.[19]

---

[19] Spencer L. Kimball, *Insurance and Public Policy* (Madison: University
of Wisconsin Press, 1960), p. 36. Italics added.

Licensing of Multiple Peril Insurance Rating Organization (MPIRO)

In the early 1950's the insurance departments of New York and
most other states, by administrative decisions, licensed MPIRO.
These decisions permitted a single national rating bureau to make
and file rates for combined multiple-line coverages involving fire,
inland marine, and casualty insurance. These decisions, which
were not appealed in the courts, facilitated the development of
multiple-line insurance because coordinating the efforts of the
traditional bureaus proved burdensome, possibly because some
of the existing bureaus (or their governing committees) were not
enamored of multiple-line developments in the first place.

Cullen v. Bohlinger[20]

Although not directly involving multiple-line policies, the case
of *Cullen v. Bohlinger* was probably instrumental in directing legal
attention away from the personal multiple-line policies to the
commercial multiple-line policies. The *Cullen* case concerned
partial subscribership by insurers to rating bureaus and independent filings of dwelling fire rates. Independent fire rating is more
readily accomplished for dwellings because they are class rated and
do not require individual inspection by company or bureau
personnel.

In the *Cullen* case the New York Fire Insurance Rating Organization (NYFIRO) contended that insurers must subscribe to the
bureau either for all of its rating services or for none of them. In
view of the impracticability of individual insurers rating all those
risks requiring inspections, the practical result, if such a contention were upheld, would be forced bureau affiliation for all
classes of business. The New York superintendent held that the
AIC Bills, upon which New York's law was patterned, provided

---

[20] *Matter of the Independent Filing of the Insurance Co. of North America,
et al.* Confirmed in the *Matter of Cullen v. Bohlinger,* 284 app. Div. 963.
Leave to appeal to Court of Appeals denied, 308 N.Y. 886, 308 N.Y. 1049,
Appeal dismissed, 350 U.S. 803.

for independent filing *and* partial subscribership. The superintendent's decision in the *Cullen* case was upheld in a New York
state court. Subsequent appeals to higher courts were dismissed.
This decision effectively blocked the rating bureaus from raising
the legal question of whether insurers had the right to use *bureau*
fire and ECE rates in *independent* homeowners filings. This
followed because generally insurers that filed homeowners independently had also previously filed the component fire and ECE
rates independently on the basis of the *Cullen* case.

Smith v. Wikler[21]

In regard to rate filings for the commercial property coverage
(CPC) policies, questions were raised as to whether the coverages
constituted a kind of insurance or a subdivision thereof, or a
subdivision or class of risk or a part thereof, or whether all perils
together represented a combination of such kind or kinds of
insurance or subdivision thereof. The interpretation of these
statutory terms was particularly important with respect to
resolving the privileges and obligations of independently filing
insurers, who often led in the development of multiple-line
coverages.

Under the AIC Casualty and Surety Bill, insurers may subscribe to rating bureaus for any kind of insurance or subdivision
thereof written by casualty or surety insurers. Under the AIC
Fire and Marine Bill, insurers may subscribe to rating bureaus for
any kind of insurance or subdivision or class of risk or part or
combination thereof written by fire or marine insurers. The exact
meaning of these two different subscribership provisions has never
been determined legally. However, similar provisions are discussed below.

The right of partial subscribership connotes the right of filing
independently those categories for which the partial subscriber has

[21] *Matter of Independent Rate Filings for Commercial Property Coverage, etc.*
Confirmed in the *Matter of Smith v. Wikler*, 10 A.D. 2nd 195, 198 N.Y.S
2d 268 (1960). *Matter of Independent Rate Filings* is reproduced in *Hearings*
pp. 2097–115. The material in the *Hearings* section is based upon that source

not authorized a rating bureau to file. However, the question was raised as to whether an insurer could file independently multiple-line coverages and rates for a class of risks and at the same time subscribe to a bureau for the fire and ECE rates for the same class of risks when written on a monoline basis.

This question gave rise to considerable controversy, particularly in connection with independent indivisible rate filings for the CPC policies in New York. CPC policies provide all-risk coverage against direct physical loss to property of mercantile risks. In September, 1957, the New York superintendent of insurance rendered a decision, without a hearing, ruling that independent CPC filings did not meet the standards contained in the New York law and should be withdrawn. A month later the independent, filers made request for hearings, which commenced in January, 1958. The New York Fire Insurance Rating Organization (NYFIRO) was allowed to intervene in the hearings. The petitioners and NYFIRO were represented by counsel, and after the hearings all these parties submitted briefs. *Amicus curiae* briefs were also submitted by the Multi-Peril Insurance Conference (MIC), the National Association of Independent Insurers (NAII), and three insurers who were not parties to the case.

The CPC policies were essentially the same as the dealers, mercantile block, and comprehensive property policies, some of which had been approved as early as October, 1955, in New York, as inland marine coverages. In January, 1956, NYFIRO filed a mercantile block policy concurrently with the National Bureau of Casualty Underwriters (NBCU) and the Inland Marine Insurance Bureau (IMIB). In March, 1956, the North America Companies, petitioners in the case, replaced their independent inland marine dealers filing with an independent multiple-line mercantile block filing and subsequently made revisions in this filing. In October, 1956, NYFIRO replaced its mercantile block with a CPC filing, made concurrently with the NBCU and the IMIB. Subsequent to this, independent and deviation filings were made by various insurers for similar coverages.

On June 20, 1957, the New York department received a letter from NYFIRO in which NYFIRO took exception to three independent CPC filings. The following day the New York department suspended all CPC filings. In September, 1957, a decision was issued ordering the independent filings withdrawn. The decision was based upon a rather narrow interpretation of the following excerpt from Subsection 4 of Section 181 of the New York law, permitting subscribership for "any kind of insurance or subdivision thereof written by casualty or surety insurers or for any kind of insurance or subdivision or class of risk or *a part or combination* thereof."[22] The narrow interpretation was based partly on the reasoning that the *italicized* words modified only "class of risk." The decision indicated, on another narrow interpretation, that the CPC was not a kind of insurance or subdivion thereof, because these terms, "under familiar rules of construction," referred to only those enumerated in Paragraphs 4 and 5 of Section 46 of the New York Insurance Law.

The hearing officer, Arthur Lamanda, stated in the August, 1958, decision reversing the September, 1957, decision that the issue was whether, within the meaning of Section 181 (4), the petitioners might exclude CPC from their subscribership to NYFIRO and at the same time continue to exercise their right to subscribe to the bureau for the rating of fire and extended-coverage insurance with respect to mercantile occupancy classes when written separately. NYFIRO's position was that the CPC filing was made on behalf of all members and subscribers, and the independent filings should be resubmitted as deviation filings under Section 185 (4) of the insurance law. However, the hearing officer noted that the provisions in the law pertaining to subscribership and deviation filings were essentially the same, and therefore, if CPC was a proper subject for deviation, it was a proper subject for independent filing.

The right of partial subscribership, which had been upheld in the *Cullen v. Bohlinger* case, connoted the alternative right of independent filing. However, NYFIRO contended that a company desiring to file the CPC independently would also have to withdraw from NYFIRO for fire and ECE rates on mercantile occupancies when written separately because those rates were a

---

[22] This wording resulted from the combination of the provisions of the two AIC Bills into a single section of the New York law in 1948. Italics added.

"component and integral" part of the CPC filing. The hearing officer noted that essentially the same argument was presented by NYFIRO in the *Cullen* case when NYFIRO asserted that for an insurer to be independent for dwelling fire rates it would have to be independent for all fire insurance. The hearing officer held this contention to be as incorrect in the present case as it was in the *Cullen* case. Mr. Lamanda was of the opinion that Section 181 (4) was sufficiently broad, *consistent with legislative intent*, to give insurers the right of partial subscribership for a kind of insurance or a subdivision of a kind of insurance or class of risk or *a part or combination of any of the foregoing*. Because CPC policies were

...distinctly separate types of contracts covering combinations of kinds of insurance and subdivisions or parts thereof for various classes of risks ... petitioners may elect to exclude ... such types of policies from their authorizations as subscribers to NYFIRO and to make such filings independently ... also ... petitioners may continue to subscribe to the rating services of NYFIRO for the ... standard forms of fire insurance and extended coverage insurance in respect to mercantile occupancy classes.[23]

The conclusions of the hearing officer, which were confirmed in *Smith v. Wikler*, are generally applicable to all multiple-line policies and have been quoted as firm precedent. The case of *Smith v. Wikler* affirmatively answered the question of whether or not an insurer could file commercial multiple-line insurance rates independently and at the same time be a subscriber to the rating services of a fire bureau for the same class of risks when the fire coverage was written separately. In effect the decision provided additional support for price and product competition by independent insurers.

SUMMARY AND CONCLUSION

Multiple-line legislation was limited in scope, being confined for the most part to permissible extension of charter powers. The fact that monoline rate-regulatory laws continued to exist caused

---

[23]*Matter of Independent Rate Filings for Commercial Property Coverage,* reproduced in *Hearings,* pp. 2114–15. Confirmed in *Smith v. Wikler, loc. cit.*

certain problems relative to the rating of multiple-line insurance policies. However, by liberal administrative and judicial decisions, the monoline rating laws were interpreted, consistent with legislative intent, in a manner that facilitated the development of multiple-line insurance policies. The upholding of the right of individual insurers in the *Cullen* and *Smith* cases to innovate with multiple-line policies without jeopardizing their bureau affiliation for the rating services for the component coverages stimulated the development of multiple-line insurance.

CHAPTER VIII

Multiple-Line
Rating Bureaus,
Filing Procedures,
and Kindred Organizations

Earlier chapters discussed the fact that the nonlife insurance industry has generally relied upon rating bureaus for the making and filing of rates for the kinds of insurance embodied in multiple-line insurance policies. Certain economies and other benefits are inherent in concerted rating, and some type of arrangement is necessary for compiling statistical data upon which to estimate loss costs. However, the practices that had become firmly established by the time multiple-line underwriting received legal sanction made it cumbersome for individual insurers to experiment with new coverages and rating plans.

Multiple-line underwriting seems to have unshackled the basic economic desires of individual insurers to determine for themselves what products they will sell and what prices they will charge. In this regard, Roger Kenney stated, "The property and liability insurance business is going through a period of great transition, transition in underwriting practices, transition in competitive and selling practices, and transition in rating methods, to say nothing about the lessening influence of the bureau as a stabilizing factor in the general rate structure."[1]   Another insurance authority commenting upon this aspect of multiple-line insurance said, "One of the definite by-products of this exile from our previous tranquil garden is the emphasis on independence of action and the competitive drive to get there first and to perhaps better survive as a result."[2]

The increase in competitive and independent actions by property and liability insurers appears to have been largely a by-product of the search for solutions to the problems involved in determining who should rate multiple-line policies.   Although the Multi-Line Insurance Rating Bureau was established by a large segment of the industry in the hope that it would bring the industry back to a more unified approach in development of multiple-line coverages and rating plans, it may be that the industry has not yet agreed upon a final resolution of the central question: Who will rate multiple-line policies?

METHODS OF FILING RATES

As was pointed out earlier the basic responsibility for pricing its products lies with the individual insurer.   The All-Industry Committee (AIC) Bills provide in Section 4a, "Rate Filings," that every insurer shall file itself the rates it proposes to use. However, in recognition of the general custom of insurers of affiliating with rating bureaus, Section 4b provides that:

An insurer may satisfy *its obligation* to make such filings by becoming a member of, or a subscriber to, a licensed rating organization which makes such filings, and by authorizing the commissioner to accept such filings on its behalf, provided that nothing contained in this Act shall be construed as requiring any insurer to become a member or of a subscriber to any rating organization.[3]

---

[1] Roger Kenney, "The Question of What a Fire or Casualty Company Is Worth," quoted in *Hearings on the Insurance Industry* (report of the Subcommittee on Antitrust and Monopoly, Committee on the Judiciary, U.S. Senate, 85th and 86th Congress, 1958–60), p. 1408.   Cited hereafter as *Hearings*.

[2] Kent H. Parker, "Multi-Peril Developments," address at 6th Annual Arizona Insurance Day, Tucson, February 8, 1963 (mimeo); reported in *Weekly Underwriter*, Vol. 188, No. 7 (February 16, 1963), p. 5 ff.

[3] AIC Bills reproduced in *Hearings*, p. 4994 and p. 5009.   Italics added.

Direct (independent) filing by individual insurers in the fire and casualty field prior to the multiple-line era was the exception, not the rule. The number of these filings has increased tremendously in the past ten years.

The AIC Bills also provide other methods of filing rates. For example, Section 7, "Deviations," and Section 8, "Appeal by Minority," of both bills provide other alternative methods of filing rates. A deviation filing by a bureau member or subscriber modifies the underlying bureau filing in some respect.[4] A minority appeal filing may result when a member or subscriber of a bureau appeals to the commissioner to overrule the decision of a bureau in approving or rejecting any proposed change or addition to the filings of the bureau. On appeal the commissioner may direct the bureau to make an addition to its filings on behalf of all members and subscribers or on behalf of specified affiliated insurers. Prior to 1950 these methods of filing rates were rarely used. Since the introduction of multiple-line insurance, deviation filings have become more common; however, minority appeals still are used only infrequently.

In the late 1950's some bureaus adopted an agency filing procedure whereby affiliated insurers could file their own programs through the bureau, which merely acted as filing agent. This method differs from the deviation approach in that agency filings need not be reapproved annually, they are more flexible in their scope, and other bureau affiliates may adopt them simply by notifying the regulatory authority through the bureau.

Thus the AIC Bills specifically provide four methods of filing rates. Use of a rating bureau is probably the most common

---

[4] The types of deviations which are allowed differ between the two bills. The Fire Bill allows insurers "to file a deviation from the class rates, schedules, rating plans or rules respecting any kind of insurance, or class of risk within a kind of insurance, or combination thereof." The Casualty Bill allows insurers "to file a uniform percentage decrease or increase to be applied to the premiums produced by the rating system so filed for a kind of insurance, or for a class of insurance which is found by the commissioner to be a proper rating unit for the application of such uniform percentage decrease or increase, or for a subdivision of a kind of insurance (1) comprised of a group of manual classifications which is treated as a separate unit for rate making purposes, or (2) for which separate expense provisions are included in the filings of the rating organization." *Ibid.*, p. 4999 and pp. 5013–14.

method of filing rates.   However, deviation and independent filings are frequently made, while minority appeals are uncommon. Today it is common for an insurer to use several combinations and variations of these methods in making filings for all of the various kinds of insurance it may write.   This enables insurers to develop and price insurance coverages in a manner that they believe will maximize their individual profits.   This is in contradistinction to a strict bureau system in which uniform contracts are developed and uniform rates are made, based upon aggregates and averages, which all bureau members must use.   The agency filing system has permitted bureau affiliates to experiment and to compete on a more equal basis with independent insurers.

It also should be noted that the rates for certain classes of inland marine risks need not be filed and approved before they are used. Therefore, if certain multiple-line property-damage coverages, such as the manufacturers output policy (MOP) and commercial property coverage (CPC), had been arbitrarily classified as inland marine, they might not have been subject to filing requirements, and possibly the pace at which they were developed might have been increased.

INDEPENDENT MULTIPLE-LINE FILINGS

Several of the early multiple-line policies were developed and filed by individual insurers.   The two most important examples of these early independent filings were the manufacturers output policy (MOP), originally filed by the Aetna Insurance Company in November, 1949, with the New York Insurance Department, and the homeowners policy, originally filed in August, 1950, with the Pennsylvania Insurance Department by the Insurance Company of North America.

Robert E. Dineen, then insurance commissioner of the State of New York, noted in a 1950 address[5] that if the MOP were handled by the various rating bureaus which rated its component

---

[5] Robert E. Dineen, "The Battle of the Bureaus," address before the New York State Association of Agents, Inc., Syracuse, May 9, 1950 (mimeo).

coverages, consideration would have been required by thirty-eight separate rating organizations and little progress had been made toward integrating or coordinating the operations of the various rating bureaus. However, Aetna's independent MOP filing met with extensive opposition regarding which Superintendent Dineen stated:

> A very sizeable amount of the opposition to the Aetna plan came from companies which had no firm convictions against multiple line or all risk underwriting. In fact ... many of these companies are prepared to introduce all risk coverages themselves, but because of long experience they are believers in standardized forms and stabilized rate structures. They know from experience that competition in forms can go to extremes. They also know that concerted activity in the field of ratemaking becomes virtually impossible because of competitive pressures when the number of independent competitors becomes unduly large in proportion to those which remain within the bureau framework.[6]

Insurers opposed to independent filings believed that, given time, the industry would develop the necessary machinery to rate multiple-line business, and everyone would benefit from the stability incidental to an orthodox evolutionary approach. Superintendent Dineen indicated that the New York department gave careful consideration to such thinking, but it believed that such an approach would result in unreasonable delay. Although the department recognized that repeated individual all-risk filings would tend to create difficulties for the rating bureaus, it felt that perhaps the existence of these problems would create the demand for their solution which might otherwise be lacking. Therefore, the department approved the MOP filing upon the merits of the filing itself.

From the outset to the present, a large segment of the industry has been opposed to independent filings. Some take this position simply because they fear competition; others fear that competition will go to extremes and will virtually destroy concerted rating. However, independent filings and filers are continually increasing. Insurers that were staunch bureau supporters have embraced the

---

[6] *Ibid.*

practice.   Independent filings have been extremely important devices in the development of multiple-line insurance.

THE MULTIPLE PERIL INSURANCE RATING ORGANIZATION (MPIRO)

As previously mentioned, rather than attempt to integrate the existing rating bureaus for the development and rating of multiple-line policies, one group of insurers organized in 1951 a national rating organization known as the Multiple Peril Insurance Rating Organization (MPIRO).[7]   MPIRO was to function "with respect to all risk, multiple peril, and other policies written for an *indivisible* premium for which members or subscribers . . . have not delegated rating and filing authority to any other rating organization."[8]   Because most of the member insurers of MPIRO were staunch supporters of the existing rating bureaus, the operation of MPIRO was to be conducted in such a manner that it would not conflict with existing bureaus.

The formation of MPIRO resulted from the recognition of a fourth category of insurance represented by multiple-line policies which do not lend themselves to ready classification as, or division into, fire, inland marine, and casualty.

MPIRO members were convinced that the near future would not bring the broadening viewpoint required of individual bureaus for the development of comprehensive line-crossing policies within the existing bureau framework.   Nor did MPIRO members believe that competition would have the patience to wait for a major reorganization of the entire rating structure.   The purpose of MPIRO was to provide leadership for the orderly development of multiple-line underwriting, by standardizing multiple-line policies

---

[7] Even before the formation of MPIRO, mutual insurers found it desirable to have a rating bureau qualify to file multiple-line coverages.   The Transportation Insurance Rating Bureau (TIRB) was the first bureau to amend its license and become qualified to file multiple-line coverages.   In 1950 TIRB also became the first bureau to file an all-risk dwelling endorsement, the comprehensive dwelling endorsement, for attachment to a fire policy.   However, since TIRB played more of a secondary role in the development of homeowners policies, no further mention of TIRB is made at this point.

[8] MPIRO, *Constitution* (June 30, 1953), p. 2.   Italics added.

on an industrywide basis and thereby avoiding the confusion which would be created if individual insurers continued to introduce widely different policies.

On the theory that multiple-line policies were new types of coverages for which no existing stock bureaus had rating authority, MPIRO assumed the function of rating policies such as the manufacturers output policy (MOP) and the homeowners. These were coverages for which insurers had not delegated rating and filing authority to other bureaus. However, individual insurers and other organizations continued to develop multiple-line coverages.[9]

Although it had become a member of MPIRO, the Insurance Company of North America (INA), the developer of the homeowners policy, continued to use its original homeowners filings and also developed new homeowners forms. This action by INA exerted competitive pressures upon MPIRO and its individual members. INA, however, eventually withdrew its affiliation with MPIRO[10] and has continued to operate independently in the homeowners categories. For various reasons, some of which are discussed below, MPIRO failed to receive enough widespread industry support to continue to function. Therefore, in an effort to gain more support, MPIRO was merged with a competing organization, Interbureau Insurance Advisory Group, which is discussed below.

INTERBUREAU INSURANCE ADVISORY GROUP (IIAG)

A group of stock insurers, actively opposed to the concept that multiple-line policies constituted a new kind of insurance, formed the Interbureau Insurance Advisory Group in March, 1953. It was the purpose of IIAG to develop multiple-line policies within the framework of the existing monoline rating bureaus. IIAG was not a rating organization, but rather a national advisory

---

[9] For example, the Eastern Underwriters Association (EUA) developed the additional extended-coverage endorsement (AECE), which was attachable to a fire policy and extended the number of perils covered by the basic fire policy. The rates and rules for the AECE were filed by the local fire rating bureaus.

[10] MPIRO, *Minutes* (Special Meeting, April 8, 1953).

organization. The founders of IIAG held a distinct belief that the proper initial approach to multiple-line policies was on a named-peril divisible-premium basis rather than on an all-risk, or even on a named-peril, indivisible-premium basis. The divisible premium would be necessary so that "flexibility as to amounts of insurance and the jurisdiction of the rating bureaus could be preserved."[11]

IIAG performed research work in cooperation with the National Bureau of Casualty Underwriters (NBCU), Eastern Underwriters Association (EAU), Western Actuarial Bureau (WAB), Southeastern Underwriters Association (SEUA), Inland Marine Insurance Bureau (IMIB), and Surety Association of America (SAA)[12] in the development of the comprehensive dwelling policy (CDP), which was designed to compete with the homeowners program. The Mutual Insurance Rating Bureau (MIRB) was also involved in the program on the basis of its cooperative arrangements with the National Bureau of Casualty Underwriters. The actual filing of the CDP, in 1954, was made on the so-called hand-in-hand basis, whereby each participating rating bureau submitted filings in their entirety to the various insurance departments. Thus, in a single state identical filings were made by the NBCU, IMIB, MIRB, and the local fire bureau. Later TIRB also participated and made similar filings.

As was previously noted, the members and subscribers of MPIRO were also affiliated with the existing monoline bureaus. Therefore, MPIRO affiliates had both CDP and homeowners filings made on their behalf. To equalize the situation for insurers affiliated with IIAG and to discourage resort to independent filings of homeowners policies by IIAG affiliates, it was requested that NBCU, IMIB, and local fire bureaus cooperatively undertake the filing of MPIRO's homeowners program.[13] This would enable

[11] IIAG, *Explanatory Material, Comprehensive Dwelling Policy* (New York, n.d.), p. 3.

[12] Although the Surety Association of America participated in the development of the CDP, it was later decided that coverages under its jurisdiction would not be included in the policy.

[13] This proposal was designed, "in essence, to avoid necessity for a number of independent filings by companies not members of MPIRO but desiring to use Homeowners policies": letter from R. M. Beckwith, manager, Inter-Regional Insurance Conference, to Roy C. McCullough, manager, MPIRO, dated January 14, 1955.

those insurers that were not affiliated with MPIRO to avail themselves of homeowners filings, if they so desired. Eventually both programs were made available to the insuring public by several insurers; however, it was the homeowners approach which captured the lion's share of the personal multiple-line insurance market. This tended to resolve the conflicting theories as to the proper rating approach of personal multiple-line coverages and helped provide the impetus for the formation of a new multiple-line advisory organization.

MULTI-PERIL INSURANCE CONFERENCE (MIC)

Generally, for competitive reasons, MPIRO and IIAG companies wrote both the homeowners and the CDP policies. In 1955, IIAG affiliates wrote over $16 million in homeowners premiums, while MPIRO affiliates wrote $43 million in homeowners premiums.[14] In 1956, committees representing MPIRO and IIAG were appointed to discuss the possibility of a consolidation of the two organizations. An agreement was made in April, 1957, to consolidate them into a new multiple-line *advisory* organization under the name of Multi-Peril Insurance Conference. The conflict among two major segments of the industry was thereby resolved, at least temporarily, through the compromise organization of MIC.

A principal objective of the consolidation was the "elimination of existing *conflict* and duplication, in the interest of greater economy and efficiency."[15] The agreement outlined the purpose, scope, and proposed plan of operation of the new organization. Provision was made for filing multiple-line policies through established rating organizations. The purpose and scope of MIC was to recommend rates, rules, and forms for all of the coverages being handled by MPIRO and/or IIAG, and all other types of

---

[14] Frederic J. Hunt, Jr., "Homeowners—The First Decade," *Proceedings of the Casualty Actuarial Society*, Vol. 49, No. 91 (May, 1962), p. 27.

[15] "Agreement of Consolidation between Interbureau Insurance Advisory Group and Multiple Peril Rating Organization under Name of Multi-Peril Insurance Conference" April 18, 1957 (mimeo), p. 4. Italics added. Cited hereafter as "Agreement."

multiple-line policies. Specifically, MIC was to be responsible for homeowners, comprehensive dwelling, manufacturers output, industrial property, commercial property, and the special office policies. It was contemplated that one form of multiple peril policy for dwellings would prevail instead of both Homeowners and the Comprehensive Dwelling Policy.

Although MIC was to operate independently of other organizations, provision was made for balanced representation on its executive and working committees of all major segments of the industry including the major rating bureaus and independent insurers.

MIC would recommend to the established stock rating bureaus for their filing, premiums, rates, rating plans, rules and forms for the policies under its jurisdiction with the understanding that members represented on committees of such rating bureaus would strive to have such recommendations implemented without delay or change.

The indivisible-premium concept, as distinguished from the premium-by-peril concept, was recognized as a "basic principle applicable to various combinations of coverages under multiple line package policies developed by MIC."[16] To help reduce the complexities of cooperative filing of multiple-line programs by several bureaus, MIC promulgated an "Inter-line Insurance Filing Procedure," which is discussed below.

Roland Lange, in his report to the first annual meeting of MIC (described as a report on the "State of the Union"), said "the industry can anticipate prompt action on the part of rating bureaus on any subject under study in the Conference, in as much as their representatives will have been a party to the study from inception."[17] Mr. Lange hoped the policies developed by MIC would become standardized packages of coverages supported by independent insurers and identified by the insurance public in a

---

[16] "Agreement," p. 6.

[17] Roland H. Lange, chairman, Executive Committee, "Report to the First Annual Meeting of the Multi-Peril Insurance Conference" October 16, 1957 (mimeo).

manner similar to that afforded the standard fire policy. The alternative to the orderly development of package policies was said to be "costly chaos which unbridled competition would bring about in a still experimental field—a circumstance which the merging of Interbureau and MPIRO recognized and determined to avoid."[18]

The hopes of Mr. Lange failed to materialize to the extent desired, and to obtain more universal backing of bureau development of multiple-line programs, MIC was consolidated with yet another advisory organization, the Inter-Regional Insurance Conference, in 1960.

INTER-REGIONAL INSURANCE CONFERENCE (IRIC)

In February, 1954, the Inter-Regional Insurance Conference was formed by stock insurers as an advisory organization to coordinate, nationwide, the practices of fire rating bureaus and regional advisory organizations. In March, 1959, IRIC held a special meeting for the purpose of discussing the advisability of functioning as a rating organization. The suggestion for this special meeting was made by the National Board of Fire Underwriters (NBFU), whose executive committee had adopted a resolution favoring a national rating organization in the field of fire and allied lines.[19] Considerable opposition developed to the proposal, and the motion to establish a national fire rating organization failed to pass.

After the defeat of the proposal for national rating, IRIC appointed a special committee to study proposals for strengthening IRIC and streamlining advisory functions in the fire and allied lines of business. Largely as a result of this committee's report, IRIC decided in July, 1959, that, subject to concurrence by the interested governing committees and memberships, IRIC would assume all the advisory functions for fire and allied lines of the

---

[18] *Ibid.*

[19] New York Insurance Department, *Report on Examination of Inter-Regional Insurance Conference* (May 1, 1962), pp. 5–7.

following organizations: Eastern Underwriters Association (EUA), Southeastern Underwriters Association (SEUA), Western Underwriters Association (WUA), Board of Fire Underwriters of the Pacific (BFUP), Western Actuarial Bureau (WAB), and Reporting Forms Service Office (RFSO). Regional advisory committees were to be appointed in order to maintain proper representation of regional interests. IRIC was to strive for closer liaison with fire rating bureaus by reviewing proposals of such organizations and thereby avoiding unnecessary duplications. In November, 1959, the advisory functions of EUA, WUA, BFUP, and SEUA were assumed by Inter-Regional.

In July, 1959, the membership of IRIC also expressed an interest in consolidating IRIC with the Multi-Peril Insurance Conference (MIC). In January, 1960, MIC was merged with IRIC and thereafter functioned as a department of Inter-Regional.[20] A primary purpose of IRIC as stated in its revised constitution (December 13, 1961) was:

... to assist in an advisory capacity *property* insurance rating and advisory organizations in the conduct of their affairs, *and other rating organizations* which cooperate *with* property insurance rating organizations in respect to all forms of multiple line coverages embracing in combination two or more lines of insurance traditionally considered fire, marine, or casualty.[21]

In accordance with this purpose, IRIC adopted in January, 1959, the "Interline Insurance Filing Procedure," which was promulgated by MIC to simplify the filing requirements relative to multiple-line insurance. This procedure provided that upon adoption of an interline rating program by two or more rating bureaus, one such bureau (referred to as the filing organization) would be designated to file the entire program on behalf of the participants, and thereby eliminate unnecessary duplicate filings by all participating bureaus. However, this was in no way to alter the jurisdiction of the participating rating bureaus over their respective portions of the interline filing. Communications to and

---

[20] IRIC previously had been active in the multiple-line field as the representative spokesman of the several fire rating bureaus.

[21] *Ibid.*, p. 198. Italics added.

from insurance departments were to be routed through the filing organization.

Under this procedure, it was not necessary for insurers to be affiliated with all of the participating rating bureaus in order to have multiple-line filings made on their behalf, because insurers could authorize the filing organization to file on their behalf those portions of the program for which they were not bureau affiliated, or they could file such portions independently.

In 1961 the members of IRIC voted to revise the IRIC constitution so that IRIC could function as a cooperating but nonfiling *rating* organization in the development of multiple-line insurances. This action led to the resignation of a number of insurer groups that had supported a national *advisory* organization but which were opposed to a national *rating* organization even on a nonfiling basis.

Ultimately IRIC secured licenses to operate as a cooperating rating organization in 27 states. However, a decision of the New York Insurance Department, holding that it would not issue a rating license to IRIC because IRIC would continue to operate in a manner that was contemplated only under the advisory-organization section of its law, was instrumental in causing the members of IRIC to re-evaluate once again the IRIC method of operation.

FIRE INSURANCE RESEARCH AND ACTUARIAL ASSOCIATION (FIRAA)

Continuing the search for the most effective and widely supported methods of organized rating activities for stock insurers in the fire and allied lines and the multiple-line areas of the insurance industry, the membership of IRIC voted in August, 1963, to reorganize IRIC into two new and separate organizations, the Fire Insurance Research and Actuarial Association and the Multi-Line Insurance Rating Bureau. As of mid-1967 these two organizations continued to function in their respective fields.

The objectives of FIRAA as set forth in its constitution (August 15, 1963) are to assist, and to coordinate the activities of, fire and allied lines rating and advisory organizations by providing a central facility for discussion, study, and research of the problems of the organizations served. FIRAA provides its members, subscribers, rating and advisory organizations, and other interested parties with information, statistics, research, and actuarial services.

FIRAA operates as a nationwide advisory organization in the fire and allied lines of insurance such as extended coverage and water damage. Although the association has a full-time staff, much of its work is done by committees largely composed of individuals employed by its member and subscriber companies. Four regional advisory committees meet with the respective territorial conference committees of the National Association of Insurance Agents (NAIA). Annual meetings are also held with the managers of the fire rating bureaus and committees of NAIA and the National Insurance Producers Conference.

MULTI-LINE INSURANCE RATING BUREAU (MLIRB)

As previously mentioned, MLIRB was created by the reorganization of IRIC in August, 1963. In September, 1963, the entire staff of the multi-peril department of IRIC was transferred to MLIRB.

The objectives of MLIRB as stated in its constitution (August 15, 1963) are to develop multiple-line coverages, rates, and premiums and to make filings therefor as authorized by member and subscriber companies; to conduct research and compile statistics for use in establishing rates; and to furnish information, statistics, recommendations, services, and advice to affiliated insurers. MLIRB represents its members and subscribers and acts as their agent in cooperative efforts with other rating or advisory organizations.

Although MLIRB is organized as a national multiple-line rating bureau, provision is made for close cooperation with those rating organizations interested in the components of multiple-line policies. The work of the bureau is conducted by a full-time staff and by committees composed of staff and employees of member insurers. In regard to indivisible-premium multiple-line programs, copies of all proposed filings and supporting information are sent to affected individual-line bureaus with a request for concurrence. This enables such bureaus to make coincident filings, with common effective dates, on behalf of their insurers who are not affiliated with MLIRB.

MLIRB makes direct filings of divisible-premium multiple-line programs, but with proposed effective dates sufficiently far in the future so that the cooperating individual-line bureaus may submit identical filings with common effective dates. MLIRB discusses the proposals for both types of programs with interested organizations before the proposals are formally submitted to such organizations for consideration. In the unlikely event that an individual-line bureau does not concur with MLIRB, the individual-line bureau may make an alternative filing for its non-MLIRB affiliates to satisfy their needs.

While there is provision for cooperative efforts with the individual-line bureaus, there is no longer reliance on the so-called interline filing procedure, a device that appeared to be "time-consuming, expensive and to involve needless duplication for the companies."[22] Thus, MLIRB is geared to proceed directly with multiple-line filings should the proposed cooperative procedures among the bureaus prove to be ineffective.

MLIRB was authorized by its executive committee to be responsible for homeowners, comprehensive dwelling, farmowners, commercial property, manufacturers output, office contents, industrial property, and the special multi-peril policy programs. The organization may research, study, and develop rates and premiums for other combinations of coverage, subject, however, to final approval of its executive committee.

NATIONAL INSURANCE ACTUARIAL AND STATISTICAL ASSOCIATION (NIASA)

One of the major problems of multiple-line insurance, as previously indicated, involved the development of satisfactory

---

[22] Multi-Line Insurance Rating Bureau, *Minutes* (first annual meeting, October 14, 1964).

statistical plans. This problem, however, was not unique to multiple-line insurance. In December, 1963, a group of executives of insurers affiliated with the actuarial bureau of the National Board of Fire Underwriters presented a statement to NAIC, indicating the nonlife insurance industry's concern with the adequacy of its statistical plans and the effectiveness of the machinery for gathering the data generated by these plans. In June, 1964, a report entitled "The Actuarial Problem," was presented to NAIC. The report concluded that there was a need for a licensed statistical and actuarial organization which would be independent of trade and rating organizations and would develop past and *prospective* loss and expense statistics for use by both bureau and *independent* insurers in rating property lines and eventually for rating all lines (presumably other than life).

The final outgrowth of the "actuarial report" was the establishment of NIASA whose constitution and bylaws were adopted on November 24, 1964. This national *advisory* organization is to provide modern statistical and actuarial facilities for collecting and processing statistics in order to assist rating bureaus and insurers in developing and substantiating rates and rating plans for fire, extended coverage and its component perils, flood, water damage, sprinkler leakage, vandalism and malicious mischief, earthquake, commercial multiple peril (including but not limited to commercial property coverage, office contents special form, public and institutional property form, industrial property policy, manufacturers output, and special multiple peril), homeowners, and farmowners; to promote and improve the actuarial techniques of collecting, processing, translating, and disseminating insurance statistics; to develop statistical plans; and to conduct studies and research appropriate to the foregoing purposes. In April, 1965, NIASA began to succeed NBFU in the various states as the official statistical agent for its affiliates.

As with virtually all of the rating, advisory, and statistical organizations, the work of NIASA is conducted by committees composed of staff and employees of member insurers. Besides an executive committee, there are standing committees of actuaries, of statisticians, and on finance. NIASA has established working relationships with other statistical agents and has encouraged them to use its statistical plans and processing facilities.

One of the first tasks confronting NIASA was the development of a personal-lines statistical plan for dwelling fire, dwelling extended coverage, and homeowners. By May 20, 1965, the plan was filed in all states, and by November 1, 1965, the plan received official approval in 42 states and unofficial approval in 9. Coding under this plan commenced on January 1, 1966.

The details of every premium and loss transaction for policies coded under the new plan will be reported monthly on an individual basis and outstanding loss reserves will be reported quarterly. This should enable NIASA to distribute its work load and to prepare consolidated reports about two months sooner than was formerly possible. Furthermore, monthly reporting will enable more accurate computation of earned premiums than the annual method.

Provision is made for obtaining the number of houses insured, amount of insurance to nearest thousand, and losses incurred, so that loss frequency and severity and pure premiums may be calculated. These items should be useful in the determination of trend and projection factors. The amount of insurance will be useful for adjusting earned premiums to current rate levels. Also the new plan employs the fiscal-accident-year method as well as the fiscal-calendar-year method. The fiscal-accident-year method does not involve estimates for unpaid losses at the start of the year in the determination of incurred losses. However, provision must be made for losses incurred but not reported as of the end of the fiscal year, and therefore the insurers will be given three months after the close of the fiscal year before they must submit their evaluation of the losses incurred during the year. This not only will enable the insurers to pay, or to establish reasonably accurate liabilities, on the incurred but not reported losses, but also will permit them to settle or re-evaluate the previously reported but unsettled losses for the year. It will be possible to re-evaluate the accident-year incurred losses one and two years after the initial reporting date to test its accuracy and to calculate development factors. These factors will reflect losses which were reported very late, the ultimate cost of closed cases, further re-evaluation of outstanding cases, and recoveries from subrogation and salvage made subsequent to the initial report.[23]

Another improvement in the new statistical plan over the 1958 statistical plan for homeowners policies is the expansion of the number of public protection codes from two to nine and of the number of construction codes from three to seven by including codes for (1) brick, stone, or masonry veneer (if used as a separate rating group), (2) aluminum or plastic siding over frame, (3) mobile homes on enclosed masonry foundations, and (4) mobile homes not on enclosed masonry foundations, in addition to the traditional frame, brick, and fire-resistive codes. Nine new codes are provided to distinguish among policies written under: bureau rates, uniform percentage deviations (5 codes), rates higher than the bureau's, independent filings, and merit rating superimposed upon bureau rates. In addition there is some refinement in the deductible codes to provide more information as to the type of deductible, the perils to which it applies, and its size. The number of cause-of-loss codes also has been increased from six to nine.

Although it will be a number of years before homeowners review-period experience can be generated entirely from the new statistical plan, ultimately the new plan should lead to more adequate and more equitable rates.

CONCLUSIONS

The dilemma of determining who should rate multiple-line insurance policies has been a difficult one for the industry to resolve. Currently it seems that MLIRB will be the vehicle for cooperative development of multiple-line insurance. However, many independents will retain their separate status and continue to be important sources of innovation in the multiple-line field of insurance.

---

[23] LeRoy J. Simon, "Statistical Support for Adequate Rates," *Best's Insurance News* (Fire and Casualty Edition), Vol. 67, No. 3 (July, 1966), p. 11 ff.

CHAPTER IX

Multiple-Line
Rating Methods

The ultimate answers to the technical problems of *how* to rate multiple-line insurance policies are interdependent with the answers to the questions studied in the previous two chapters relating to *what* the legal framework should be and *who* should perform the rating within this framework. It was thought by many, for instance, that the initial approach to multiple-line rating would be on a schedule-policy, named-peril, divisible-premium basis because existing coverages were generally rated on this basis.[1] Such an approach would facilitate multiple-line rating without "disrupting" existing rating practices.

However, it appears that the technical rating problems were subordinate to the practical problems involved in obtaining effective cooperative action among existing bureaus. Cooperative bureau rating does not necessarily preclude an indivisible-premium integrated-policy approach, but it is more conducive and logically applied to the divisible-premium schedule-policy approach. There are desirable relationships, then, between policy format and rating method, with some combinations of policy format and rating method being more compatible than others.

---

[1] See, for example, James M. Cahill, "Multiple Line Underwriting," *Proceedings of the Casualty Actuarial Society*, Vol. 36, No. 66 (November 18, 1949), p. 4.

There are many interrelationships that may affect the final determination of the technical rating methods used. The legal framework, while always subject to amendment, is usually the determining or limiting factor. For example, the insurance law of at least one state required that premiums be set forth separately for each kind of insurance within a multiple-line policy. Such a legal framework tends to preclude the indivisible-premium integrated-policy approach, as would a framework that did not authorize a multiple-line rating bureau.

METHODS OF PROVIDING MULTIPLE-LINE COVERAGES

There are essentially three, though not mutually exclusive, methods of providing multiple-line coverages: endorsement, schedule policy, and integrated policy.

Endorsements which include casualty coverages, such as householders limited theft, residence glass, comprehensive personal liability, and additional extended coverage, may be written in conjunction with fire policies to provide multiple-line policies. This is probably the simplest way of providing multiple-line coverage, and it does not directly disrupt the existing fire and casualty rating structures. However, this approach generally fails to achieve the basic purposes of multiple-line insurance— providing broader coverage and/or reducing rates.

A higher level of coverage integration may be achieved with a schedule policy, such as the comprehensive dwelling policy (CDP), which includes optional coverages within the body of the contract. This method is relatively simple, and it can be employed without directly disrupting existing rating structures. However, this approach, as experience with the CDP illustrated, and as will be explained below, also fails to achieve the benefits possible from multiple-line policies to the extent possible with an integrated-policy indivisible-premium approach, such as is employed in the homeowners programs.

A completely integrated approach, such as that used in the homeowners programs, is probably the most satisfactory method of providing multiple-line coverages, because, among other reasons, it reduces adverse selection by type of coverage, by peril, and by amount of insurance purchased. Although the integrated-policy format may be combined with divisible-premium rating, it is better suited than a scheduled-policy or the use of endorsements to indivisible-premium rating.

METHODS OF DETERMINING ORIGINAL MULTIPLE-LINE RATES

There are several methods of calculating the original rates to be charged for a new multiple-line coverage. However, regardless of the method used to provide the coverage or the ultimate method of rating, some consideration is generally given to the cost of the component coverages when they are purchased separately. The rate for a multiple-line coverage should bear some reasonable and justifiable relation to the sum of the existing rates for the component coverages. When there is no broadening of coverage within the multiple-line policy, the rate for the multiple-line policy certainly should not exceed the sum of the component rates[2]; however, there are several reasons which justify a lower rate for a multiple-line policy even when there is a broadening of coverage. These reasons will be discussed fully later in the chapter. In any event, the sum of the gross rates for the component coverages generally becomes a point of departure for determining the multiple-line rate. When casualty endorsements *selected* by the insured are simply attached to a fire policy, the sum of the fire and casualty endorsement rates usually is not modified. There have been situations where a broadening of coverage has occurred in the packaging of coverages, but where the sum of the rates for the unmodified component coverages was used. In other words, the anticipated savings due to the packaging were passed on to the insured in the form of broadened protection in lieu of a rate

---

[2] Harry F. Perlet, "Multiple-Peril Trends," *Proceedings of the Thirteenth Annual Insurance Conference* (College of Commerce Conference Series; Columbus: Ohio State University Publications, 1962), p. 152. The term "package" is frequently used by the industry as a synonym for a multiple-line insurance policy. That will also be the practice herein.

reduction. On the other hand, an additional charge or loading may be added to the sum of component rates to reflect broadened coverage and the possibility of including unthought-of perils or types of losses which may occur when all-risk coverage is provided.

Whether or not a loading is added for broadening protection, the sum of the rates for the component coverages is usually modified to reflect differences that arise between writing the coverages separately and combining them in a single policy. The differences effect both loss and expense experience. For example, the modification might reflect increased insurance to value and economies resulting from handling one policy instead of several. If these differences did not justify a multiple-line rate lower than the sum of the component rates, there would be little incentive for insureds to buy the multiple-line coverages. Fortunately, there are several factors which justify a favorable differential. The size of the modifications is largely a matter of informed underwriting judgment. However, after the new coverage is launched, "the judgment is tested by the reception in the marketplace, by what competitors do and ultimately the experience of the package itself ... you rarely have to worry about the premiums on a new package being excessive; if they are the contract simply will not sell in volume and there will be a rapid revision."[3]

After the methods of providing and rating a multiple-line coverage are determined, it is necessary to decide whether insureds will be shown divisible or indivisible rates and/or premiums. If divisible, premiums are apportioned on the policy among its component coverages, whereas if they are indivisible, only the aggregate rate and premium are shown.

The preceding chapters revealed that generally the legal framework, constructed on a liberal interpretation of the All-Industry Committee (AIC) Bills, permitted cooperative bureau rating, multiple-line bureaus, and independent rating. Also both the divisible-premium schedule-policy and indivisible-premium integrated-policy approaches were permitted. The indivisible-

---

[3] Roy C. McCullough, "Multiple Line Rates and Rating," address before Insurance Regulation Institute, East Lansing, Michigan, February 11, 1958 (mimeo).

premium integrated-policy approach, which was adopted by the Insurance Company of North America (INA) and later by the Multiple Peril Insurance Rating Organization (MPIRO), received an early and successful trial.   Later the Interbureau Insurance Advisory Group (IIAG) was formed, and it adopted the divisible-premium schedule-policy approach.   However, when MPIRO and IIAG were merged into the Multi-Peril Insurance Conference (MIC), that organization adopted the indivisible-premium integrated-policy approach.   For homeowners policies, the indivisible-premium integrated-policy approach seems firmly established; and therefore, while certain comparisons will be made with other approaches, this approach will receive primary consideration in this chapter.

The approach used is not merely a matter of technique, since it tends to affect the insurer's ability to reduce adverse selection against it by the insured as to perils, types of coverages, and amount of coverage.   The least opportunity for adverse selection arises with the integrated-policy approach.   The basis also affects the ability to reduce the expense of rating, collecting experience data and selling the multiple-line coverage.   "There is very little case for allowing much credit, except for that to be expected from expense savings, when the same *selection* by the insured is available in the package policy as in the plan which provided the data for the original cost of the optional coverage."[4]   The full measure of possible expense savings cannot be achieved by the divisible-premium schedule-policy or endorsement methods.

ECONOMIC MOTIVATION FOR MULTIPLE-LINE INSURANCE AND PACKAGE DISCOUNTS

Before studying the reasons given in rate filings to justify package discounts, one should understand two important economic motivations for multiple-line insurance, which also justified

---

[4] L. H. Longley-Cook, "Development and Rating of Package Policies," address before All-Industry Luncheon, Pacific Northwest Chapter, Chartered Property Casualty Underwriters, Seattle, Washington, October 24, 1961 (mimeo).   Italics added.

package discounts; namely, rate redundancies and disproportionate agents' commissions rates. Rate redundancies result when rates are higher than they need be to cover losses and to provide reasonable amounts for expenses and profits. Disproportionate agents' commissions result from using the same percentage rate of commission on both large and small-premium policies.

Rate Redundancies

When insurance rates become redundant because of favorable loss experience, economically it is generally better (for insurers and insureds) to broaden coverage than to reduce rates. This enables insurers to maintain their premium income and insureds to obtain better insurance protection with no increase in cost. This situation arose in 1943, when insurers affiliated with the Board of Fire Underwriters of the Pacific (BFUP) were contemplating rate and/or coverage changes on California dwellings which had experienced very favorable loss ratios for several years. Dwellings produced 35 to 40 percent of the California fire premiums, and therefore it was believed that "reductions in rate commensurate with experience would involve a loss in premium income, which should, if possible, be avoided."[5] Furthermore, favorable loss ratios "made the dwelling house business particularly attractive to nonaffiliated carriers,"[6] which could profitably pay commission rates 5 to 10 points higher (sometimes with contingents) than the 30 percent rate which BFUP companies were paying.

To help alleviate this situation, agents recommended broadening coverage by (1) making a 10 percent extension of coverage on outbuildings; (2) allowing automatic reinstatement; (3) including coverage for cost of debris removal; (4) including $100 coverage on trees and shrubbery; (5) allowing removal to *any* new location for 120 days; (6) extending the rental-value endorsement to cover additional living expenses up to 10 percent of the basic coverage; and (7) eliminating the electrical exemption clause.[7] While it

---

[5] Special Subcommittee of the Executive Committee on the Board of Fire Underwriters of the Pacific, "Report on Dwelling House Forms and Rates" (March 11, 1943, mimeo). Cited hereafter as "1943 report."

[6] *Ibid.*

[7] *Ibid.*

was believed that these concessions could be made with very little increase in loss ratios, it was felt that granting concessions would not solve the competitive problem because they would afford little, if any, sales motivation to the public. Conditions seemed to indicate that major revisions were necessary to cure the competitive situation. Therefore, in 1943, a special committee of the BFUP recommended that several broadening features be incorporated into a comprehensive dwelling house form. With minor exceptions, these features could have been provided by endorsements under BFUP rules. This implied that the broadening of coverage would be limited to that allowable under a fire insurer's charter powers. The committee also recommended that the existing dwelling rates be continued without material changes and the rate for the proposed named-peril policy be low enough to make it desirable for the agent to try to sell the comprehensive form exclusively. The insurers preferred to broaden coverage in the new form rather than give a rate reduction on the existing coverages. Because of the new form's attractiveness they also hoped premium income would increase rather than decrease.

The subcommittee also recommended that the form be offered only on an 80 percent coinsurance basis with a loading of $.08 per year per $100 of insurance applicable to both building and contents, regardless of the class of fire protection. Although contents are usually more susceptible to physical damage than buildings and therefore generally have a higher fire rate than buildings, it was felt the same loading could be charged because the coinsurance requirement would have greater force in correcting underinsurance of contents than of buildings. Dwelling buildings generally had substantial mortgagee insurance requirements and therefore were more nearly insured to their value than were their contents. A differential would still remain in total rate because of the differential in the fire rate. Also it was felt that, while a loading which did not vary with the class of public fire protection would undoubtedly discriminate to a degree against the better protected cities, the simplicity it would achieve in rating the initial program would outweigh that disadvantage.

Rate redundancy was also the precipitant that led the EUA to promulgate the additional extended-coverage endorsement

(AECE).   One member of the EUA committee considering the problems created by rate redundancies thought that broadened coverage might help meet the competition of local mutuals which had successfully specialized on profitable classes for many years.

It may be surmised that great impetus is provided for multiple-line insurance where rate redundancies exist in component rates. Broadening of coverage within a single line of insurance had reached practical limits for some classes of risks.   The economic inefficiencies resulting from rate reductions and the inroads made by competitors when rates were redundant prompted the introduction of multiple-line coverages.   Redundancies in component coverage rates also provided a margin with which to absorb package discounts.

Disproportionate Agents' Commissions

Disproportionate agents' commissions also provided economic motivation for multiple-line insurance and could be used to justify package discounts.   Since agents' commissions are usually determined as a flat percentage of the premium, they tend to become disproportionate to the economic value of the agents' services as the premium increases.   Before the acquisition-cost conferences, insurance price competition took the form of bidding up commission rates.   After the *SEUA* decision and the resulting demise of the cost conferences, it was again possible for price competition to take the form of bidding for agency favor through increased commissions.

Price (and form) competition had not been important *at the consumer level* until quite some time after the *SEUA* decision. Rather strict bureau control continued to be maintained over the rating process and the thought persisted that bureau rating required uniform rates and forms.   Also, the vast majority of insurers still operated on the basis of the American agency system (AAS), under which agents represented several insurers rather than a single insurer.   This also precluded, to a large degree, effective advertising (with or without a price advantage) at the consumer level because agents might nullify the advertising efforts by placing the business with an insurer other than the one doing the advertising. After the *SEUA* decision unilateral commission cuts by individual insurers would have been impolitic, to say the least. Nor was it thought advisable for bureau affiliates, as a group, to lower agents' commission rates, because such action might violate antitrust laws.

Multiple-line insurance facilitated the paying of lower commission rates by many insurers, at least for multiple-line policies. Even though multiple-line rating formulas made no reference to commission rates, even a superficial analysis of the total-expense provision made it obvious that lower commission rates were contemplated. This was justified because premiums per multiple-line policy were generally much larger than premiums per monoline policy. One sales effort and policy replaced three or more monoline sales efforts and policies. Although agents did not like having their commission rates lowered, they nevertheless sold multiple-line policies, such as the homeowners. Insurers maintained that agents' aggregate commission income would be greater, even with lower commission rates, because unit and aggregate premiums would be much larger for multiple-line policies. Many agents believed that in order to compete pricewise with direct writers and mutuals, lower commission rates were necessary as long as they were reflected in lower rates to insureds. Homeowners advertising campaigns were so effective that many insureds would not settle for anything but a homeowners policy, because they realized it provided more complete protection at a lower price than would a collection of monoline policies. In many instances, therefore, agents had to sell homeowners policies at lower commission rates or lose the business altogether. The lower commission rates on multiple-line policies provided another margin for package discounts because they reduced the expense factor in the rating formula.

The relationship between multiple-line insurance rates and agents' commission rates can be explained best by way of a representative illustration. Assume, for example, that prior to the introduction of multiple-line insurance the allowable expense and profit ratios for the fire, casualty, and marine policies which were eventually combined in a homeowners policy were 50 percent. This meant the permissible loss ratios were also 50 percent. Further assume that prior to the introduction of multiple-line insurance, (1) agents' commission rates on component coverages were 25 percent and (2) premiums for each of the three traditional policies were $10. In this case the agents' total commission on the three policies would be $7.50 ($30 × 25%). The insurers' net premium income would be $22.50, allocated as follows: $7.50 ($30 × 25%) for insurers' expenses and profit and $15 ($30 × 50%) for losses.

Now assume that the permissible loss ratio for homeowners was 55 percent, based upon a reduction in agents' commission rates from 25 percent to 20 percent, and that a package discount of 20 percent was applied to component rates. Then if the insured replaced the three policies with a homeowners but did not increase the face amount of coverage, the total premium would be $24 ($30 × 80%). The agents' total commission would be $4.80 ($24 × 20%) and the insurers' net premium income would be $19.20, allocated as follows: $6 ($24 × 25%) for insurers' expenses and profit, and $13.20 ($24 × 55%) for losses. The result is 36 and 14.6 percent reductions in dollar income for agents and insurers, respectively. Of the $6 reduction in premium, the agents and insurers absorb 45 percent and 55 percent, respectively. In order for agents to *earn* the same dollar amount of commission income as previously, because of lower premium rates *and* a lower commission rate, they must *sell* 56 percent more coverage. This represents a 25 percent increase in premium outlay by the insured over that expended on the three monoline policies. On the other hand, a premium of only $28.13, which is less than the previous total, is all that is required for the insurers to obtain the same dollar income as before.

The picture was not as gloomy for the agents, however, as the foregoing analysis may appear. As subsequent discussion will explain more fully, several factors tended to increase the coverages purchased on homeowners as contrasted with component policies. Also certain agents' expenses were eliminated entirely or transferred to the insurers (such as through direct billing) in the process. Although competitors of insurers operating within the framework of a rating bureau also sell homeowners, it is more difficult for them to maintain a competitive price and/or commission rate advantage because the homeowners programs have tended to eliminate any redundancies in rates for the eligible householders.

Many agents were strongly opposed to multiple-line policies, mainly because of the decreased commission rates associated with them. In this regard a California insurance commissioner stated:

> We should ... effect economies and pass the resultant savings on to the policyholders. There will be little sympathy given to objections or obstructions based exclusively or principally upon a resulting reduction in commissions to producers unless it can be clearly proved by facts and figures that such result is improper and unfair.[8]

JUSTIFICATION FOR "PACKAGE" DISCOUNT

Two factors—rate redundancies and disproportionate agents' commissions—that justify package discounts already have been discussed. Before considering other factors, the term "package discount" should be explained. Package discounts are generally expressed as percentage credits, which are to be deducted uniformly from all component rates. However, actual savings depend on many technical factors that vary among coverages within each package; and the uniform percentage represents a carefully weighted average which provides a simple end result for easy application.[9]

Justifications for package discounts arise from anticipated expense or loss savings. MPIRO's original homeowners' discount of 20 percent was evenly divided between the two.[10] Rate redun-

---

[8] John R. Maloney, welcoming address before 45th Annual Convention of the California Association of Insurance Agents, November 17, 1952. For agents' points of view see Robert P. Battles, quoted in *National Underwriter*, November 13, 1952, p. 6, and W. M. Sheldon, quoted in *Eastern Underwriter*, February 27, 1953, p. 32.

[9] Longley-Cook, *op. cit.*

[10] MPIRO, "Report of Householders' Comprehensive Dwelling Policy Rating Committee," June 11, 1952. Cited hereafter as "1952 MPIRO report."

dancies may relate to losses or expenses or both. Disproportionate agents' commissions provide room for expense savings.

Expense Savings

The estimation of possible expense savings in MPIRO's homeowners policies was based upon various assumptions "as to commission rates, reasonable allocation of certain expenses on a per-policy basis, average policy size, savings in loss experience, etc."[11]

Expense savings were based on a comparison of the costs of one policy and premium with the several policies and premiums which would otherwise be required to duplicate the coverage, with consideration having been given to the savings to be realized in the areas of policy writing; premium transmittal and collection; checking, accounting and filing; statistical premium cards; and premium calculation.[12]

Elimination of Unnecessary Duplication

The homeowners, just as the extended-coverage endorsement (ECE) and the comprehensive personal liability policy (CPL), replaced several relatively small-premium policies for which the costs of issuance and processing were high in relation to the total premium received. For example, a homeowners policy could replace a fire policy with the ECE, a CPL policy, a theft policy, and a glass policy. Where these four policies were written on an annual basis, *one* homeowners written for a three-year term would replace *twelve* policies. Certain expense factors which are duplicated when coverages are written separately are eliminated by packaging coverages into single multiple-line policies.

Costs that are relatively fixed per policy become less significant, proportionally, as the size of the policy and total premium increase. The integration of several coverages into a homeowners policy tended to increase the number of perils, the types of coverages, and the amount of dollar limit per policy, thereby increasing the

---

[11] *Ibid.*

[12] Frederic J. Hunt, Jr., "Homeowners—The First Decade," *Proceedings of the Casualty Actuarial Society*, Vol. 49, No. 91 (May, 1962), p. 21.

total premium per policy. Generally, even the premium for the smallest homeowners was much larger than that for any of the policies it replaced. Therefore, a much smaller percentage of the premium was required for expense purposes. This resulted in a more efficient use, i.e., for losses, of the insureds' premium dollars.

Depending upon the assumptions made, estimates of expense savings ranged up to 25 percent. Therefore, the MPIRO committee studying the problem believed that an expected expense saving of 10 percent was properly conservative.

Loss Savings

Loss savings result in part from differences in coverages and in conditions relating to coverage when the coverages are written separately and when they are written in an integrated package. There is a reduction in adverse selection when the insured is required to purchase all coverages in an integrated policy. Loss savings also are derived from eligibility rules and other factors which tend to attract the better risks from the component classifications.

Differences in Coverage and Conditions. Differences in coverage and in conditions relating to coverage in the original MPIRO homeowners program were reflected both through modification of component rates, before application of a package discount, and through the discount itself. For instance, the coverage and the conditions relating to the coverage of theft differed between homeowners contracts and policies on residence and outside theft. Although multiple-line coverages were generally broader than monoline coverages, certain high-loss coverages were restricted on some multiple-line coverages. The homeowners theft coverage was not so broad in certain respects as that provided in residence and outside-theft policies. Mysterious disappearance was not covered in the homeowners, but it was covered in theft policies.[13]

---

[13] The discussion of theft premiums is based upon the minutes of the MPIRO Householder's Comprehensive Dwelling Policy Rating Committee meetings of February 6, 13, 28, and 29, 1952.

An example of differing conditions was the variation in dollar amounts of coverage available. In a theft policy insureds could select amounts, but in a homeowners the amount of theft coverage was a fixed percentage (subject to a $1,000 minimum) of the amount of fire coverage on the dwelling building. This reduces adverse selection by amount of insurance purchased. Because of the differences between the two theft coverages, a formula was devised for determining the homeowners theft premium component.

Since most insureds usually carried only a nominal amount of theft insurance and an analysis of one insurer's theft experience revealed relatively few losses in excess of $1,000, it was decided that the theft rate for on-premises coverage should not be applied to the full theft limit of liability. After considerable discussion, it was agreed that a charge based upon 20 percent of the on-premises coverage (which was fixed at 40 percent of the building coverage), subject to a minimum of $1,000, would be reasonable. Concurrently, after making several comparisons, it was decided that the National Bureau of Casualty Underwriters (NBCU) rates for 100 percent blanket residence and outside-theft rates would be used as a starting point in determining what theft rate to charge. The NBCU rates were to be reduced 10 percent because of the absence of mysterious-disappearance coverage in the homeowners. This rate was then to be increased 10 percent to take account of the fact that the rate would be applied to only 20 percent of the premises limits of coverage. For the off-premises coverage the residence and outside rate would also be used as a starting point and be reduced 10 percent because of the absence of the mysterious-disappearance coverage. This rate was to be increased 10 percent because some unattended-automobile coverage was in the homeowners but not in the NBCU policy. The off-premises theft rate was to be applied to the entire off-premises coverage (which was fixed at 10 percent of the premises coverage, i.e., 4 percent of the building coverage), subject to a minimum of $1,000. This relatively small amount of coverage more closely reflected possible off-premises exposure.

Since application of the foregoing formula produced a rate only 1 percent less than the NBCU rate (NBCU rate × 90% ×

110% = 99% NBCU rate), it was decided, for simplicity, to use the NBCU rates but to take into account the one percent surplus in the theft component when considering the overall policy discount.

The foregoing is typical of the consideration given by the MPIRO Rating Committee to the modifications that might be needed in component rates because of differences between the separate component policies and homeowners. There was not always complete agreement within MPIRO committees as to how the new product should be priced. The final result represented the evaluation and compromise of particular groups of bureau personnel and insurer representatives. Other groups of individuals quite likely would have reached a different result. This serves to underscore once again the importance of judgment in the rating process.

The Householders' Comprehensive Dwelling Policy Rating Committee[14] believed that contents would be insured more closely to their actual value in the homeowners than in individual fire policies because in the homeowners program contents were automatically insured for an amount equal to 40 percent of the building coverage. The minimum amount of contents coverage was $3,200, and there was a bracketing of dwelling buildings coverage from $1,000 amounts in the lower valued dwellings to $2,500 in the higher valued dwellings. The review of values that took place when a homeowners replaced coverages that had often been renewed without change during a period of inflation encouraged the purchase of more adequate amounts of insurance. Lower rates (much the same as the coinsurance principle), the increased consciousness of the possibility of loss arising out of the intensive homeowners advertising programs, and the stimulus given agents by the large unit premium and the advertising campaigns helped attain better insurance to value. Since most property and liability insurance losses, such as those occurring under a homeowners policy, are partial (i.e., less than the limit of liability under the policy), increases in the ratio of insurance purchased to insurable value tend over time to reduce the *rates* charged.

---

[14] 1952 MPIRO report.

The MPIRO Rating Committee believed that requiring a core of perils and coverages for certain amounts would eliminate much of the adverse selection that existed when the perils and coverages were purchased separately in amounts optional with insureds. By tying several mandatory coverages, in essence, to the fire coverage, which was more universally and adequately bought than the other coverages, a greater spread of risk, by type of coverage, peril, and amount, was achieved.

Also, it was felt that exclusion of mysterious disappearance in the theft coverage, restriction of coverage on property in automobiles, and limitation of coverage on valuable objects would eliminate or reduce many of the losses occurring under similar coverages when sold separately. These provisions were designed to eliminate those types of losses which are often due to carelessness and those which could be insured more appropriately and more adequately under separate policies for an additional premium.

Refinement of Classification. The committee felt that the following factors tended to result in the writing of better risks from the component classifications under homeowners policies. Only owner-occupied, one- or two-family dwellings were eligible for homeowners coverage. Owner occupants were expencted to have better loss experience than rental occupants because of the natural tendency for owners to be more careful with the use and maintenance of their properties. One- and two-family dwellings were not considered so hazardous as multiple-occupancy dwellings. Also, a self-refinement of classification was expected since it was thought that the homeowners would appeal to the prudent type of insured. People who wanted and could afford the several highly integrated coverages available in the homeowners were considered better risks than those who desired or only could afford less coverage.

There has been both a designed and a subtle subclassification of risks by the introduction of homeowners policies. In fact, a former manager of the Multi-Peril Insurance Conference once said that "packaging essentially is a refinement of classifications."[15] He felt that this was fully demonstrated by the

---

[15] Perlet, *op. cit.*, p. 153.

homeowners experience. The loss ratios for dwelling fire and extended coverage averaged 40 percent for the five-year period 1947-53. This fairly favorable loss ratio was offset by a comparatively high expense ratio incurred in handling policies with average premiums from $20 to $30. Then there was the advent of homeowners into the field, with certain eligibility restrictions. These dwelling policies were written at rate levels as much as 40 percent or more below the manual rates of the component coverages, and yet homeowners produced a favorable loss ratio. This was possible because the 40 percent loss ratio referred to above reflected the experience for all types of dwellings. The homeowners, because of eligibility and other requirements, created a subclass which had a lower loss ratio than the entire class. That homeowners resulted in a subclassification of better risks is also illustrated by the fact that the experience for risks not eligible for homeowners has been consistently deteriorating. This indicates that the less desirable insureds were left in the component classifications, and that if eligibility for multiple-line package policies were not restricted, the same loss ratio would result for the package as for the overall original class.

The view that homeowners resulted in a refinement of rating classifications cannot be disputed logically because now there are all of the homeowners rating classifications *plus* the component classifications. It must be emphasized nevertheless that differences in loss ratios between homeowners and the component coverages are not due entirely (and maybe not even primarily) to the difference in hazards among insureds in the various classifications. In support of this position is the fact that eligibility requirements are the same for fire risks whether they are written with or without coinsurance or a deductible. Nevertheless, the loss ratios on coinsurance and deductible business generally are lower than on no-coinsurance and no-deductible business. This is true even though risks written with coinsurance and deductibles have lower rates than those not so written.[16] Identically hazardous insureds may have different loss ratios because of the differences in

---

[16] See New York Insurance Department, *Report on Examination of the Inland Marine Insurance Bureau* (March 1, 1955), p. 96.

conditions under which monoline and multiple-line coverages are written. Also, lower rates and/or higher balance point loss ratios may be justified on the basis of expense savings with multiple-line coverages.

However, even if the difference in loss ratios between home-owners and the component coverages were due mainly to the different eligibility requirements, it seems that the advantages inherent in multiple-line policies could be made available to a larger percentage of the insuring public by creating more homeowners rating classifications. For example, if nonowner-occupied and multiple-family dwellings are more hazardous, it is not necessary to prohibit them from obtaining a homeowner type of policy; it is only necessary to charge them higher rates than the owner-occupied one- and two-family dwellings.

CHAPTER X

Rating Procedures for Homeowners Coverage

At the time of MPIRO's formation, its organizers decided that the indivisible-premium concept would be adopted as a basic rating principle. However, this concept may have presented some difficult problems in regard to exposure units, because the exposure units employed in rating the component coverages differed. Also coverages which used the same exposure unit were rated by different techniques.

PRELIMINARY PROBLEMS

Variation in Exposure Units

Although the unit of exposure, $100 of insurance protection, was the same for theft and fire, theft rates became smaller as the amount of coverage was increased beyond a certain minimum, whereas fire rates were a constant regardless of the amount of coverage purchase.

If $100 of insurance protection were used as the exposure unit, there was a question as to whether the indivisible rate would be applied to the amount of protection on the building or the basic comprehensive personal liability (CPL) limit of $10,000. It seemed inappropriate to apply an indivisible homeowners rate to a fixed amount of liability protection, such as $10,000, because the resulting premium would not properly reflect the property values exposed to loss.

Except for the occasional purchase of excess limits, CPL protection was written for the combined basic limit of $10,000 bodily injury and property damage liability per occurrence. The amount of CPL coverage that could be purchased was not a continuous function in the sense that any dollar amount between $10,000 and $1,000,000 or more could be bought, as was true for fire insurance, for example. Generally, additional amounts of insurance could be purchased only in multiples of $5,000. Advantages associated with limiting the purchase of CPL protection to discrete amounts include simplification of rating, reduction of "underinsurance" problems, and administrative expense savings.

Premium Table

A new rating concept was necessary to solve the problems relating to the variations in rating approaches and exposure units among the component coverages. In retrospect the concept was obvious and simple. Instead of trying to find an exposure basis that would be suitable for all of the homeowners coverages, MPIRO decided to use the traditional exposure units but with modified rates. In this manner the premium contributions of the components coverages were determined. However, instead of revealing component rates and premiums, even to agents or insurer personnel, total *indivisible* premiums were precomputed and presented in a premium table. Although this entailed a considerable amount of preliminary work for the bureau, it greatly simplified the application of the rating structure for insurers and agents, and eliminated a vast amount of unnecessary duplication.

It was not so difficult a task to precompute homeowners premiums for the various coverage and amount combinations as might at first have been expected, because homeowners policies were sold with predetermined amount relationships among the component coverages. Aside from the CPL coverage, which was for the basic $10,000 limit, the amount of coverage on the dwelling building determined the amounts of protection afforded under the various component coverages. Therefore, the premium chart was designed to show the total policy premium based upon the amount of dwelling-building coverage.

The minimum amount of insurance which could be purchased on the dwelling building was $8,000. Premiums were precomputed for 20 different amounts of insurance between the minimum and $50,000. The increments between the different amounts increased from $1,000 at the smaller amounts to $1,500 starting at $12,000 and to $2,500 starting at $15,000. Within the $8,000-to-$50,000 range the amount of insurance which could be purchased on the dwelling building originally was restricted to one of the 20 round-figure amounts shown in the basic premium chart.

Considerable simplification and reduction in the size of the basic premium chart resulted from the use of premium groupings in the construction of the premium tables. After premiums were calculated for the various combinations of coverages, they were grouped within certain ranges, and an average premium was calculated for each group. The average premium for each group was used in the premium table in place of the several premiums within a group. Generally, the average premium used in the premium chart would be within plus or minus 5 percent of each premium it replaced and represented. Premiums were developed for every purchasable combination of construction, protection, and territory; and the resulting premiums were grouped, averaged, and rounded to the nearest multiple of $3 for ease in calculating three-year installment premiums.[1] For each additional amount of $5,000 of building protection, up to $100,000 total building protection, additional premium *loadings* were also precomputed and incorporated into the basic premium chart.

This rating approach resulted in fewer homeowners rating classifications than would have been the case if a separate home-owners rating classification were created for each combination of component coverage classifications. Therefore, although the total number of home-related insurance rating classifications was

---

[1] 1952 MPIRO report.

increased because of the superimposing of homeowners classifications over the existing classifications, there was a broadening
effect *within* the homeowners classifications.

Many dwelling fire-classification rate differentials are as small
as $.01 per $100 of insurance. When rates are $.10 or less, as
some dwelling fire rates are, a $.01 rate differential produces at
least a 10 percent premium differential. There is justification for
such refined subclassification when fire coverage is written separately. However, a $.01 fire rate differential tends to become
relatively insignificant when the fire premium is but a component
of a homeowners premium. When homeowners premiums were
averaged for premium chart groupings, dwellings which would be
rated in different fire classifications were merged into a single
homeowners rating classification.

Critique of MPIRO's Original Procedures

The $8,000 minimum restriction, the discrete minimum amount
increment of $1,000 in the premium table, and the predetermined
amount relationships tended to encourage the purchase of more
adequate amounts of insurance in relation to insurable values
than is the situation with the component coverages when they
are purchased separately. The various limitations in the premium
table should not have resulted in any grave injustices because
the determination of insurable values is subject to greater variations than that resulting from the use of a limited number of
round figures in the premium table. The economies derived from
the use of the premium tables should have completely offset any
occasional injustices involved.

The premium tables also reflected the fact that the dwelling
contents were automatically insured for an amount equal to 40
percent of the amount of dwelling-building protection. It might
be thought that those insureds whose contents were worth less than
40 percent of their dwellings were being *unfairly* discriminated
against. However, this may well be a case where discrimination
resulted in lower rates, and even lower premiums, for *all* concerned
since rating practices prevented underinsurance and facilitated

rating economies. The rating practices used may have resulted in lower rates and total premiums for those being discriminated against than the rates and premiums that would result if the discrimination were removed. In other words, the elimination of the discrimination resulting because some insureds were being charged for more contents protection than they needed might cost more than the savings in premium which would result if the premiums were based upon the exact values of each insured's contents.

An oversimplified example may demonstrate how discrimination may result in lower rates and premiums for all concerned. Assume a group of homeowners policyholders are identical except that some have contents worth exactly 40 percent of the value of their dwellings and some have contents worth less. Assume that the homeowners rates and premiums for all insureds in the group, based upon the described premium tables, are $.50 and $50, respectively. However, without discrimination, because of the increased expenses involved and the tendency to underinsure, the rates and premiums for those who have a 40 percent relationship between contents and dwelling may be $.60 and $60, respectively, whereas the rates and premiums for those whose contents are worth less than 40 percent of their dwelling buildings may be $.60 and $54, respectively. The *rates* are the same for both groups in either case, because the physical hazards are assumed identical; however, the *premiums* for the latter group are less when exact contents values are used to determine premiums because their insured values are less. Nevertheless, when exact contents values are used to determine premiums, both groups pay larger premiums than when the premium table is used. Thus discrimination may result in lower rates and premiums for all concerned. Furthermore, those insureds who feel that they are being unfairly discriminated against may purchase their coverages separately on a monoline basis in any combinations and amounts they choose and thus avoid the alleged discrimination.

The premium table was constructed in such a manner that premiums within certain ranges were grouped and averaged so that the average premium calculated for each group would be within plus or minus 5 percent of the premiums it represented. This averaging produces no great injustice because it is unlikely that the rates for the component rating classifications are accurate within a 5 percent tolerance. In fire rating, for instance, the differentials based upon fire-protection classifications are based largely upon judgment and are designed to maintain an incentive for improvement in fire-protection gradings. As a result of the use of premium tables in homeowners rating, it is not readily apparent when rates for eighth- and ninth-class towns, for example, are identical. Also, the fact that such rates are identical may be due to offsetting differences in fire and theft rates, for example. Therefore, the incentive for improvement in fire-protection grading is not jeopardized. The above discussion justifying "discrimination" because of the assumed 40 percent contents ratio applies also to discrimination resulting from premium averaging. The foregoing discussion justifying "discrimination" because of the assumed 40 percent contents ratio applies in a similar manner to discrimination which may result from premium averaging.

RATE REVISIONS BY MPIRO AND MIC

Proposed Statistical Plan

The MPIRO Rating Committee felt that after the homeowners policies had "been on the market for a period long enough to provide a credible mass of experience," they could "be rated largely on the basis of that experience."[2] Such rate revisions required a statistical plan under which the experience would be collected. The following discussion is based largely upon minutes of MPIRO Rating Committee meetings held in 1952; however, the first uniform homeowners statistical plan was not adopted until 1956. Although the 1956 plan was jointly devised by MPIRO and IIAG in conjunction with the NBFU, its foundations were laid in the 1952 MPIRO committee meetings.

The Rating Committee proposed a statistical plan under which premiums were to be reported on an indivisible basis, coded as to

---

[2] *Ibid.*

type of policy form, amount of insurance on the dwelling, term, limits of liability for CPL and medical payments, optional coverages, state, construction, protection, and rating zone.

In addition, losses were to be coded as to cause, coverage, and size, and whether a deductible was applicable. Such cause-of-loss codes aid in evaluating trends or peculiarities in loss experience. They indicate where deductibles are required and whether certain coverages need modification to eliminate relatively uninsurable occurrences. Windstorm catastrophe problems exist with the homeowners just as with the extended-coverage endorsement (ECE). The cause-of-loss codes have helped in finding suggested solutions to these problems.

The proposed statistical plan was designed to provide certain advantages over existing plans. For example the quantity of statistical records under the proposed plan would be considerably less than that required if the coverages were artifically divided into their components and recorded accordingly. As the number of premium and loss classifications increase, it becomes more difficult to obtain meaningful and accurate data because of clerical errors in coding and the fact that the volume of data in many classes is too small to have much credibility. Although experience under comprehensive dwelling policies (CDP) was coded so that data could be compiled for the entire policy separately, as well as be fed back into the statistical plans for its component coverages, no compilation was made because the experience was reported to several statistical agencies under several statistical plans rather than to a single agency under a single plan.

The CDP statistical plan involved increased processing costs without a commensurate increase in information usable for rating purposes. Whereas the CDP plan entailed use of separate premium codes for each component coverage plus one for the policy as a whole, the homeowners plan required only one premium code. Under the proposed homeowners plan, experience would be collected by policy form with the idea of making rates for each type of multiple-line policy as a whole rather than making rates for each component of each policy and then adding these rates together to determine the policy rates. The latter method might require a change in the multiple-line rate discount each time a component rate was changed. This was an important reason why self-rating was contemplated for homeowners, i.e., eventually homeowners rates were to be based upon homeowners experience regardless of the experience on component coverages when written separately.

As was pointed out in conjunction with the commercial property coverage (CPC) policies:

> To break down the premiums into arbitrary percentages and to include them in with fire, extended coverage ... etc., would result in mixing the statistics without obtaining any conclusive indications. There would be no means of determining the adequacy of the rates for these package policies unless the experience on these types of risks is maintained separately for such packages.[3]

The proposed homeowners statistical plan allowed a great deal of flexibility. Since the rating plan involved premiums which varied according to the size of policy, separate statistics by amounts of insurance were to be maintained. The proposed statistical plan would produce current experience data on a calendar-year basis. The policy-year basis was not favored by the Committee because it required too long a period of time to develop. However, the proposed plan was designed to develop experience on either a calendar-year or policy-year basis, so that experience could be tabulated on a policy-year basis if and when required.

The statistics developed would compare incurred losses in any calendar or policy year with the premiums earned and mean exposures developed during the same period. Provision was made for obtaining exposure data (to calculate pure premiums) not then available in the field of property insurance; however, homeowners were never rated by the pure-premium method. The information

---

[3] Arthur F. Lamanda, *Opinion and Decision in the Matter of Independent Rate Filings for Commercial Property Coverage by the North American Companies and the American Casualty Company* (New York Insurance Department, August 8, 1958), reproduced in *Hearings on the Insurance Industry* (report of the Subcommittee on Anti-trust and Monopoly, Committee on the Judiciary, U.S. Senate, 85th and 86th Congress, 1958–60), p. 2102. Cited hereafter as *Hearings*.

necessary to develop policy-year data was subsequently eliminated from the plan as were the provisions for breaking out liability or medical-payments limits, optional coverages, and coding losses by size.[4]

It was contemplated that a statistical plan for expenses might be required in the future, but at the start only a limited amount of expense data would be requested.

Revisions Based upon Rate Changes in Component Coverages

While the homeowners statistical plan was designed to enable homeowners to become "self-rating," this required a credible volume of experience, which would take a period of years to accumulate. Before such experience was accumulated, homeowners rate revisions were based upon changes in the rates for the component coverages. It was not until 1959 that bureau homeowners rates were based upon homeowners experience. However, in New York, although homeowners were originally filed in 1954, homeowners "rate changes ... were ... based entirely on changes in the rates for component coverages—mostly liability insurance. The Homeowners experience itself was not employed for rate making purposes until ... November 1962."[5]

As early as January, 1953, MPIRO had to decide what action to take when there was a rate reduction in a component coverage since at that time a reduction in dwelling fire rates was made in California.[6] Although it was decided to revise homeowners premiums to reflect the fire reduction, the revision was not to be considered a firm precedent, each case being considered on its merits. The desire to eventually self-rate homeowners was again expressed; however, during the years between 1952 and 1956 "there were a number of premium changes, many reflecting changes in the component rates. Others, however, were the result of the competitive situations, with MPIRO responding to the

---

[4] Hunt, *op. cit.*, p. 23.

[5] Letter to the author from Robert C. Hayden, assistant manager, New York Fire Insurance Rating Organization, October 4, 1963.

[6] MPIRO, "Minutes," Rating Committee, January 14, 1953.

pressure of both the independent market and increases in discount in the CDP program."[7]

Rate Revisions by Multi-Peril Insurance Conference (MIC)[8]

During the time homeowners were rated by MPIRO, various "package discounts," ranging up to 25 percent, were used in calculating homeowners premiums. Between November, 1958, and April, 1959, MIC promulgated the so-called "new" homeowners program in about 20 states. The premiums for this program were determined in a more formularized fashion than those for MPIRO rate revisions.

Combined Discount Modification Factor. A combined discount modification factor of 40 percent, reflecting both term and packaging credits, was used countrywide in the calculation of premiums for the "new" program. In several states this factor reflected a 10 percent three-year term discount and a package discount of $33^1/_3$ percent.

A combined discount modification factor of 40 percent meant that the three-year premium would equal 1.8 annual premiums ($3 \times 60\%$ equals 1.8). The homeowners premiums were calculated on the basis of a three-year term discount. Application of the 10 percent term discount reduces the three annual premiums to 2.7 annuals. Application of a $33^1/_3$ percent package discount reduces the 2.7 annual premiums to 1.8 annual premiums. This is the same premium which is produced by application of the 40 percent combined discount modification factor.

Basic Premiums. The annual tariff or manual rates for the component coverages were reflected in MIC's rating procedure by so-called basic premiums. Basic premiums were equal to the result obtained by multiplying the annual tariff rates by three, discounting that product by the 40 percent combined modification factor, multiplying the resulting rates by their corresponding exposure units, and then summing the resulting premiums. The

---

[7] Hunt, *op. cit.*, p. 27.

[8] The material in this section is based upon MIC, "Report of the Dwelling Committee," n.d.

foregoing procedure was used in calculating the basic premiums for all homeowners forms, except Form 5, in which the three-year $50 deductible personal property floater premium reflecting the personal property premium component was discounted only 10 percent because of the poor experience with the all-risk PPF policy.

Credibility Table. A credibility table used in fire rating was applied to determine the weights to be given component-coverages rates (as reflected in basic premiums) and homeowners experience in determining homeowners premium levels. The nature of the credibility table is indicated by the following condensed version of the actual table, and the use of the table is explained subsequently.

Earned Experience Premium	Credibility Factor
500	0.01
50,000	0.10
200,000	0.20
450,000	0.30
800,000	0.40
1,250,000	0.50
1,800,000	0.60
2,450,000	0.70
3,200,000	0.80
4,050,000	0.90
5,000,000	1.00

Fully credible premium volume was set at $5 million of earned homeowners premiums. Credibility factors for selected premium volumes of less than $5 million are shown above. However, all credibility factors were subject to application of a "seasoning" factor, described below.

Initially MIC used the experience developed under homeowners A and B, along with such comprehensive dwelling policy (CDP) experience as was available, to calculate the premiums for Forms 1, 2, 3, and 4. This was intended to give due recognition to the experience developed under similar types of policies. However, no homeowners experience was to be reflected initially in Form 5 premiums, for which the basic premiums only, as explained above, were to be used.

"Seasoning" Factors. If less than five years' experience had been accumulated, the factors found in the credibility table were to be multiplied by the following "seasoning" factors:

Experience Period	Factor
	(%)
a. Less than two years............................	20
b. More than 2 years, less than 3...................	40
c. More than 3 years, less than 4...................	60
d. More than 4 years, less than 5..................	80
e. Five years or more............................	100

"Seasoning" factors were introduced because homeowners was considered to be a relatively new kind of coverage and it was subject to the possibility of relatively low frequency but high severity losses, such as those due to windstorms. The seasoning factors were intended to prevent extreme changes in premiums, either upward or downward, on the basis of inadequate experience timewise, regardless of premium volume.

After premium volumes became fully credible, and five or more years of experience was available, homeowners premium revisions would become a matter of adjusting existing premium levels, in essentially the same manner as fire rate revisions are made, based upon the experience for the new kind of insurance. However, when earned homeowners premiums were less than $5 million or the experience period was less than five years, basic premiums would continue to receive some weight in the rating formula. Indicated adjustments in premiums would be limited to a 25 percent change and adjustments would be waived when the indicated net change was negligible.

"Modified" Homeowners Premiums. So-called "modified" homeowners premiums were calculated to reflect both the basic premiums and actual homeowners experience. For states with fully credible homeowners experience, the "modified" homeowners premiums were determined in essentially the same manner that fire rate levels were revised, by using the experience data and a 54 percent balance-point (or permissible) loss ratio.[9] In those

---

[9] An important difference between fire and homeowners rate-level adjustments is that for fire the balance-point loss ratio is largely determined from previous expense date while for homeowners the ratio was based upon a somewhat arbitrary "budgetary" allowance for losses. In other words, in fire insurance the balance-point loss ratio is determined as a residual by subtracting the actual expense ratio and the anticipated profit margin from 100 percent, while with homeowners the appropriate loss ratio is established first, and thus the expense allowance becomes the residual figure after the loss ratio and the anticipatory profit margins are subtracted from 100 percent.

states with partially credible premium volume, "modified" premiums would be calculated as follows:

1. Determine credibility factor, based upon premiums earned, from credibility table.
2. Determine seasoning factor, based upon length of experience period, from seasoning table.
3. Determine adjusted credibility factor by multiplying tabular credibility factor by tabular seasoning factor.
4. Adjust homeowners premium to the indicated rate level, using a balance-point loss ratio of 54 percent earned premiums (adjusted to current rate levels) and incurred losses as derived from use of the homeowners statistical plan.
5. Compute basic premiums using annual tariff rates for component coverages multiplied by 3 and discounted 40 percent.
6. Compute the "modified" premium by the following formula:

$$\text{Modified Premium} = Z\,(AP) + (1-Z)\,(BP)$$

where:

Z = Adjusted credibility factor (from 1, 2, and 3 above)

AP = Adjusted homeowners premium (from 4 above)

BP = Basic premium (from 5 above)

The result produced under step 6 above was to "be the basis of Committee consideration for possible further adjustment to reflect factors that cannot be formularized."[10]

The 54 percent balance-point loss ratio was based upon a loading for all expenses (excluding loss-adjustment expenses) of 34 percent, 6 percent for loss-adjustment expense, and 6 percent for profit and catastrophes. The balance-point loss ratio was determined on a judgment basis; the 34 percent expense ratio was presumably selected as the maximum MIC companies could allow and still maintain competitive premiums.

"Trend" Factors. Consideration was given to using "trend" (weighting) factors in homeowners premium-level revisions. Such factors give the more recent years' experience more weight than the earlier years' experience in the rate-revision formula. However, since there was a rapidly increasing homeowners premium

---

[10] MIC, "Report of the Dwelling Committee."

volume, it was decided at the time that a trend factor was unnecessary because the more recent experience automatically received more weight than less recent experience. The following table illustrates this reasoning by comparing the weighting factors which had been recommended by the Inter-Regional Insurance Conference (IRIC) for use in fire rate-level revisions and the approximate distribution of total countrywide earned premiums for the six-year period 1955 to 1960 inclusive.

Year	IRIC Recommended Fire Factor (%)	Annual Homeowners Premiums as a Percent of the Total 6-year Premium[11] (%)
1	10	1.7
2	10	5.7
3	10	10.7
4	15	17.4
5	25	27.0
6	30	37.5

The IRIC factors are used to give greater weight to the more recent experience. The fire factors are applied to the premiums earned and losses incurred for each corresponding year in the experience period. Then the resulting premiums and losses are totaled for the six-year period in order to calculate the weighted average loss ratio. Since earned fire premiums are relatively constant, the sixth or most recent year's experience would account for about 30 percent of the final result. According to the above countrywide distribution of earned homeowners premiums, the sixth year's earned premiums would account for about 37.5 percent of the earned premiums for the six-year period. That the fire factors did not correspond exactly with the homeowners distribution is not too important because the fire factors used were a matter of judgment. The relevant point here is that more recent experience should receive more weight than less recent experience in the rating formula. The running six-year distribution of earned homeowners premiums has changed yearly. The earned premiums have tended to become more evenly distributed, and therefore

---

[11] Calculations based upon earned premiums as shown in Exhibits III and IV in Hunt, *op. cit.*, pp. 35–36. Also see Harry F. Perlet, "Ratemaking in Multiple Line Insurance," in John D. Long and Davis W. Gregg (eds.), *Property and Liability Insurance Handbook* (Homewood, Ill.: Richard D. Irwin, Inc., 1965), p. 783.

"trend" factors have been introduced into the homeowners rating procedure.

Rate Relativities. The credibility procedure described earlier was useful for determining premium levels; "however, for the purpose of adjusting rate relativities with respect to town grading, construction, building amount, territory and other rating variables, the individual package premiums were recomputed from components using rating methods very similar to those in the original Homeowners."[12]

IMPACT OF COMPETITION ON HOMEOWNERS RATING

Deductibles

In general the Multiple Peril Insurance Rating Organization (MPIRO) favored the use of mandatory windstorm deductibles in homeowners. However, local fire-bureau practice did not always require them. As a consequence of this fact, along with opposition by agents and especially competitive conditions, the principle was compromised.

In Pennsylvania, for example, the local fire bureau did not require a deductible under the extended-coverage endorsement (ECE), nor did the Insurance Company of North America (INA) require one in conjunction with its independent homeowners program. In Pennsylvania "there had been continued and widespread opposition by the agents to the deductible feature. Regardless of their position on the question, most companies ... indicated that the deductible" was "a serious obstacle to wider sales."[13] The problem was aggravated not only by the unfavorable competitive position with existing competitors, but also by reports that other rating bodies and individual insurers would soon introduce policies similar to homeowners.

There was also the immediate problem of acting upon requests by two insurers affiliated with MPIRO for deviations from

---

[12] Hunt, *op. cit.*, p. 28.

[13] MPIRO, "Report of Rating Committee for Dwelling Policies," January 29, 1953.

MPIRO filings which would allow elimination of deductibles. It was thought that providing for the elimination of deductibles would not resolve the entire problem unless action was "also taken toward bringing the Homeowners premium level in line with that of the North America."[14] An evaluation was made of the appropriate charge to be made for waiving the deductible. It was recommended that in Pennsylvania full coverage be provided on wind and hail without an increase in premium because it was believed that MPIRO affiliates desired "to reach so far as possible a condition of competitive equality in Pennsylvania."[15] It was noted that even if the proposal were adopted, MPIRO's premium level would still be higher than INA's, but the disparity would be reduced.[16]

Revision of the Floor Plan

In the summer of 1952 a "floor plan" was adopted by MPIRO in regard to homeowners premiums. The "floor plan" provided that no homeowners premiums would be less than the premium charged for coverage of specific building and contents under fire and allied lines plus a percentage loading.[17] This feature of the rating plan soon became a problem, especially in those states which had relatively high fire rates.[18] In those states MPIRO's premiums were much higher than those of some competitors. There was considerable opposition to eliminating the floor plan; however, in 1954 it was decided that the floor plan would include only the premium obtained by using specific fire rates on the contents.[19] By 1955, the floor plan was apparently dropped, since in September of that year the Executive Committee instructed the Rating Com-

---

[14] *Ibid.*

[15] *Ibid.*

[16] It is interesting that one of the five companies on the committee did not concur in the recommendation, but concurring, as chairman of the committee, was a representative of the INA.

[17] MPIRO, "Minutes," Rating Committee for Dwellings, July 24 and August 1, 1952.

[18] MPIRO, "Minutes," Executive Committee, January 14, 1954.

[19] *Ibid.*, September 22, 1954.

mittee to derive *competitive premiums,* keeping cognizant of NBFU town gradings.[20]

Multi-Peril Insurance Conference (MIC) "New New" Homeowners

Most of the independent insurers did not adopt the "new" homeowners program promulgated by MIC; many "in fact soon acted to re-establish their competitive advantages by reducing premiums and broadening coverages."[21]

In light of these competitive conditions, bureau homeowners filings were discontinued in the spring of 1959 in order to provide time for MIC to re-evaluate the situation. In the summer of 1959, MIC promulgated the so-called "new new" homeowners program, which provided essentially the same coverages as were available under the previous MIC "new" homeowners program but at generally lower premiums. The major revision in coverage related to the introduction of a mandatory franchise deductible on Form 5 and optional franchise deductibles on all perils except fire on the other forms.

New York Homeowners Filings[22]

The impact of competition on the rating of homeowners is illustrated further by various interline homeowners rate filings made by the New York Fire Insurance Rating Organization (NYFIRO) with the New York Insurance Department and the hearings and decision arising therefrom.

Homeowners A, B, and C were originally filed in New York during 1954 by MPIRO and were revised by MPIRO in 1956.

---

[20] *Ibid.,* September 22, 1955.

[21] Hunt, *op. cit.,* p. 29.

[22] The material in this section is based primarily upon Newall Alford, Jr., *Opinion in the Matter of New York Fire Insurance Rating Organization–National Bureau of Casualty Underwriters–Inland Marine Insurance Bureau Hearing Pursuant to Section 186 of the Insurance Law Relating to Homeowners Policies* (New York Insurance Department, August 28, 1962), p. 10 (mimeo). Cited hereafter as *1962 Opinion.*

Starting as early as March, 1960, NYFIRO had proposed introduction in New York of the "new new" program which encompassed rate changes that purported to reflect Homeowners loss experience in New York. The proposed filings were disapproved by the department in each instance because of disagreement between the department and NYFIRO over what permissible or balance-point loss ratio should be used in the rate-revision formula.

In November, 1961, the department directed NYFIRO, National Bureau of Casualty Underwriters (NBCU), Inland Marine Insurance Bureau (IMIB), and Transportation Insurance Rating Bureau (TIRB) to show cause why rates then in effect for homeowners should not be adjusted as indicated in an experience exhibit prepared by the department for the years 1955 to 1960 inclusive. In response to the directive, a filing was made later in the month, but this too was unacceptable to the department. Therefore, the superintendent convened formal hearings on the matter in December, 1961.

Proposals for homeowners rate revisions require evaluation of loss experience, evaluation of the effect of coverage changes (if any), and selection of a permissible loss ratio. Disagreement between NYFIRO and the department mainly centered on the selection of a permissible loss ratio and the extent to which past and prospective expense experience should be used as guides in determining the permissible loss ratio for the "new new" program. There was also disagreement as to the application of the unique "Barrett-Russo" statute, which was in effect at that time. This is discussed in more detail later in this chapter.

According to the department, the "new new" filings had not included sufficient data to support the 54 percent balance-point loss ratio proposed by NYFIRO, nor were sufficient supplementary data provided. The department concluded, upon examination of insurers' expense exhibits filed with the department by the insurers affiliated with the participating bureaus, that the proposed permissible loss ratio was unsupportable and therefore unwarranted.

On the basis of *past expense experience*, as reported in the expense exhibits, the department developed a 50 percent balance-

point loss ratio, as the complement of the following total expense
and profit ratio:

Loss adjustment	6.2%
General	5.6
Taxes, licenses, and fees	2.8
Commissions	25.0
Other acquisition	5.4
Profit (including allowance for catastrophes)	5.0
Total expenses and profit	50.0%

According to the department, the difference in coverage between
the old and the "new new" programs did not warrant adoption of
a permissible loss ratio based upon the assumption that *future*
expenses under the proposed program would be materially different
from past expenses.   The department's position was somewhat
unusual, because a 50 percent permissible loss ratio results in a
higher premium level, other things being equal, than a 54 percent
ratio.   This results since a smaller permissible loss ratio in the
denominator of the rate-level adjustment factor (actual divided
by permissible loss ratio) increases the adjustment factor.

As a result of actions taken by independent insurers, NYFIRO
took the position that if its affiliated insurers were to retain their
proportion of the market and if reasonable competition were to be
preserved, it was not practical for the bureau to make a premium
charge that was based on any permissible loss ratio less than
54 percent.[23]   The 54 percent ratio would have required approximately a 10 percent reduction in expense costs, i.e., a reduction
in expenses from 45 to 40 percent of the gross rate.   However,
NYFIRO offered no concrete statistical justification for the
reduction in expenses.   In its filing of March 30, 1961, NYFIRO
stated that:

The ... expense allowance in the rate filing is prospective in nature
and is but one of several factors incorporated into the formula.   It has no
statistical foundation and, in fact, as in the case with any prospective
matter, is not capable of prior statistical justification.   There is no way of
telling what the expense is, or for that matter what the losses will be,
under a given program until actual experience is accumulated. ... The

---

[23] NYFIRO, "Filing Letter, November 22, 1961," p. 4.

specific distribution of this 40% for any one company is entirely within its individual discretion and underwriting practices. No bureau filing can in any way influence or control such company decision. It follows, therefore, that it is incumbent upon the individual company to decide the manner and the place whereby it will effect reduction in expense, if such reduction is necessary in order to come within the 40%.[24]

The department maintained that, although the expense allowance proposed by NYFIRO was based upon the interested underwriters' best judgment, the administration of the Insurance Law also requires exercise of judgment by the superintendent in reviewing proposed filings and the related factual data. Therefore it was incumbent upon the superintendent, if he were to approve the filing, to reconcile the proposed and actual expense allowances. This he was unable to do. The department also pointed out that the general precepts laid down in the law cannot always be applied identically to independent insurers and rating bureaus. It was stated in this regard that neither the bureaus nor the superintendent have authority to fix commissions, but individual insurers have power to control their own expenses (especially commissions) to a large degree, and the implication was that this must be taken into consideration when reviewing filings.

In other words, the New York Insurance Department's position is that bureau rate filings must largely reflect actual average commissions paid during the experience-review period. Bureau insurers are placed in an inflexible position in New York because their *prospective* expenses may not receive the same weight as those of an independent insurer, and therefore they cannot reduce their rates on the basis of anticipated expense savings. This tends to emphasize that the real need and purpose of rating bureaus, from an economic pricing viewpoint, lies in the calculation of expected losses or the pure-premium portion of the rate. This would allow each insurer to determine its own expense needs and to charge rates more consistent with its own methods of operation. Also this should foster more meaningful rate regulation by

---

[24] *1962 Opinion.* The 40 percent expense allowance was based upon the 54 percent permissible loss ratio and a 6 percent profit factor.

directing attention to individual insurers rather than broad industry aggregates and averages.

The New York Homeowners "Market."   The *1962 Opinion* in the New York homeowners case was particularly interesting because it included an economic analysis of the competitive situation in New York and related the analysis to statutory requirements and rating principles.   NYFIRO's presentation regarding competition emphasized lower initial rates, i.e., price competition.   However, the *Opinion* pointed out that it is difficult to interpret data regarding price competition, because "even when coverages are absolutely standardized in property and casualty insurance, the 'products' of different insurers are not necessarily fungible and completely comparable.   Performance of the contract is inevitably varied."[25]

Factors significantly affecting an insurer's premium volume and its relative share of the market include (1) date of entry into the market; (2) company policy with respect to rate of expansion of its agency and sales force; (3) underwriting policy; (4) merchandising and advertising methods; (5) condition of coverage, e.g., coinsurance requirements; (6) commission rates; and (7) the initiative of its agents.   According to the department, there appeared to be at least two homeowners markets in New York. The market for homeowners C seemed very different from that for A and B; however, there were very little meaningful data on the record regarding the nature and impact of competition.

Responsiveness to Experience.   If insurers affiliated with bureaus were actually less successful in competing for homeowners than independent insurers, it could have been due to the failure of the rating bureaus to keep rates in a reasonable relationship to the experience.   The experience had indicated that rates for the C policy were "at a clearly inadequate level," and therefore "the writing of such coverage would hardly be rapidly expanded, indeed it would likely be reduced."[26]   On the other hand, it appeared that

---

[25] *Ibid.*
[26] *Ibid.*

rates for the A and B policies were "somewhat excessive," and therefore "competitors ... naturally tended to make their own rates on a more reasonable basis and aggressively push for a larger share of sales."[27] It was suggested that bureau insurers could compete more effectively if the bureau were more responsive to the experience indications.

Barrett-Russo Amendment. The New York Insurance Department did not believe bureau affiliates should be entitled to decrease the price of their insurance simply to remain competitive and retain a certain proportion of the business. The department thought its position was also in accord with the Barrett-Russo amendment, which added the following italicized words to Section 183 (1) of the New York law:

> Consideration shall be given ... *to commissions paid during the most recent annual period in this state,* to past and prospective *other* expenses both country-wide and those specifically applicable to this state.[28]

The department noted that like all provisions of the law, this provision:

> ... must be read and applied in specific situations so that it is in harmony with other requirements of law and with the general legislative purposes. ... Literally read it means that no consideration shall be given to 'prospective commissions' and that consideration of commissions as an expense shall be confined to the commissions paid in New York 'in the most recent annual period.'[29]

Functional duplications exist between certain tasks that may be remunerated on either a commission or a noncommission basis. While the desired end result was "to establish a permissible loss ratio based upon a *proper allowance for all expenses of the bureau stock companies on an average basis,*"[30] the Barrett-Russo amendment required consideration of actual commissions paid. Furthermore, commissions were the only expense components susceptible to sufficient control to effect the necessary reduction in overall

---

[27] *Ibid.*

[28] *Ibid.*

[29] *Ibid.*

[30] *Ibid.* Italics added.

expenses anticipated by NYFIRO's proposed permissible loss ratio. However, "the Barrett-Russo amendment was intended to prevent insurers making rates in concert from, in the rate-making process, mandating collective departure from commission ratios of those insurers during the 'most recent annual period'."[31]   In other words, the amendment was intended to prevent a commission rate change simply because a bureau filing provided for a different commission rate than that contemplated by those actually paid in the most recent annual period.

According to the department, NYFIRO failed to demonstrate that the provision of the Barrett-Russo amendment had been met, or that the proposed rates would be adequate, not excessive, not unfairly discriminatory, and not otherwise unreasonable. The department ordered the participating bureaus to comply with its recommendations for adjusting homeowners rates on the basis of a 50 percent permissible loss ratio. The order was subsequently complied with by the bureaus.

Filings in States Other than New York

In other states, however, the 54 percent permissible loss ratio has been used in homeowners rate revisions. An examination of the 1962 loss and expense ratios (compiled from insurance expense exhibits as of December 31, 1962, by the New York Insurance Department) shows that many insurers were unable to keep their expenses within the 40 percent expense allocation (exclusive of 6 percentage points for profit and catastrophe factors). Although the trend of expense ratios has been downward, the data seem to indicate that competitive pressures forced the use of unrealistic expense assumptions to justify lower rates.

Competition also has resulted in the practice of making annual reviews of experience and making indicated revisions where necessary. In this regard, the time involved in consolidating the experience has resulted in something of a problem, because there have been situations where catastrophic losses occurred after the

---

[31] *Ibid.*

period covered by the *consolidated* experience. Inclusion of such losses would have indicated rate adjustments counter to those indicated by the consolidated experience. This problem, however, is not unique to multiple-line rating, but exists for many kinds of insurance, because there is a relatively long lag between the generation and processing of experience data.

Fixed versus Variable Costs

In regard to the problem of functional duplication and allocation of expenses, it can be shown that, other things being equal, an insurer that transfers variable costs (such as commissions for which the total increases directly with sales) to fixed costs (such as salaries for insurer personnel, for which the total is relatively constant over wide ranges of sales) will tend to have a profit maximization position that has a lower price and a greater sales volume than an insurer that has fewer fixed costs and more variable costs. This occurs because the transfer of variable costs to fixed costs lowers the marginal-cost curve, making its intersection with the marginal-revenue curve lower and to the right of the former intersection. Competition in all kinds of insurance has resulted in such a transfer of costs; for example, part of the reduction in agents' commission rates may be due to the presently increasing practice of direct billing, i.e., the billing of insureds by insurers rather than by agents. Thus, certain accounting costs become fixed (represented by salaries of insurer accounting personnel) rather than variable (represented by agents' commissions). This tendency to shift costs seems to have had an impact upon homeowners rating. Not only has there been a shifting of functions so that they entail fixed rather than variable costs, but, possibly more importantly, there has resulted an increase in the efficiency of performing these operations because of increased specialization and the greater utilization of electronic data processing made possible by the shifting of functions.

CHAPTER **XI**

Rating Procedures for Homeowners Coverage (Continued)

MULTI-LINE INSURANCE RATING BUREAU (MLIRB) PROCEDURES FOR RATING HOMEOWNERS COVERAGE

MLIRB assumed rating jurisdiction over homeowners policies for its affiliated companies in August, 1963. In the first annual report of the general manager of the bureau, the late Elmer Twaits referred to this function as having "a tiger by the tail."[1] The company executives who established MLIRB anticipated a need for higher rate levels for homeowners business. Considering the proper rating of homeowners to be the single most pressing problem to face the new bureau, its executive committee recommended that the staff give immediate consideration to the problems involved in adjusting experience-review-period loss data to current cost levels by the use of trend factors, determining the proper expense allowances to be used in the determination of the permissible or balance-point loss ratio, providing for catastrophic losses in the

---

[1] Elmer A. Twaits, "Annual Report," MLIRB, October 14, 1964. The material in this paragraph is based upon this report.

rating formula, restricting replacement-cost coverage, increasing the factor used in the calculation of installment premiums, and introducing mandatory disappearing deductibles applying to all Section I property-damage losses. The extent to which these considerations have been adopted by MLIRB will become apparent in the subsequent discussion of its current procedures. Before any of these innovations in homeowners rating were introduced, however, the bureau felt it was desirable to establish its jurisdiction over homeowners by refiling the existing bureau homeowners programs in its own name.

In its second year of operation[2] MLIRB introduced the use of trend factors for the purpose of adjusting experience-review-period loss data to current cost levels. Nationwide relativities by policy amount or size were also introduced to develop consistent loss ratios for the various policy amounts. At the same time, weighting factors were introduced to give more weight to the loss ratios of the most recent year in determining the experience-review-period weighted loss ratio. Also, in its second year MLIRB received approval in 29 states for rate-level increases which represented an annual increase in premium income of $65 million. Furthermore, mandatory deductible programs were introduced in some states, charges for elimination or reduction of deductibles were increased in some states, and provisions for replacement-cost coverage were restricted in most states.

ELEMENTS OF MLIRB HOMEOWNERS RATE REVISION

Underwriting Unit and Time Reference

Homeowners rate revisions are based upon the loss-ratio approach. The earned-incurred underwriting unit is used in the determination of the actual adjusted experience-review-period weighted loss and loss-adjustment expense ratio. The time refer-

---

[2] Lewis R. Plast, "Report of General Manager," MLIRB, October 14, 1965. The material in this paragraph is based upon this report.

ence is the calendar year. The experience review period consists of the most recent six calendar years for which data are available. When the classified data are not available for the most recently completed calendar year, the latest data on page 14 of the annual statement are used. Otherwise the data for all six years are as reported under the 1956 and 1958 Homeowners Statistical Plans.[3] Collected written premiums[4] under these plans are reported by bureau stock insurers to the National Insurance Actuarial and Statistical Association (NIASA), by mutual insurers to the Transportation Insurance Rating Bureau (TIRB), and by independent insurers to the National Association of Independent Insurers (NAII). Earned premiums are developed from written premiums by distributing the written premiums into premiums earned in the year of writing and those earned in subsequent years, using the standard earned-premium factors of $1/2$ - $1/2$ and $1/6$ - $1/3$ - $1/3$ - $1/6$ for one- and three-year policies, respectively. The earned premiums are then adjusted to the current rate level by applying percentage rate-level adjustment factors. When a rate-level adjustment has been made during a calendar year, its effect is prorated for the number of months in the year which elapsed prior to its effective date.

The aforementioned statistical plans provide for the reporting of losses paid during the year and the unpaid loss liability, or outstanding losses, as of the end of the year. From these data incurred losses are calculated by adding the unpaid loss liability at the end of the year to the losses paid during the year and subtracting therefrom the unpaid loss liability at the start of the year, i.e., at the end of the previous year. Catastrophic losses caused by windstorms and hurricanes are spread forward over a

---

[3] In subsequent years the data to be used will be reported under the New Personal Lines Statistical Plan (Dwellings and Homeowners), which became effective January 1, 1966, in most states.

[4] Collected written premiums include premiums developed under deviation and independent filings, as well as manual premiums, without reforming the nonmanual premiums to manual. That is, nonmanual premiums are not adjusted to determine what they would have been had the manual premium been charged rather than a deviated or independently filed premium.

period of ten years, beginning with the year of occurrence, to avoid sharp fluctuations in rate levels. However, the bureau is considering the adoption of an approach to the catastrophe-loss problem which will incorporate loadings for catastrophes on the basis of each state's catastrophe experience in a manner similar to that used in the rating of the extended-coverage endorsement.

The provision for loss-adjustment expenses is based upon a percentage of incurred losses. The percentage is determined periodically by reviewing the appropriate data in the insurance expense exhibits of a representative group of bureau insurers. Since loss-adjustment expenses in a given state may vary considerably from one year to the next, a countrywide average is used in all states. Currently a factor of 13.3 percent of incurred losses is being used to provide for loss-adjustment expenses.

Incurred losses and loss-adjustment expenses are adjusted to the current cost level by trend factors known as composite current cost-index factors. These factors relate current cost levels to those of the past. The index is a weighted average. The United States Department of Commerce Composite Cost Index, which is representative of construction costs, is given a weight of 60 percent and the Bureau of Labor Statistics' Consumer Price Index, which is representative of the prices of goods and services, is given a weight of 40 percent. Both indices are computed monthly. The composite current cost-index factor was used only as a trend factor until mid-1966, at which time the procedure was revised so that the factors are projected twelve months beyond the proposed effective date of a filing by a least-squares projection method.

Loss-Ratio Weighting Factors

After all of the foregoing adjustments are made in the earned premiums and incurred losses, actual adjusted earned-incurred loss ratios are determined separately for each year of the six years in the experience-review period. The actual adjusted experience-review-period loss ratio is a weighted average of the six aforementioned loss ratios. Because of the tendency for homeowners premium volume either to level off or to increase at smaller rates than in the past, the same weighting factors used in fire insurance rating have been adopted for homeowners rating in order to give greater weight to the experience of the more recent years. The latest year receives a weight of 30 percent and weights of 25, 15, 10, 10, and 10 percent are assigned to each preceding year, respectively.

Indicated Overall Rate-Level Adjustment Factor

In the determination of the indicated overall rate-level adjustment factor, use is currently made of the 60 percent balance-point loss and loss-adjustment expense ratio introduced by the Multi-Peril Insurance Conference (MIC) in July, 1959. This ratio is based upon a budgetary allowance of 34 percent for insurer operating and administrative expenses and a profit and contingency allowance of 6 percent. Interim revisions were made on the basis of a 54 percent balance-point loss ratio, exclusive of loss-adjustment expenses. Use of the 54 percent ratio was tantamount to using a loss-adjustment expense factor of 11.11 percent of incurred losses rather than the current factor of 13.3 percent, which is reviewed annually.

The actual adjusted weighted average experience-review loss and loss-adjustment expense ratio (A) is used with the 60 percent balance-point ratio in the following manner to calculate the indicated overall rate-level adjustment factor:

$$\text{Indicated Overall Rate-Level Adjustment Factor} = \left(\frac{A-.60}{.60}\right)100$$

This factor shows the overall increase or decrease required in the current premium level to make the actual adjusted weighted average experience-review-period loss and loss-adjustment ratio equal to the balance-point ratio of 60 percent.

Credibility and Seasoning Factors

MLIRB continues to use the credibility and seasoning factors which were introduced into homeowners rating by MIC, as was discussed previously. In many states, especially for the MIC Forms 1, 2, and 3 with 4, both factors equal unity because $5 million of earned homeowners premiums and five or more years of homeowners experience are available. Fewer states, however, receive full credibility with MIC Form 5 because of the smaller aggregate of premiums earned under this form.

Relativities of Premium by Policy Amount and Form

A review by the bureau of loss ratios by policy amount (size or limit) revealed that the homeowners premiums which were developed from the component-coverage rates produced considerable variations in loss ratios by policy size. It was felt that the homeowners experience volume was entirely adequate for refining premium relativities among the major classifications within the various homeowners forms. The need for the use of classifications which more clearly defined variation in loss potential under the homeowners program than those paralleling the component-coverage classifications of construction, protection, and wind and theft territories was recognized. However, the bureau has not been prepared to introduce refinements other than those establishing basic relativities of premiums by policy limit.

A comparison of the existing premium relativities by policy limits in all states in which the MIC 1–5 homeowners program was in effect showed very little variation among the states for Forms 1, 2, and 3 with 4. Although Form 5 relativities by policy limits showed greater variation, uniform countrywide relativities were established for all forms. In the establishment of policy-size premium relativities, a policy amount of $15,000 was selected as a base for Forms 1, 2, and 3 with 4 and a policy size of $22,500 was selected for Form 5. The study showed, for example, that the following relativities should be used.

Policy Amount (000 omitted)	Proposed Premium Relativities (%)	
	Forms 1, 2, and 3 with 4	Form 5
$ 8	.82	—
10	.86	—
12	.90	—
15	Unity — 100	80
20	124	93
22.5	138	Unity — 100
25	155	107
30	190	122
35	230	140
40	270	160
50	350	209
each additional $5	40	26

Relativities were determined for all policy sizes appearing in the homeowners manual.

In a similar manner countrywide relativities were established among Forms 1, 2, and 3 with 4. Their relativities to Form 5, however, vary by state. Using the combined loss ratios for all forms except 5 as a base, the form relativities are as shown below:

Form	Relativity Percent
1	94.3
2	100.5
3 with 4	103.2

Using the policy size and form relativities, premium levels are adjusted in accordance with actual homeowners experience by policy size and form so that essentially the same loss ratios may be expected of each homeowners rating classification. The bureau felt that this would produce more equitable premiums for each classification, however, no mention was made of the possibility that the balance-point loss ratio should tend to decrease with policy size because some expenses are relatively constant regardless of policy or premium size.[5] As of July 15, 1965, the new rating approach had been approved in 26 jurisdictions.[6] An example of

---

[5] P. G. Buffinton, "The Low Value Risk. A Study of the Premium Required for Habitational Risks of Various Policy Amounts," *Proceedings of the Casualty Actuarial Society*, Vol. 49, No. 92 (1962), p. 119.

[6] "New Rating Approach for HO Gaining Acceptance: MLIRB," *Insurance Advocate* (July 17, 1965), p. 5.

a typical result of the combination of an overall rate-level increase and the redistribution of premiums by policy size and form is shown graphically below:[7]

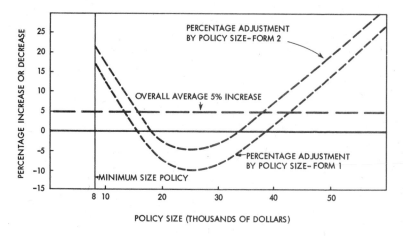

POLICY SIZE (THOUSANDS OF DOLLARS)

When premiums are redistributed without an overall rate-level change, a factor is applied to correct for any off balance which might have developed due to the redistribution. In this manner the overall premium level is not changed.

Mandatory Disappearing All-Perils Deductible

The practices regarding deductibles vary among the states. For example, in some states Loss Deductible Clause No. 1, which is applicable to loss by windstorm or hail to buildings, structures, or personal property in the open, is mandatory, while in other states the clause is voluntary, since there are provisions to eliminate or to "buy back" this deductible. There also is variation regarding the maximum loss for which the insurer is completely relieved of liability, $50 or $100, and the perils to which the deductibles apply. Loss Deductible Clause No. 1 applies to wind and hail only, but Loss Deductible Clause No. 2 also may be added, covering all other perils except fire and lightning that may

---

[7] *Ibid.*, p. 21.

cause loss to the dwelling, its appurtenant structures, and personal property. With a $50 disappearing deductible, as used in many states, the insurer is not liable for paying any part of a loss of $50 or less. The insurer pays an increasing percentage of all losses between $50 and $500, while payments for losses of $500 or more are not reduced because of the deductible. The $50 disappearing deductible clause states that the insurer is liable only when loss in any occurrence exceeds $50. When loss is between $50 and $500, the insurer is liable for 111 percent of the amount of the loss in excess of $50; when the loss is $500 or mo.c, the loss-deductible clause does not apply, i.e., the loss is paid in full subject to the limits or any other controlling provision of the policy. A $100 disappearing deductible applies in a similar manner, except that the insurer is liable for 125 percent of the amount of loss in excess of $100. Thus the insurer is not liable for losses of $100 or less and the insurer makes no deductible offset for losses of $500 or more.

The disappearing type of deductible has the advantage of eliminating not only the payments for losses less than $50 or $100, but also the disproportionate loss-adjustment expenses associated with such losses. Furthermore, insurer payments for losses of $500 or more are not reduced because of the deductible. This is as it should be, because insurance should be designed to protect against losses which are significant to the insured and not small budgetable losses. The disappearing feature also eliminates the inequity that would result from a $500 franchise deductible, in which the insurer is relieved of liability for losses of $500 or less but makes no deduction for losses greater than $500. With such a clause a loss of $499 would be borne entirely by the insured, while a loss of $501 would be paid in full by the insurer.

In 1965 the bureau undertook a study of deductibles based upon a special experience call for countrywide homeowners statistics for the last quarter of 1964 for six of the largest bureau members. Two nonbureau insurers also submitted data. The data encompassed approximately 174,000 claims valued in excess of $24 million. In order to determine the effect of a mandatory disappearing deductible, the data were coded to reflect policy form, deductible (if any), policy limit, cause of loss, and size of loss. The formula used to calculate the credit to be given for the disappearing-deductible is explained below.

Maine Filing.[8]   The results of the 1965 special deductible study and other interesting aspects of homeowners rating are discussed for convenience, and for a point of reference, in relation to a homeowners filing in Maine under date of December 30, 1965. The filing requested approval of an automatic or disappearing deductible applicable to all perils under Section I of Forms 1, 2, and 3 with 4 at premium levels equivalent to those that were currently in effect for the use of Deductible Clause No. 1.   It was requested that the $100 disappearing deductible under Form 5 be extended to include all perils.   A provision to reduce the deductible amount to $50 would be retained.   The premium levels for the mandatory all-perils disappearing $100 deductible would be equivalent to those currently in effect for the basic $100 deductible applicable to all perils except fire and lightning.   These requests were made in lieu of indicated rate increases.   The filing also proposed amendment of the basic premium relativities by policy size to the countrywide factors previously discussed.

The filing was based upon the six-year experience-review period from 1959 through 1964 inclusive.   Loss ratios, average size losses overall and for various causes, and composite cost indices were calculated for each calendar year in the experience-review period to illustrate the continuation of unfavorable trends for each of these items.   Loss ratios for Forms 1, 2, and 3 with 4 over the six-year period were as follows:

Year	Loss Ratio (%)
1959	52.5
1960	57.9
1961	53.1
1962	57.7
1963	76.8
1964	61.1

The large 1963 loss ratio was caused by an unusual number of water and freezing losses in that year.   Otherwise the 1963 loss

---

[8] Based upon *Filing: MLIRB H 65-3 Maine* and letter dated December 30, 1965, from MLIRB to the insurance commissioner, State of Maine, accompanying the filing.

ratio would have been between those produced in 1962 and 1964. Increases in the average size of losses were shown as follows:

Cause of Loss	Average Size of Loss in Dollars by Year						
	1959	1960	1961	1962	1963	1964	1959–64
Fire...............	$168	$206	$216	$260	$238	$282	$241
Wind..............	80	102	109	108	121	152	125
Water.............	94	98	106	120	138	131	127
Theft..............	75	65	82	73	72	86	77
Other.............	51	60	47	48	69	47	55
Liability..........	66	65	94	107	131	95	102
All Causes Combined..	105	116	119	123	130	129	125

The composite cost index showed a similar increase, as follows:

COMPOSITE COST INDEX IN PERCENT BY YEAR

Year	(%)
1957–59...........	100
1959..............	101.8
1960..............	103.0
1961..............	104.1
1962..............	106.4
1963..............	108.1
1964..............	110.4
1965..............	112.4 (June)

All three series and a knowledge of the present economic situation indicate that continued increases in the cost of those items insured under homeowners policies may be expected. Considering this and the fact that the experience review indicated an increase in premium levels in excess of 10 percent, the bureau explored other corrective measures. The data used to develop the tabulation of losses shown above also revealed that during the period reviewed the number of homeowners claims increased by more than 500 percent while premium volume increased by only 150 percent. The average fire loss, with no deductible applying, was $241 during the period, while the average wind and hail loss, with a $50 disappearing deductible applying, was $125. The other perils, excluding liability losses, caused average losses ranging from $55 (miscellaneous property losses) to $127 (water losses) and accounted for about 55 percent of the total number of all Section I losses. Furthermore, for the most recent four years for which such data were available, the study showed that less than

5 percent of the premiums were written with Loss Deductible Clause No. 2. Thus, the losses caused by perils other than wind and hail largely represented first-dollar losses. Therefore, the bureau felt that the introduction of mandatory franchise deductibles would significantly improve the homeowners loss ratios and thereby stabilize homeowners premiums.

Calculation of $50 Disappearing-Deductible Credits. The deductible credit for Maine was computed to be applicable to the Deductible Clause No. 1 premiums, with all Section I coverages subject to the $50 disappearing deductible. Since Maine required Loss Deductible Clause No. 1, the $50 disappearing-deductible wind losses were eliminated from the state experience and the credit was calculated to apply to existing Deductible Clause No. 1 premiums on the basis of the elimination of losses caused by all perils except wind and hail.

With a straight or flat deductible, where the insurer is relieved of liability for losses equal to the deductible amount or smaller and the insurer's liability for all other losses is reduced by the deductible amount, the losses eliminated because of the deductible clause equal the sum of all losses up to the deductible amount plus the number of losses above the deductible amount times the amount of the deductible. With a disappearing deductible, the losses eliminated equal the sum of all losses up to the deductible amount plus the amount of the deductible times the number of losses that are above the deductible amount but are not in excess of the amount where the deductible disappears minus the amount of loss payment, due to the operation of the disappearing-deductible clause, for losses within the ranges where the deductible disappears. This latter amount equals, in the case of the $50 deductible disappearing at $500, 11 percent of the sum of the losses between $50 and $500 after each loss within the range has been reduced by $50. Since the disappearing deductible does not eliminate any portion of the losses in excess of $500, such losses are not included in determining the amount of loss eliminated because of a $50 disappearing deductible.

The proportion of total losses eliminated because of a deductible, known as the loss-elimination ratio (LER), is stated in a mathematical formula as follows:

$$LER = \frac{L_1 + 50\,N_1 - .11\,(L_2 - 50\,N_1)}{L_T} = \frac{L_1 - .11\,L_2 + 55.5\,N_1}{L_T}$$

Where: L_1 = Total dollars of losses of \$50 or less

L_2 = Total dollars of losses greater than \$50 but less than \$500

L_T = Total dollars of losses regardless of the size of loss (equals $L_1 + L_2$ + losses of \$500 or more)

N_1 = Number of losses greater than \$50 but less than \$500

Applying the above formula separately for each cause-of-loss code other than the one for liability, which is not affected by the deductible, to the countrywide special experience call discussed above, loss-elimination ratios were calculated as follows:

Cause of Loss	Loss-Elimination Ratio (%)		
	Form 1	Form 2	Form 3 with 4
Fire	9.2	9.5	9.3
Wind and Hail............	47.1*	36.0*	23.0*
Water	—	22.7	20.3
Theft	33.9	30.9	22.1
Other	42.7	36.4	31.5

* For policies written without a wind and hail deductible, i.e., full cover.

A review of loss-elimination ratios, by policy limit and cause of loss, revealed considerable similarity within each policy form. Therefore, uniform deductible credits are used for each policy form, regardless of policy limit. In the calculation of the proposed deductible credits, a tempering factor was applied to the loss data which increased the losses by about 21 percent. This was done in anticipation of the effect that the disappearing deductible was likely to have on the loss severity of the gross losses with a mandatory deductible. Since the cause-of-loss distributions varied among the states, the deductible credit proposed in a particular state is calculated to reflect the loss distribution in such state.

In Maine, for example, the average credit for Forms 1, 2, and 3 with 4 was based upon weighting the tempered countrywide loss-elimination ratios for each cause of loss by the percent of the total loss in Maine, as indicated by the data for the most recent three-year period, due to the respective cause of loss separately for

each form.   The resulting weighted state loss-elimination ratios
for each form were weighted by the percent of Maine premium
writings for each form, in the most recently available year,
to determine the overall weighted state average mandatory
disappearing-deductible credit.

The calculations for Maine were as follows:

	National		Maine			
Cause of Loss	Tempered LER	Percent of Losses*	Weighted LER	Percent of Premiums*	Weighted Credit	
			Form 1			
Fire	.083	× .641	= .053			
Water	—	—	—			
Theft	.250	× .041	= .010			
Other	.213	× .096	= .020			
			.083	× .123	= .010	
			Form 2			
Fire	.085	× .527	= .045			
Water	.185	× .067	= .012			
Theft	.213	× .064	= .015			
Other	.219	× .164	= .036			
			.108	× .193	= .021	
			Form 3			
Fire	.086	× .454	= .039			
Water	.174	× .141	= .025			
Theft	.182	× .054	= .010			
Other	.210	× .173	= .036			
			.110	× .684	= .075	
					.106*	

* As a decimal fraction.

As previously mentioned, the bureau recommended that the
indicated 10.6 percent credit be used to offset the increase in
premiums that was indicated by the experience-review-period
results.   Because of the small premium volume under Form 5,
about $125,000 in 1964, the bureau felt that evaluation of the
experience would not be credible, and therefore recommended that
the existing premiums for the $100 deductible applicable to all

perils except fire and lightning be used for the mandatory $100 all-peril deductible coverage.

Critique of Mandatory Disappearing Deductibles.   The MLIRB felt that the potential effect of small losses was recognized by the broad deductible options, with their lower premiums, that were offered in the MIC 1–5 program.   However, the bureau maintained that since less than 5 percent of the premiums were written with policies having Loss Deductible Clause No. 2, a mandatory approach to deductibles was necessary.   Although from strictly an insurance-theory viewpoint, based upon the large-loss principle,[9] mandatory deductibles may be justified, the freedom of choice which we cherish calls for another approach.

As was discussed in Chapter VI, the way the options are presented in the policy to the insuring public greatly influences the acceptance or rejection of the option, as does the extent to which insurers publicize the premium savings which result from the use of deductibles.   It is unfortunate that a more positive approach was not taken in presenting the deductible options in the policy. Such an approach would not only require the insured to request the elimination of any deductibles otherwise applicable, but also prominently indicate the *additional* premium required to eliminate said deductibles.   The policy should be designed in a manner indicating that the deductibles are a part of the *standard* package and their elimination is a modification of the standard which requires additional premium.   If insureds were shown the cost per $100 of protection with the deductibles applying and the cost per $100 of *deductible eliminated*, there would be greater purchase of deductible policies.   It is likely that the same result would be achieved as with the mandatory deductibles, but with freedom of choice preserved.

---

[9] Herbert S. Denenberg, *et al., Risk and Insurance* (Englewood Cliffs, N.J.: Prentice-Hall, Inc., 1964), pp. 188 ff.

CHAPTER **XII**

Summary and Conclusions

SUMMARY

Between 1849, when New York became the first state to give statutory recognition to and enforcement of the monoline principle, and the late 1940's, when multiple-line legislation began to break down the walls of compartmentalization, most states limited the kinds of insurance which an insurer could write to those comprising only one of three broad duo-classifications: life and health, fire and marine, and casualty and surety. In 1955 Ohio became the last state to enact multiple-line legislation which allowed financially qualified insurers to write all types of fire, marine, casualty and surety coverages. Since the integration of coverages had reached a limit on the monoline basis, a natural result of multiple-line legislation was the writing of coverages in a single multiple-line policy which formerly had been segregated into either the fire and marine or the casualty and surety duo-classifications.

Premium volume attributed to multiple-line policies has grown significantly since 1956, the first year in which separate categories were established in the annual statement for the multiple-line equivalents: homeowners and commercial multiple peril. In 1956 multiple-line premiums, as reflected by these two categories, amounted to less than $200 million and accounted for only 2 percent of all fire and casualty premiums. By 1965 the corresponding figures exceeded $2 billion and 10 percent, respectively. During this period multiple-line premiums increased at an average annual rate of 30 percent, whereas the increase for the entire fire and casualty business, including multiple line, was only 7 percent annually. These figures should leave little doubt as to the importance of multiple-line insurance to either the insurance industry or the insuring public.

One may readily imagine that multiple-line insurance was not introduced without problems, since it directly controverted doctrines, practices, and traditions that had been nurtured in this country for more than a century. In order to understand more completely the problems involved in the rating of homeowners policies and other multiple-line coverages, it was desirable to examine first the fundamentals of insurance rating. This involved the entire process by which the prices of insurance contracts are determined. This process must, under governing law, produce rates that are adequate, equitable, and not excessive. As a practical matter, rates must be stable yet responsive, consistent, easy to apply and to understand, and conducive to motivating loss prevention. The manner in which these objectives are interrelated and stated precludes a unique solution to the problem of simultaneously achieving the conflicting objectives; rather it is necessary that the resulting rates fall within a "zone of reasonableness."

Since the rate and premium charged for a particular contract depend upon the system of classifications used in the rating method, there is no "proper" rate for a particular insured, exposure, or risk. Also, judgment is fundamental to all rating systems and varies among individuals. Although insurance rating is ideally based upon the law of large numbers, the practicalities of issuing new coverages and changing economic conditions often require the application of large doese of informed underwriting judgment. For these reasons one cannot expect the objectives of insurance rating to be achieved on a year-by-year basis for each classification but must hope they will be achieved on the average over a reasonable number of years.

In pursuit of the foregoing objectives, rates are revised periodically. The mechanism used for these revisions is a rate filing which frequently involves a change in both the overall rate-level and the rate relativities among classes—or the classification system itself. The objectives of adequacy and nonexcessiveness receive primary emphasis in the consideration of the rate-level, whereas equity is of paramount importance in classification changes. To a large degree the nonexcessiveness standard focuses on the determination of the allowable expense and profit ratio from which the balance-point loss ratio is derived. The adequacy of the existing rate level is then tested by comparing an adjusted actual loss ratio with the balance-point loss ratio. For example, in the loss ratio method, an experience-review-period loss ratio is determined using adjusted incurred losses and earned premiums. The experience-review-period combines a number of time references such as policy year, calendar year, and/or accident year. If the adjusted actual experience-review-period loss ratio is greater than the balance-point loss ratio an increase in rate level is indicated and vice versa.

Even in the pure-premium method in which specific consideration is given to the expected loss per unit of exposure, the rate-level adjustment often is based upon a comparison of adjusted-actual and balance-point loss ratios while classification changes usually are made after examination of classification pure premiums. With the pure-premium method, as opposed to the loss-ratio method, the exposure units usually are more reliable but still less than ideal standards of measurement. In both methods, however, rates usually are applied to exposure or insurance coverage units to determine the premium or total price of an insurance contract. The variety of these units used to rate the coverages integrated into the homeowners contracts was the source of a potentially serious multiple-line rating problem. There also were problems due to the variations found in the statistical plans and time references applicable to the component coverages.

There were other problem areas besides the actuarial. For example, in the legal area, questions were raised as to the applicability of the persisting monoline rating laws to multiple-line policies. These problems were placed in better perspective by examining the fundamentals and tracing the development of rate regulation in this country. Rate regulation is only one aspect of insurance regulation; but, in the name of solvency, there seems to have been an unwarranted preoccupation with rate regulation, at least since the late 1940's. In this country the regulation of prices generally has been left to the forces of open competition in the market place. This attitude was reflected in the anticompact statutes which were enacted between 1885 and 1912 and applied to the business of insurance. These statutes subsequently were supplemented or supplanted, depending upon the state, with antidiscrimination statutes. Finally, commencing in 1909 all of these types of statutes were replaced with rate regulatory laws. Several state legislative committees, convened in the early 1900's, concluded that concerted action in the area of insurance rating was justified but that the public should be protected through supervision against the possibility that excessive or unfairly discriminatory rates might emanate from such monopolistic-type price setting. The adequacy standard apparently was included in recognition of the fact that previous insurer insolvencies were thought to have been due, in part at least, to the charging of clearly inadequate rates. Unfortunately, because of rate regulation, insurers have not been permitted to innovate, as much as they could or would, in satisfying the needs of the insuring public on a sound and logical basis.

Another problem area pertained to the so-called jurisdictional functions of the monoline rating bureaus and related organizations. Cooperative rating began in the fire field at least as early as 1819 in the form of loose local associations of insurer agents. These associations evolved into the more formal, scientific, and regulated rating bureaus that operate today. The historical development of rating bureaus gave rise to a seemingly endless chain of amalgamation and division of jurisdictional functions, which should make it clear that the scope of any bureau's jurisdiction either geographically or by type of insurance is largely a matter of accommodating, in the most efficient manner under existing circumstances, the needs of its constituency—member and subscriber insurers. A rating bureau may obtain legal authority to rate any type of insurance for which it has qualified personnel.

Hence, the question of bureau jurisdiction is not one of preemption. In some states the only constraint is that an insurer is not permitted to have more than one bureau file rates on its behalf for one particular kind of insurance. This restriction need not have been an impediment to multiple-line rating.

Additional insight into the problems involved in rate making for homeowners insurance was provided by a study of three multiple-line forerunners which became components of the homeowners policies. The extended-coverage endorsement (ECE), comprehensive personal liability policy (CPL), and personal-property floater policy (PPF) exemplified the advantages to be gained from broadening (and integrating) coverages from the fire, casualty and inland-marine lines, respectively, even when the coverages were limited to monoline components. For the most part each of these coverages was treated as an inseparable core of components which were rated on an indivisible premium basis; the expense savings inherent in the packaging concept and the loss reductions resulting from diminished adverse selection were passed on to the insuring public in the form of lower rates. The sales success of these coverages provided valuable precedent, experience, and stimulus for multiple-line insurance. The ECE and the PPF also illustrated the desirability of encouraging the use of deductibles with comprehensive property coverages to prevent them from becoming extremely expensive maintenance contracts.

Although final impetus for the passage of multiple-line legislation was provided by the 1944 NAIC Diemand Committee Report, eleven years elapsed before all states enacted such legislation. Multiple-line legislation was narrow in scope in the sense that it only pertained to the charter power section of the various insurance codes; virtually all other sections of the codes continued to be couched in monoline terms. Although it was obvious that the legislators foresaw the use of the new charter authority for providing multiple-line policies, the remaining monoline rate regulatory laws, for example, allowed those opposed to multiple-line underwriting—and the independent filings which it spawned—to create obstacles to their use. Fortunately, most of the insurance commissioners who were charged with administering the resulting conglomerate of insurance laws proceeded on the assumption that the legislators deemed the monoline aspects of the laws flexible enough to allow the writing and rating of multiple-line coverages. This view was sustained in the courts in two landmark cases—*Cullen v. Bohlinger* and *Smith v. Wikler.*

After multiple-line coverages had been firmly established, controversy developed as to the agencies that would rate these coverages and the procedures that would be followed. The question of *who* would rate these policies revolved aroung independent versus cooperative rating. Those in the cooperative camp were further divided into two groups, one favoring rating by a single multiple-line bureau and the other preferring joint rating by the existing monoline bureaus. Homeowners originally was developed, rated, and filed by an independent insurer, the Insurance Company of North America (INA). For a short time INA joined the ranks of those favoring a single national multiple-line rating bureau by becoming a member of the Multiple Peril Insurance Rating Organization (MPIRO). INA and other independents continue to be very significant factors in the multiple-line field, while MPIRO has vanished from the scene. However, after several mergers and reorganizations of a succession of cooperative multiple-line rating organizations, the single national bureau concept seems to be prevailing, at least since the establishment of the Multi-Line Insurance Rating Bureau (MLIRB) in 1963.

The fundamental question of *how* to rate multiple-line policies as it pertains to homeowners has been resolved in favor of the indivisible-premium integrated-policy approach as opposed to the divisible-premium schedule-policy approach. While the technical details represent a blending of practices from the component lines, it is not surprising that fire techniques dominate the result, since the predominant coverages are from the fire and allied lines. Although homeowners rates originally were based directly upon appropriately modified rates for its component coverages, the present practice is for the homeowners experience to be the basis of homeowners rate changes, with little or no regard being given to the changes which occur in component coverage rates. However, rather than publish rates, per se, the bureau precomputes and publishes premiums. Homeowners rating has resulted in more equitable rates and premiums. As experience data are complied under the latest and most refined statistical plan, further improvements can be expected.

CONCLUSIONS

The rating process had two opposite impacts upon the development of multiple-line insurance. One was negative, in that certain problems involved in rating multiple-line coverages tended to retard development. It seems, however, that the technical rating problems received attention out of proportion to their real importance and complexity. The technical problems of homeowners rating are little different from those encountered in rating the component coverages and they involve primarily methods of classification and revising rates. Although the technical problems involved in rating multiple-line insurance were complex, it may well be true that inertia, vested interests, and psychological resistance to change were greater impediments to the development of multiple-line insurance than were the technical rating problems.

The positive impact of the rating process was derived from the integrated-policy indivisible-premium technique used in rating homeowners. Therein lies the ability of insurers to reduce expenses absolutely and to reduce losses incurred in relation to premiums earned. This approach encourages purchase of a basic core of coverages, in adequate amounts, for which the insured has a reasonable need.

Multiple-line insurance has resulted in a refinement of classification to the extent that multiple-line rating classifications have been superimposed upon the various monoline rating classifications. This has resulted in a tendency toward more equitable rating. However, a problem has been created because of the delay involved in increasing the rates for the residual business still being written under specific coverages. If it is true that, generally, only the less hazardous insureds are attracted to, or eligible for, multiple-line coverages, then the insureds being written under the specific monoline coverages are being charged inadequate rates. While the idea of more equitable rating is generally commendable, it may lead to problems of "no market" during the transition and "unreasonableness" afterward for the more hazardous insureds.

On the other hand, with "imperfectly homogeneous classes . . . some risks become 'desirable' and much sought after . . . while others become 'undesirable' . . . to be avoided by almost any means."[1] Both heterogeneous and "overrefined" rating classifications involve problems. However, the refinement of classification approach used in homeowners rating is more in harmony with pricing according to anticipated costs. This approach also tends to eliminate the anomalous practice of "underwriting" (except for moral hazard), i.e., rejecting insureds because rates are inadequate. It is unfortunate that insurers must turn down as many prospective buyers as they do because of rating systems that do not produce adequate rates.

Homeowners insurance has tended to make insureds, who are heterogeneous as to specific monoline coverages, homogeneous with respect to a mandatory package of multiple-line coverages. This occurs because there are considerably fewer homeowners rating classifications than component classifications. To the extent that multiple-line insurance fosters more accurate rating, it also reduces the need for so-called selective underwriting. Insurers have been spending large sums on underwriting because monoline and multiple-line rating classifications still are not homogeneous. Greater efficiency and service to the insuring public would result, it would seem, if these expenses were used instead for the refinement of rating classifications.

It is questionable whether those insureds who would have "unreasonable" rates if the refining process were carried to extremes should be provided "reasonable" rates through subsidization by less hazardous insureds simply because insurance is affected

---

[1] Statement of Ingolf H. E. Otto, quoted in *Hearings*, Vol. II, p. 1050.

with a public interest. The physical hazards of some insureds may be so great that public policy should be directed toward reducing the hazards rather than compelling insurers to provide protection against them.

Homeowners insurance seems representative of a fundamental trend pervading our whole economy—namely, greater efficiency, increased sales volume, and lower profits per unit of sales. This trend toward mass merchandising with a concomitant profit squeeze has been bitterly resisted by many segments of the insurance industry. It may be that competition for homeowners business has gone to extremes. However, this is no reason to condemn either multiple-line insurance or multiple-line rating, since both rest upon sound economic and actuarial foundations. Multiple-line rating problems are problems of degree rather than kind. In fact, on the whole multiple-line rating has been an effective rationalization of monoline rating techniques and methods, mostly those used in rating fire lines.

When placed in proper perspective, multiple-line coverages and rating may be viewed as logical and progressive evolutionary developments which are inevitable in the business of insurance. With multiple-line insurance, as with any other human endeavor, improvement will always be possible. Just as the extended-coverage endorsement, comprehensive personal liability, and personal-property floater coverages and rating methods fore-shadowed current homeowners coverages and rating methods, it is likely that the present situation will foreshadow all-lines coverages and rating methods.

APPENDIXES

APPENDIX A. HOMEOWNERS POLICY AND FORM 2

HOMEOWNERS POLICY

No. H

TYPE OF COMPANY

DECLARATIONS

Named Insured and P.O. Address   (No., Street, Town, County, State)

Policy Term: _____ Years _____ Inception _____ Expiration

The described premises covered hereunder are located at the above address, unless otherwise stated herein: (No., Street, Town, County, State)

Insurance is provided only with respect to those of the following coverages which are indicated by a specific limit of liability applicable thereto.

Coverages	Limit of Liability		Premium		
A. Dwelling	$		Basic Policy Premium	$	
B. Appurtenant Private Structures	$		Additional Premium	$	
C. Unscheduled Personal Property	$		Total Policy Premium	$	Premium for Scheduled Property
D. Additional Living Expense	$		Credit, if any, for existing insurance	$	
E. Personal Liability (Bodily Injury and Property Damage)	$	Each occurrence	Net Prepaid Premium	$	$
F. Personal Medical Payments	$	Each person	Total Premium if paid in installments	$	
	$25,000.	Each accident	Payable: At Inception (and)	$	$
G. Physical Damage to property of others	$250.	Each occurrence	At each subsequent anniversary	$	$

Subject to the following Forms and Endorsements: INSERT NO. AND EXPIRATION DATE

The described dwelling of _____ construction is occupied by not more than two families and not more than two roomers or boarders per family.

_____ Approved Roof _____ Unapproved Roof   Not more than _____ feet from Hydrant

Protection _____ Class _____ Zone _____ Premium Group No.   Not more than _____ miles from Fire Dept.

Special provisions applicable only in State(s) indicated: $ _____ South Carolina — Valuation Clause

Southern States: _____ Inside City Limits _____ Inside Fire District _____ Inside Protected Suburban Area

N. Y. Coinsurance Clause applies: _____ Yes _____ No _____ Fire District

Applicable when only Form 4 is attached to this policy: $ _____ Annual fire and extended coverage contents rate; Number of apartments in building _____

Described dwelling is not seasonal and no business pursuits are conducted at the premises thereof. Exceptions, if any:* (ENTER BELOW):

Business of Named Insured: Less Deductible Clause No. 1 (Loss by windstorm or hail) is _____ applicable.

Less Deductible Clause No. 2 (Loss by other perils) is _____ applicable.

Section II Only: (a) The described premises are the only premises where the Named Insured or spouse maintains a residence other than business property and farms; (b) Insured employs not more than two full-time residence employees; (c) There are at the premises no swimming or wading pools capable of being filled to a depth of more than thirty inches at any point; (d) The Insured owns no outboard motors rated at more than 10 hp for which coverage is desired. Exceptions, if any, to (a), (b), (c) or (d):*

First Mortgagee: NAME AND ADDRESS

Countersignature Date   Agency at:

_____ Agent

In Consideration of the Provisions and Stipulations Herein or Added Hereto and of the Premium Above Specified (or specified in endorsement attached hereto), this Company, for the term shown above from inception date shown above (At Noon Standard Time) to expiration date shown above (At Noon Standard Time) at location of property involved, to an amount not exceeding the amount(s) above specified, does insure the Insured named in the declarations above and legal representatives, to the extent of the actual cash value of the property at the time of loss, but not exceeding the amount which it would cost to repair or replace the property with material of like kind and quality within a reasonable time after such loss, without allowance for any increased cost of repair or reconstruction by reason of any ordinance or law regulating construction or repair, and without compensation for loss resulting from interruption of business or manufacture, nor in any event for more than the interest of the Insured, against all DIRECT LOSS BY FIRE, LIGHTNING AND OTHER PERILS INSURED AGAINST IN THIS POLICY INCLUDING REMOVAL FROM PREMISES ENDANGERED BY THE PERILS INSURED AGAINST IN THIS POLICY, EXCEPT AS HEREINAFTER PROVIDED, to the property described herein while located or contained as described in this policy, or pro rata for five days at each proper place to which any of the property shall necessarily be removed for preservation from the perils insured against in this policy, but not elsewhere. Assignment of this policy shall not be valid except with the written consent of this Company.

This policy is made and accepted subject to the foregoing provisions and stipulations and those hereinafter stated, which are hereby made a part of this policy, together with such other provisions, stipulations and agreements as may be added hereto, as provided in this policy.

*Absence of an entry means "No Exceptions."

HP 1001-0-A (Ed. 7-62-Standard)

231

#		
1	**Concealment,**	This entire policy shall be void if, whether
2	**fraud.**	before or after a loss, the insured has wil-
3		fully concealed or misrepresented any ma-
4	terial fact or circumstance concerning this insurance or the
5	subject thereof, or the interest of the insured therein, or in case
6	of any fraud or false swearing by the insured relating thereto.
7	**Uninsurable**	This policy shall not cover accounts, bills,
8	**and**	currency, deeds, evidences of debt, money or
9	**excepted property.**	securities; nor, unless specifically named
10		herein in writing, bullion or manuscripts.

Perils not included. Lines 11–24: This Company shall not be liable for loss by fire or other perils insured against in this policy caused, directly or indirectly, by: (a) enemy attack by armed forces, including action taken by military, naval or air forces in resisting an actual or an immediately impending enemy attack; (b) invasion; (c) insurrection; (d) rebellion; (e) revolution; (f) civil war; (g) usurped power; (h) order of any civil authority except acts of destruction at the time of and for the purpose of preventing the spread of fire, provided that such fire did not originate from any of the perils excluded by this policy; (i) neglect of the insured to use all reasonable means to save and preserve the property at and after a loss, or when the property is endangered by fire in neighboring premises; (j) nor shall this Company be liable for loss by theft.

Other Insurance. Lines 25–27: Other insurance may be prohibited or the amount of insurance may be limited by endorsement attached hereto.

Conditions suspending or restricting insurance. Unless otherwise provided in writing added hereto this Company shall not be liable for loss occurring Lines 28–37: (a) while the hazard is increased by any means within the control or knowledge of the insured; or (b) while a described building, whether intended for occupancy by owner or tenant, is vacant or unoccupied beyond a period of sixty consecutive days; or (c) as a result of explosion or riot, unless fire ensue, and in that event for loss by fire only.

Other perils or subjects. Lines 38–41: Any other peril to be insured against or subject of insurance to be covered in this policy shall be by endorsement in writing hereon or added hereto.

Added provisions. Lines 42–48: The extent of the application of insurance under this policy and of the contribution to be made by this Company in case of loss, and any other provision or agreement not inconsistent with the provisions of this policy, may be provided for in writing added hereto, but no provision may be waived except such as by the terms of this policy is subject to change.

Waiver provisions. Lines 49–55: No permission affecting this insurance shall exist, or waiver of any provision be valid, unless granted herein or expressed in writing added hereto. No provision, stipulation or forfeiture shall be held to be waived by any requirement or proceeding on the part of this Company relating to appraisal or to any examination provided for herein.

Cancellation of policy. Lines 56–67: This policy shall be cancelled at any time at the request of the insured, in which case this Company shall, upon demand and surrender of this policy, refund the excess of paid premium above the customary short rates for the expired time. This policy may be cancelled at any time by this Company by giving to the insured a five days' written notice of cancellation with or without tender of the excess of paid premium above the pro rata premium for the expired time, which excess, if not tendered, shall be refunded on demand. Notice of cancellation shall state that said excess premium (if not tendered) will be refunded on demand.

Mortgagee interests and obligations. Lines 68–83: If loss hereunder is made payable, in whole or in part, to a designated mortgagee not named herein as the insured, such interest in this policy may be cancelled by giving to such mortgagee a ten days' written notice of cancellation. If the insured fails to render proof of loss such mortgagee, upon notice, shall render proof of loss in the form herein specified within sixty (60) days thereafter and shall be subject to the provisions hereof relating to appraisal and time of payment and of bringing suit. If this Company shall claim that no liability existed as to the mortgagor or owner, it shall, to the extent of payment of loss to the mortgagee, be subrogated to all the mortgagee's rights of recovery, but without impairing mortgagee's right to sue; or it may pay the mortgage debt and require an assignment thereof and of the mortgage. Other provisions relating to the interests and obligations of such mortgagee may be added hereto by agreement in writing.

Pro rata liability. Lines 86–89: This Company shall not be liable for a greater proportion of any loss than the amount hereby insured shall bear to the whole insurance covering the property against the peril involved, whether collectible or not.

Requirements in case loss occurs. Lines 90–122: The insured shall give immediate written notice to this Company of any loss, protect the property from further damage, forthwith separate the damaged and undamaged personal property, put it in the best possible order, furnish a complete inventory of the destroyed, damaged and undamaged property, showing in detail quantities, costs, actual cash value and amount of loss claimed; and within sixty days after the loss, unless such time is extended in writing by this Company, the insured shall render to this Company a proof of loss, signed and sworn to by the insured, stating the knowledge and belief of the insured as to the following: the time and origin of the loss, the interest of the insured and of all others in the property, the actual cash value of each item thereof and the amount of loss thereto, all encumbrances thereon, all other contracts of insurance, whether valid or not, covering any of said property, any changes in the title, use, occupation, location, possession or exposures of said property since the issuing of this policy, by whom and for what purpose any building herein described and the several parts thereof were occupied at the time of loss and whether or not it then stood on leased ground, and shall furnish a copy of all the descriptions and schedules in all policies and, if required, verified plans and specifications of any building, fixtures or machinery destroyed or damaged. The insured, as often as may be reasonably required, shall exhibit to any person designated by this Company all that remains of any property herein described, and submit to examinations under oath by any person named by this Company, and subscribe the same; and, as often as may be reasonably required, shall produce for examination all books of account, bills, invoices and other vouchers, or certified copies thereof if originals be lost, at such reasonable time and place as may be designated by this Company or its representative, and shall permit extracts and copies thereof to be made.

Appraisal. Lines 123–140: In case the insured and this Company shall fail to agree as to the actual cash value or the amount of loss, then, on the written demand of either, each shall select a competent and disinterested appraiser and notify the other of the appraiser selected within twenty days of such demand. The appraisers shall first select a competent and disinterested umpire; and failing for fifteen days to agree upon such umpire, then, on request of the insured or this Company, such umpire shall be selected by a judge of a court of record in the state in which the property covered is located. The appraisers shall then appraise the loss, stating separately actual cash value and loss to each item; and, failing to agree, shall submit their differences, only, to the umpire. An award in writing, so itemized, of any two when filed with this Company shall determine the amount of actual cash value and loss. Each appraiser shall be paid by the party selecting him and the expenses of appraisal and umpire shall be paid by the parties equally.

Company's options. Lines 141–147: It shall be optional with this Company to take all, or any part, of the property at the agreed or appraised value, and also to repair, rebuild or replace the property destroyed or damaged with other of like kind and quality within a reasonable time, on giving notice of its intention so to do within thirty days after the receipt of the proof of loss herein required.

Abandonment. Lines 148–149: There can be no abandonment to this Company of any property.

When loss payable. Lines 150–156: The amount of loss for which this Company may be liable shall be payable sixty days after proof of loss, as herein provided, is received by this Company and ascertainment of the loss is made either by agreement between the insured and this Company expressed in writing or by the filing with this Company of an award as herein provided.

Suit. Lines 157–161: No suit or action on this policy for the recovery of any claim shall be sustainable in any court of law or equity unless all the requirements of this policy shall have been complied with, and unless commenced within twelve months next after inception of the loss.

Subrogation. Lines 162–165: This Company may require from the insured an assignment of all right of recovery against any party for loss to the extent that payment therefor is made by this Company.

IN WITNESS WHEREOF, this Company has executed and attested these presents; but this policy shall not be valid unless countersigned by the duly authorized Agent of this Company at the agency hereinbefore mentioned.

INSERT SIGNATURES AND
TITLES OF PROPER OFFICERS

OTHER PROVISIONS APPLICABLE TO SECTIONS I AND II
EXCEPT AS OTHERWISE INDICATED

1. War Risk Exclusion: Under Section I as respects all perils insured against hereunder except the perils of fire and lightning (which are otherwise provided for on page 2 of this policy) and under Section II as respects liability assumed by the Insured under any contract or agreement, as to expenses under any Medical Payments coverage, or under any Supplementary Payments provision relating to immediate medical or surgical relief, or as to Coverage F, this policy shall not apply to loss, bodily injury or property damage caused directly or indirectly by:

    (a) hostile or warlike action in time of peace or war, including action in hindering, combating or defending against an actual, impending or expected attack, (1) by any government or sovereign power (de jure or de facto), or by any authority maintaining or using military, naval or air forces; or (2) by military, naval or air forces; or (3) by an agent of any such government, power, authority or forces, it being understood that any discharge, explosion or use of any weapon of war employing nuclear fission or fusion shall be conclusively presumed to be such a hostile or warlike action by such a government, power, authority or forces;

    (b) insurrection, rebellion, revolution, civil war, usurped power, or action taken by governmental authority in hindering, combating or defending against such an occurrence; seizure or destruction under quarantine or Custom's regulations, confiscation by order of any government or public authority, or risks of contraband or illegal transportation or trade.

2. Nuclear Clause—(Not Applicable in New York) Section I: The word "fire" in this policy or endorsements attached hereto is not intended to and does not embrace nuclear reaction or nuclear radiation or radioactive contamination, all whether controlled or uncontrolled, and loss by nuclear radiation or radioactive contamination is not intended to be and is not insured against by this policy or said endorsements, whether such loss be direct or indirect, proximate or remote, or be in whole or in part caused by, contributed to, or aggravated by "fire" or any other perils insured against by this policy or said endorsements; however, subject to the foregoing and all provisions of this policy, direct loss by "fire" resulting from nuclear reaction or nuclear radiation or radioactive contamination is insured against by this policy.

3. Nuclear Exclusion—(Not Applicable in New York) Section I: This policy does not insure against loss by nuclear reaction or nuclear radiation or radioactive contamination, all whether controlled or uncontrolled, or due to any act or condition incident to any of the foregoing, whether such loss be direct or indirect, proximate or remote, or be in whole or in part caused by, contributed to, or aggravated by any of the perils insured against by this policy; and nuclear reaction or nuclear radiation or radioactive contamination, all whether controlled or uncontrolled, is not "explosion" or "smoke". This clause applies to all perils insured against hereunder except the perils of fire and lightning, which are otherwise provided for in the Nuclear Clause contained above.

4. Nuclear Exclusion—Section II: This policy does not apply, under Coverage E, to bodily injury or property damage with respect to which an Insured under this policy is also an Insured under a nuclear energy liability policy issued by Nuclear Energy Liability Insurance Association, Mutual Atomic Energy Liability Underwriters or Nuclear Insurance Association of Canada, or would be an Insured under any such policy but for its termination upon exhaustion of its limit of liability.

GENERAL CONDITIONS

1. MODIFICATION OF TERMS: The provisions on page 2 of this policy as respects uninsurable and excepted property, the exclusion of loss by theft and suspension of insurance are hereby waived. Provisions on page 2, other than those pertaining to theft, cancellation, concealment and fraud and subrogation, do not apply to Section II of this policy. With respect to subrogation, the provisions are not applicable to Coverage F — Personal Medical Payments.

2. DEFINITIONS:

    (a) **Insured:** The unqualified word "Insured" includes (1) the Named Insured and (2) if residents of his household, his spouse, the relatives of either, and any other person under the age of twenty-one in the care of an Insured.

    The word "Insured" also includes, under Coverages E and F, (1) with respect to animals and watercraft owned by an Insured, any person or organization legally responsible therefor, except a person using or having custody or possession of any such animal or watercraft without the permission of the owner, and (2) with respect to farm tractors and trailers and self-propelled or motor or animal drawn farm implements, any employee of an Insured while engaged in the employment of the Insured.

    The insurance afforded under Coverage E applies separately to each Insured against whom claim is made or suit is brought but the inclusion herein of more than one Insured shall not operate to increase the limit of the Company's liability.

    (b) **Premises:** Means the premises described in the Declarations, including grounds, garages, stables and other outbuildings incidental thereto, and private approaches thereto.

    (c) **Residence Employee:** Means an employee of an Insured whose duties are in connection with the ownership, maintenance or use of the premises, including the maintenance or use of automobiles or teams, or who performs elsewhere duties of a similar nature not in connection with an Insured's business.

    (d) **Business:** Includes trade, profession or occupation.

3. OTHER INSURANCE: Other insurance covering the described dwelling building (except existing insurance for which credit is given in this policy) is not permitted.

4. APPORTIONMENT:

    (a) **Section I—Loss by fire or other perils not provided for in 4b) below:** This Company shall not be liable for a greater proportion of any loss from any peril or perils included in this policy than (1) the applicable limit of liability under this policy bears to the whole amount of fire insurance covering the property, or which would have covered the property except for the existence of this insurance, whether collectible or not, and whether or not such other fire insurance covers against the additional peril or perils insured hereunder, (2) nor for a greater proportion of any loss than the applicable limit of liability under this policy bears to all insurance whether collectible or not, covering in any manner such loss, or which would have covered such loss except for the existence of this insurance.

    (b) **Section I (Coverage C)—Loss by theft or loss of personal property covered on an unspecified peril basis:** Insurance under this policy shall apply as excess insurance over any other valid and collectible insurance which would apply in the absence of this policy.

    (c) **Section II (Coverage E)—Loss under Personal Liability:** If the Insured has other insurance against a loss covered by this policy, this Company shall not be liable under this policy for a greater proportion of such loss than the applicable limit of liability stated in the Declarations bears to the total applicable limit of liability of all valid and collectible insurance against such loss, provided that with respect to loss arising out of the ownership, maintenance, operation, use, loading or unloading of (1) any automobile or midget automobile at the premises or the ways immediately adjoining or (2) watercraft, this insurance shall not apply to the extent that any valid and collectible insurance, whether on a primary, excess or contingent basis, is available to the Insured.

    (d) When loss under this policy is subject to a deductible, this Company shall not be liable for more than its pro rata share of such loss in excess of the deductible amount.

5. DEATH OF NAMED INSURED: Upon the death of the Named Insured, this policy shall cover the Named Insured's spouse, if a resident of the same household at the time of such death, and legal representative as Named Insured's from the date of such death; provided, (a) under Section I, if such legal representative is not a person who was a permanent member of the Named Insured's household at the time of the death of the Named Insured, this policy shall apply as it applied prior to such death but shall not apply to loss of property owned or used by such person, a member of his household or a residence employee thereof, unless such loss occurs at a part of the premises occupied exclusively by the original Named Insured's household, and (b) under Section II, if such legal representative was not an Insured at the time of the death of the Named Insured, this policy shall apply to such person only with respect to the premises of the original Named Insured and those of his spouse, and shall cover as Insured, while a resident of said premises, any person who was an Insured at the time of the death.

6. LIBERALIZATION CLAUSE: If during the period that insurance is in force under this policy, or within 45 days prior to the inception date thereof, on behalf of this Company there be adopted, or filed with and approved or accepted by the Insurance supervisory authorities, all in conformity with law, any changes in the form attached to this policy by which this form of insurance could be extended or broadened without increased premium charge by endorsement or substitution of form, then such extended or broadened insurance shall inure to the benefit of the Insured hereunder as though such endorsement or substitution of form had been made.

7. CONFORMITY WITH STATUTE: The terms of this policy and forms attached hereto which are in conflict with the statutes of the state wherein this policy is issued are hereby amended to conform to such statutes.

8. CANCELLATION: The words "five days" in the cancellation provision on page 2 of the policy are deleted and the words "ten days" are substituted therefor.

9. POLICY TERM: This policy applies only to losses or occurrences during the policy term.

CONDITIONS APPLICABLE ONLY TO SECTION I

1. PERMISSION GRANTED: (a) for such use of the premises as is usual or incidental to a dwelling; (b) for the premises to be vacant or unoccupied without limit of time, except as otherwise provided in this policy for certain specified perils; however, a building in the course of construction shall not be deemed vacant; and (c) for Named Insured to make alterations, additions and repairs, and to complete structures in course of construction.

In the event of loss hereunder, the Insured is permitted to make reasonable repairs, temporary or permanent, provided such repairs are confined solely to the protection of the property from further damage and provided further that the Insured shall keep an accurate record of such repair expenditures. The cost of any such repairs directly attributable to damage by any peril insured against shall be included in determining the amount of loss hereunder. Nothing herein contained is intended to modify the policy requirements applicable in case loss occurs, and in particular the requirement that in case loss occurs the Insured shall protect the property from further damage.

2. CONTROL OF PROPERTY: This insurance shall not be prejudiced by any act or neglect of any person (other than the Named Insured) when such act or neglect is not within the control of the Named Insured.

3. SUBROGATION: This insurance shall not be invalidated should the Named Insured waive in writing prior to a loss any or all right of recovery against any party for loss occurring to the property covered herein.

4. BENEFIT TO BAILEE: The insurance afforded by this policy shall not inure directly or indirectly to the benefit of any carrier or other bailee for hire.

5. PAIR AND SET CLAUSE: If there is loss of an article which is part of a pair or set, the measure of loss shall be a reasonable and fair proportion of the total value of the pair or set, giving consideration to the importance of said article, but such loss shall not be construed to mean total loss of the pair or set.

6. LOSS PAYABLE CLAUSE: Loss, if any, shall be adjusted with the Named Insured and shall be payable to him unless other payee is specifically named hereunder.

CONDITIONS APPLICABLE ONLY TO SECTION II

1. LIMITS OF LIABILITY: The limit of liability stated in the Declarations for Coverage E is the limit of this Company's liability for all damages, including damages for care and loss of services, as the result of one occurrence.

The limit of liability stated in the Declarations for Coverage F as applicable to "each person" is the limit of the Company's liability for all expenses incurred by or on behalf of each person who sustains bodily injury as the result of any one accident; the limit of liability stated in the Declarations for Coverage F as applicable to "each accident" is, subject to the above provision respecting each person, the total limit of the Company's liability for all expenses incurred by or on behalf of two or more persons who sustain bodily injury as the result of any one accident.

2. LIMITS OF LIABILITY; SETTLEMENT OPTIONS — COVERAGE G: The limit of this Company's liability for loss of property arising out of any one occurrence shall not exceed (a) the actual cash value of the property at time of loss, nor (b) what it would then cost to repair or replace the property with other of like kind and quality, nor (c) the applicable limit of liability stated in the Declaration for Coverage G.

This Company may pay for the loss in money or may repair or replace the property and may settle any claim for loss of property either with the Insured or the owner thereof. Any property so paid for or replaced shall, at the option of this Company, become the property of this Company. Payment hereunder shall not constitute an admission of liability of the Insured or, except hereunder, of this Company.

3. NOTICE OF OCCURRENCE — COVERAGES E AND F: When an occurrence takes place, written notice shall be given by or on behalf of the Insured to this Company or any of its authorized agents as soon as practicable. Such notice shall contain particulars sufficient to identify the Insured and also reasonably obtainable information respecting the time, place and circumstances of the occurrence, the names and addresses of the injured and of available witnesses.

4. NOTICE OF CLAIM OR SUIT — COVERAGE E: If claim is made or suit is brought against the Insured, the Insured shall immediately forward to this Company every demand, notice, summons or other process received by him or his representative.

5. ASSISTANCE AND COOPERATION OF THE INSURED — COVERAGE E: The Insured shall cooperate with the Company and, upon the Company's request, assist in making settlements; in the conduct of suits, and in enforcing any right of contribution or indemnity against any person or organization who may be liable to the Insured because of bodily injury or property damage with respect to which insurance is afforded under this policy, and the Insured shall attend hearings and trials and assist in securing and giving evidence and obtaining the attendance of witnesses. The Insured shall not, except at his own cost, voluntarily make any payment, assume any obligation or incur any expense other than for such immediate medical and surgical relief to others as shall be imperative at the time of the accident.

6. MEDICAL REPORTS; PROOF AND PAYMENT OF CLAIM — COVERAGE F: As soon as practicable, the injured person or someone on his behalf shall give to this Company written proof of claim, under oath, if required, and shall, after each request from this Company, execute authorization to enable this Company to obtain medical reports and copies of records. The injured person shall submit to physical examination by physicians selected by this Company when and as often as this Company may reasonably require.

This Company may pay the injured person or any person or organization rendering the services and such payment shall reduce the amount payable hereunder for such injury. Payment hereunder shall not constitute admission of liability of the Insured or, except hereunder, of this Company.

7. INSURED'S DUTIES WHEN LOSS OCCURS — COVERAGE G: When loss occurs, the Insured shall give written notice as soon as practicable to the Company or any of its authorized agents, file sworn proof of loss with the Company within ninety-one (91) days after the occurrence of loss, exhibit the damaged property, if within his control, and cooperate with the Company in all matters pertaining to the loss or claims with respect thereto.

8. ACTION AGAINST COMPANY — COVERAGE E: No action shall lie against this Company unless, as a condition precedent thereto, the Insured shall have fully complied with all the terms of this policy applicable to Section II, nor until the amount of the Insured's obligation to pay shall have been finally determined either by judgment against the Insured after actual trial or by written agreement of the Insured, the claimant and this Company.

Any person or organization or the legal representative thereof who has secured such judgment or written agreement shall thereafter be entitled to recover under said Section II to the extent of the insurance afforded by this policy. No person or organization shall have any right under this policy to join the Company as a party to any action against the Insured to determine the Insured's liability, nor shall the Company be impleaded by the Insured or his legal representative.

Bankruptcy or insolvency of the Insured or of the Insured's estate shall not relieve this Company of any of its obligations hereunder.

9. ACTION AGAINST COMPANY — COVERAGES F AND G: No action shall lie against this Company unless, as a condition precedent thereto, there shall have been full compliance with all the terms of this policy applicable to Section II, nor until 30 days after the required proofs of claim have been filed with this Company.

HOMEOWNERS POLICY — BROAD FORM
PROVISIONS APPLICABLE TO SECTION I
DESCRIPTION OF PROPERTY AND INTERESTS COVERED

MIC-2
(Ed. 12-66)
Central—T

COVERAGE A — DWELLING.

This policy covers: (a) the building described including additions in contact therewith, occupied principally for dwelling purposes; (b) if the property of the Insured and when not otherwise covered, building equipment, fixtures and outdoor equipment, all pertaining to the service of the premises and while located thereon or temporarily elsewhere; and (c) materials and supplies located on the premises or adjacent thereto, intended for use in construction, alteration or repair of such dwelling. Trees, shrubs, plants or lawns are not covered, except as provided elsewhere in this form.

COVERAGE B — APPURTENANT PRIVATE STRUCTURES.

This policy covers private structures appertaining to the premises and located thereon, including materials and supplies located on the premises or adjacent thereto, intended for use in construction, alteration or repair of such structures. This coverage does not include: (a) any structure used in whole or in part for commercial, manufacturing or farming purposes; or (b) any structures (except structures used principally for private garage purposes) which are wholly rented or leased to other than a tenant of the described dwelling.

COVERAGE C — UNSCHEDULED PERSONAL PROPERTY.

1. On premises: This policy covers unscheduled personal property usual or incidental to the occupancy of the premises as a dwelling, owned, worn or used by an Insured, while on the premises, or at the option of the Named Insured, owned by others while on the portion of the premises occupied exclusively by the Insured.

This coverage does not include: animals, birds, automobiles, vehicles licensed for road use and aircraft; the property of roomers or boarders not related to the Insured; articles carried or held as samples or for sale or for delivery after sale or for rental to others; and property which is separately described and specifically insured in whole or in part by this or any other insurance.

2. Away from premises: This policy also covers unscheduled personal property as described and limited, while elsewhere than on the premises, anywhere in the world, owned, worn or used by an

Insured, or at the option of the Named Insured, owned by a guest while in a temporary residence of, and occupied by an Insured or owned by a residence employee while actually engaged in the service of an Insured and while such property is in the physical custody of such residence employee or in a residence temporarily occupied by an Insured. Property pertaining to a business is not covered.

The limits of this Company's liability for such property while away from premises shall be an additional amount of insurance equal to 10% of the amount specified for Coverage C, but in no event less than $1,000.

COVERAGE D — ADDITIONAL LIVING EXPENSE.

This policy covers the necessary increase in living expense resulting from loss by a peril insured against hereunder incurred by the Named Insured to continue as nearly as practicable the normal standard of living of the Named Insured's household for the applicable period described in (a) or (b) below:

(a) The time required, with the exercise of due diligence and dispatch, to repair or replace such damaged or destroyed property;

(b) The time required for the Named Insured's household to become settled in permanent quarters.

This coverage includes the fair rental value of the described dwelling and appurtenant private structures with respect to any portion thereof rented or held for rental by an Insured and, as furnished by the owner, for the period of time required with the exercise of due diligence and dispatch to restore same to tenantable condition, less such charges and expenses as do not continue.

The periods described above shall not be limited by the expiration of this policy.

This Company shall also be liable under Coverage D for the period of time, not exceeding two weeks, while access to the premises is prohibited by order of civil authority, but only when such order is given as a direct result of damage to neighboring premises by a peril insured against.

PERILS INSURED AGAINST

This policy insures under Section I against direct loss to the property covered (and additional living expense resulting from such loss) by the following perils as defined and limited herein:

1. Fire and lightning.

2. Removal, meaning loss by removal of the property covered hereunder from premises endangered by the perils insured against, including coverage pro rata for 30 days at each proper place to which such property must necessarily be removed for preservation from or for repair of damage caused by the perils insured against.

3. Windstorm or hail, excluding:

(a) loss caused directly or indirectly by frost or cold weather or ice (other than hail), snowstorm or sleet, all whether driven by wind or not;

(b) loss to the interior of the building(s), or the property covered therein caused by rain, snow, sand, or dust, all whether driven by wind or not, unless the building(s) covered or containing the property covered shall first sustain an actual damage to roof or walls by the direct force of wind or hail and then this Company shall be liable for loss to the interior of the building(s) or the property covered therein as may be caused by rain, snow, sand, or dust entering the building(s) through openings in the roof or walls made by direct action of wind or hail.

4. Explosion.

5. Sudden and accidental tearing asunder, cracking, burning, or bulging of a steam or hot water heating system, except appliances for heating water for domestic consumption, and excluding loss resulting from freezing while the described building(s) is vacant or unoccupied, unless the Insured shall have exercised due diligence with respect to maintaining heat in the building(s), or unless the plumbing and heating systems and domestic appliances had been drained and the water supply shut off during such vacancy or unoccupancy.

6. Riot, riot attending a strike, and civil commotion, including direct loss from pillage and looting occurring during and at the immediate place of a riot, riot attending a strike or civil commotion.

7. Aircraft.

8. Vehicles, but excluding loss to driveways and walks, caused by any land vehicle owned or operated by any occupant of the premises.

9. Sudden and accidental damage from smoke, other than smoke from agricultural smudging or industrial operations.

10. Vandalism and malicious mischief, meaning only the wilful and malicious damage to or destruction of the property covered, but excluding as respects this peril loss if the described dwelling had been vacant beyond a period of 30 consecutive days immediately preceding the loss.

11. Theft, meaning any act of stealing or attempt thereat and, as to Coverage C (on premises), including theft of property covered from within any bank, trust or safe deposit company, public warehouse, or occupied dwelling not owned or occupied by or rented to an Insured, in which the property covered has been placed for safekeeping.

Upon knowledge of loss under this peril or of an occurrence which may give rise to a claim for such loss, the Insured shall give notice as soon as practicable to this Company or any of its authorized agents and also to the police.

General Exclusions applicable to theft: This policy does not apply as respects this peril to loss: (a) if committed by an Insured; or (b) in or to a dwelling under construction or of materials or supplies therefor until completed and ready for occupancy.

Exclusions applicable while the described dwelling is rented to others: While the portion of the described dwelling customarily occupied exclusively by an Insured is rented to others, this policy does not apply, as respects this peril, to loss from the described dwelling: (a) of money, numismatic property and bank notes; (b) of accounts, bills, deeds, evidences of debt, letters of credit, notes other than bank notes, passports, railroad and other tickets, securities, and stamps including philatelic property; and (c) of jewelry, watches, necklaces, bracelets, gems, precious and semiprecious stones, or articles of gold or platinum; or (d) caused by a tenant of such portion of the described dwelling or any of his employees or members of his household.

Exclusions applicable to property away from described premises: This policy does not apply as respects this peril to loss away from the premises of: (a) property while in any dwelling or premises thereof, owned, rented or occupied by an Insured, except while an Insured is temporarily residing therein; (b) property while unattended in or on any automobile, motorcycle or trailer, other than a public conveyance, unless the loss is the result of forcible entry either into such vehicle while all doors and windows thereof are closed and locked or into a fully enclosed and locked luggage compartment, of which entry there are visible marks upon the exterior of said vehicle.

12. Falling objects, but excluding loss to (a) the interior of the building(s) or the property covered therein, caused by falling objects unless the building(s) covered or containing the property covered shall first sustain an actual damage to the exterior of the roof or walls by the falling object; (b) outdoor equipment, cloth awnings, fences, all except as the direct result of the collapse of a building.

13. Weight of ice, snow or sleet which results in physical injury to the building(s) covered or containing the property covered, but excluding loss to (a) outdoor equipment, cloth awnings, fences, all except as the direct result of the collapse of a building; (b) fences, pavements, patios, swimming pools, foundations, retaining walls, bulkheads, piers, wharves or docks, when such loss is caused by freezing, thawing, or by the pressure or weight of ice or water whether driven by wind or not; all except as the direct result of the collapse of a building.

14. Collapse (not settling, cracking, shrinkage, bulging or expansion) of building(s) or any part thereof, but excluding loss to (a) outdoor equipment, gutters and downspouts, cloth awnings and fences, all except as the direct result of the collapse of a building; (b) fences, pavements, patios, swimming pools, foundations, retaining walls, bulkheads, piers, wharves or docks, when such loss is caused by freezing, thawing, or by the pressure or weight of ice or water whether driven by wind or not; all except as the direct result of the collapse of a building.

EXTENSIONS OF COVERAGE

1. Trees, shrubs, plants and lawns: The Named Insured may apply up to 5% of the limit of liability for Coverage A, subject otherwise to the limitations and exclusions applicable thereto, to cover trees, shrubs and plants on the premises (except those grown for commercial purposes), against loss by fire, lightning, explosion, riot, civil commotion, vandalism, malicious mischief, theft, aircraft or vehicles not operated by an occupant of the described premises, but this Company shall not be liable for more than its proportion of $250 on any one tree, shrub or plant, including expense incurred for removing debris thereof. Coverage A shall also apply to lawns. This Company shall not be liable under this Extension of Coverage for loss from the perils (as defined in this policy) of windstorm or hail; or vehicles owned or operated by an occupant of the premises, falling objects; or weight of ice, snow or sleet.

2. Debris removal: This policy covers expenses incurred in the removal of all debris of the property covered hereunder occasioned by loss thereto for which coverage is afforded.

3. Replacement cost — Coverages A and B: This Extension of Coverage shall be applicable only to a building structure covered hereunder, but excluding carpeting, cloth awnings, domestic appliances and outdoor equipment, all whether permanently attached to the building structures or not.

(a) If at the time of loss the whole amount of insurance applicable to said building structure for the peril causing the loss is 80% or more of the full replacement cost of such building structure, the coverage of this policy applicable to such building structure is extended to include the full cost of repair or replacement (without deduction for depreciation).

(b) If at the time of loss the whole amount of insurance applicable to said building structure for the peril causing the loss is less than 80% of the full replacement cost of such building structure, this Company's liability for loss under this policy shall not exceed the larger of the following amounts (1) or (2):
 (1) The actual cash value of that part of the building structure damaged or destroyed; or
 (2) That proportion of the full cost of repair or replacement (without deduction for depreciation) of that part of the building structure damaged or destroyed, which the whole amount of insurance applicable to said building structure for the peril causing the loss bears to 80% of the full replacement cost of such building structure.

(c) This Company's liability for loss under this policy including this Extension of Coverage shall not exceed the smallest of the following amounts (1), (2), or (3):
 (1) The limit of liability of this policy applicable to the dam-

15. Accidental discharge, leakage or overflow of water or steam from within a plumbing, heating, or air conditioning system or domestic appliance, including the cost of tearing out and replacing any part of the building(s) covered required to effect repairs to the system or appliance from which the water or steam escapes, but excluding: (a) loss resulting from freezing while the described building(s) is vacant or unoccupied, unless the Insured shall have exercised due diligence with respect to maintaining heat in the building(s), or unless the plumbing and heating systems and domestic appliances had been drained and the water supply shut off during such vacancy or unoccupancy; (b) loss if the described property had been vacant beyond a period of 30 consecutive days immediately preceding the loss; and (c) loss to the system or appliance from which the water or steam escapes.

16. Sudden and accidental tearing asunder, cracking, burning, or bulging of appliances for heating water for domestic consumption but excluding loss resulting from freezing while the described building(s) is vacant or unoccupied, unless the Insured shall have exercised due diligence with respect to maintaining heat in the building(s) or unless the plumbing and heating systems and domestic appliances had been drained and the water supply shut off during such vacancy or unoccupancy.

17. Breakage of glass constituting a part of the building(s) covered hereunder, including glass in storm doors and storm windows, but excluding loss if the dwelling had been vacant beyond a period of 30 consecutive days immediately preceding the loss.

18. Freezing of plumbing, heating and air conditioning systems and domestic appliances, but excluding loss resulting from freezing while the described building(s) is vacant or unoccupied, unless the Insured shall have exercised due diligence with respect to maintaining heat in the building(s), or unless the plumbing and heating systems and domestic appliances had been drained and the water supply shut off during such vacancy or unoccupancy.

19. Sudden and accidental injury from artificially generated electric current to electrical appliances, devices, fixtures and wiring, except tubes, transistors and similar electronic components.

aged or destroyed building structure;
 (2) The replacement cost of the building structure or any part thereof identical with such building structure on the same premises and intended for the same occupancy and use;
 (3) The amount actually and necessarily expended in repairing or replacing said building structure or any part thereof intended for the same occupancy and use.

When the full cost of repair or replacement is more than $1,000 or more than 5% of the whole amount of insurance applicable to said building structure for the peril causing the loss, this Company shall not be liable for any loss under paragraph (a) or sub-paragraph (2) of paragraph (b) of this extension of coverage unless and until actual repair or replacement is completed.

(d) In determining if the whole amount of insurance applicable to said building structure is 80% or more of the full replacement cost of such building structure, the cost of excavation, underground flues and pipes, underground wiring and drains and brick, stone and concrete foundations, piers and other supports which are below the under surface of the lowest basement floor, or where there is no basement, which are below the surface of the ground inside the foundation walls, shall be disregarded.

(e) The Named Insured may elect to disregard this Extension of Coverage in making claim hereunder, but such election shall not prejudice the Named Insured's right to make further claim within 180 days after loss for any additional liability brought about by this Extension of Coverage.

4. Fire Department Service Clause (Not applicable in New Mexico): This insurance also covers for an amount not exceeding $100 the Named Insured's liability, assumed by contract or agreement for fire department charges where fire department is called because of a fire in, on or exposing property insured hereunder, while located on the premises described. This extension does not cover Named Insured liability, by contract or otherwise, to indemnify either a city, municipality or fire protection district, or any other person, firm or corporation against loss, claim or liability arising by reasons of the movement or functioning of fire apparatus or members of a fire department; or by reason of any accident arising out of the performance of service to Insured by any fire department. Coverage afforded under this clause applies only if the property is not located within the limits of the city, municipality or fire protection district furnishing such fire department response.

5. The foregoing Extensions of Coverage shall not increase the limit of liability applying under this policy to the property damaged or destroyed.

SPECIAL LIMITS OF LIABILITY

1. Loss Deductible Clause (No. 1 and No. 2) — With respect to loss by any of the perils insured against, this Company shall be liable only when such loss in each occurrence exceeds $50. When loss is between $50 and $500 this Company shall be liable for 111% of loss in excess of $50 and when loss is $500 or more, this loss deductible clause shall not apply.

This loss deductible clause shall not apply to Coverage D (Additional Living Expense).

2. Under Coverage C, this Company shall not be liable in any one loss with respect to the following named property:

(a) for more than $100 on money, bullion, numismatic property and bank notes;

(b) for more than $500 on accounts, bills, deeds, evidences of debt, letters of credit, notes other than bank notes, passports, railroad and other tickets, securities, and stamps including philatelic property;

(c) for more than $1,000 on manuscripts;

(d) by theft for more than $1,000 on any single article of jewelry including watches, necklaces, bracelets, gems, precious and semiprecious stones and any article of gold or platinum or any article of fur or any article containing fur which represents its principal value;

(e) for more than $500 on watercraft, including their trailers, whether licensed or not, furnishings, equipment and outboard motors, nor for any loss by windstorm or hail to such property not inside fully enclosed buildings (except rowboats and canoes on the premises).

SPECIAL EXCLUSIONS

This Company shall not be liable:

(a) as respects Perils 5, 12, 14, 15, 16 and 18: for loss caused by, resulting from, contributed to or aggravated by any earth movement, including but not limited to earthquake, landslide, mud flow, earth sinking, rising or shifting; unless loss by fire or explosion ensues, and this Company shall then be liable only for such ensuing loss; but this exclusion does not apply to loss by theft;

(b) as respects Perils 3, 5, 12, 13, 14, 15, 16, 17 and 18: for loss caused by, resulting from, contributed to or aggravated by any of the following:

(1) flood, surface water, waves, tidal water or tidal wave, overflow of streams or other bodies of water, or spray from any of the foregoing, all whether driven by wind or not;

(2) water which backs up through sewers or drains;

(3) water below the surface of the ground including that which exerts pressure on or flows, seeps or leaks through sidewalks, driveways, foundations, walls, basement or other floors, or through doors, windows or any other openings in such sidewalks, driveways, foundations, walls or floors;

unless loss by fire or explosion ensues, and this Company shall then be liable only for such ensuing loss; but these exclusions do not apply to loss by theft;

(c) for loss occasioned directly or indirectly by enforcement of any local or state ordinance or law regulating the construction, repair, or demolition of building(s) or structure(s) unless such liability is otherwise specifically assumed by endorsement hereon;

(d) for consequential loss of any nature except that loss, to unscheduled personal property covered hereunder, due to change of temperature shall be limited to such loss resulting from physical damage to the described building(s) or to equipment therein or to equipment on the described premises caused by a peril insured against.

SPECIAL CONDITIONS

1. Loss Clause: Loss hereunder shall not reduce the limit of liability under this Policy.

2. Occupancy Clause: It is a condition of this policy that if the described dwelling is associated with and in proximity to farming operations (1) the agricultural products produced on the land are incidental to the occupancy of the dwelling and are principally for home consumption, or (2) that the occupants of the dwelling and buildings appurtenant thereto are not engaged in the operation of the farm and said buildings are in addition to a complete set of farm buildings on the farm and are not exposed within 200 feet by any farm building.

3. Mortgage Clause — Coverages A and B only — (This entire clause is void unless name of Mortgagee(s) (or trustee(s)) is inserted in the Declarations): Loss or damage, if any, under this policy, shall be payable to the mortgagee (or trustee), named on the first page of this policy, as interest may appear, under all present or future mortgages upon the property herein described in which the aforesaid may have an interest as mortgagee (or trustee) in order of precedence of said mortgages, and this insurance as to the interest of the mortgagee (or trustee) only therein, shall not be invalidated by any act or neglect of the mortgagor or owner of the within described property, nor by any foreclosure or other proceedings or notice of sale relating to the property, nor by any change in the title or ownership of the property, nor by the occupation of the premises for purposes more hazardous than are permitted by this policy; provided, that in case the mortgagor or owner shall neglect to pay any premium due under this policy, the mortgagee (or trustee) shall, on demand, pay the same.

Provided also, that the mortgagee (or trustee) shall notify this Company of any change of ownership or occupancy or increase of hazard which shall come to the knowledge of said mortgagee (or trustee) and, unless permitted by this policy, it shall be noted thereon and the mortgagee (or trustee) shall, on demand, pay the premium for such increased hazard for the term of the use thereof, otherwise this policy shall be null and void.

This Company reserves the right to cancel this policy at any time as provided by its terms, but in such case this policy shall continue in force for the benefit only of the mortgagee (or trustee) for ten days after notice to the mortgagee (or trustee) of such cancellation and shall then cease, and this Company shall have the right, on like notice, to cancel this agreement.

Whenever this Company shall pay the mortgagee (or trustee) any sum for loss or damage under this policy, and shall claim that, as to the mortgagor or owner, no liability therefor existed, this Company shall, to the extent of such payment, be thereupon legally subrogated to all the rights of the party to whom such payment shall be made, under all securities held as collateral to the mortgage debt, or may at its option pay to the mortgagee (or trustee) the whole principal due or to grow due on the mortgage, with interest and shall thereupon receive a full assignment and transfer of the mortgage and of all such other securities; but no subrogation shall impair the right of the mortgagee (or trustee) to recover the full amount of said mortgagee's (or trustee's) claim.

4. Installment Payment — Not applicable if policy is written on a Continuous Renewal basis: If the Insured elects to pay the premium in equal annual payments as indicated on the first page of this policy the premium for this policy is hereby made so payable.

If the Insured is in default of any such premium payment and this Company elects to cancel this policy, notice of cancellation shall be in accordance with the provisions of this policy, but in such case any portions of the premium previously paid shall be earned by this Company.

(OVER)

PROVISIONS APPLICABLE TO SECTION II

THIS COMPANY AGREES WITH THE NAMED INSURED:

INSURING AGREEMENTS

1. COVERAGE E — PERSONAL LIABILITY:

(a) **Liability:** To pay on behalf of the Insured all sums which the Insured shall become legally obligated to pay as damages because of bodily injury or property damage, and the Company shall defend any suit against the Insured alleging such bodily injury or property damage and seeking damages which are payable under the terms of this policy, even if any of the allegations of the suit are groundless, false or fraudulent; but the Company may make such investigation and settlement of any claim or suit as it deems expedient.

(b) **Fire Legal Liability:** Coverage E also applies with respect to all sums which the Insured shall become legally obligated to pay as damages because of property damage to the premises or house furnishings therein if such property damage arises out of (1) fire, (2) explosion, or (3) smoke or smudge caused by sudden, unusual and faulty operation of any heating or cooking unit.

2. COVERAGE F — PERSONAL MEDICAL PAYMENTS: To pay all reasonable expenses incurred within one year from the date of accident for necessary medical, surgical, X-ray and dental services, including prosthetic devices, and necessary ambulance, hospital, professional nursing and funeral services, to or for each person who sustains bodily injury caused by accident,

(a) while on the premises with the permission of an Insured, or
(b) while elsewhere if such bodily injury, (1) arises out of the premises or a condition in the ways immediately adjoining, (2) is caused by the activities of an Insured, (3) is caused by the activities of or is sustained by a residence employee and arises out of and in the course of his employment by an Insured, or (4) is caused by an animal owned by or in the care of an Insured.

3. COVERAGE G — PHYSICAL DAMAGE TO PROPERTY: To pay for loss of property of others caused by an Insured. "Loss" means damage or destruction but does not include disappearance, abstraction or loss of use. This coverage shall not apply if insurance is otherwise provided in Section I of this policy.

4. SUPPLEMENTARY PAYMENTS: With respect to such insurance as is afforded by this policy for Coverage E, this Company shall pay, in addition to the applicable limits of liability:

(a) all expenses incurred by this Company, all costs taxed against the Insured in any defended suit and all interest on the entire amount of any judgment therein which accrues after entry of the judgment and before this Company has paid or tendered or deposited in court that part of the judgment which does not exceed the limit of this Company's liability thereon;
(b) premiums on appeal bonds required in any such suit, premiums on bonds to release attachments for an amount not in excess of the applicable limit of liability of this policy, but without any obligation to apply for or furnish any such bonds;
(c) expenses incurred by the Insured for such immediate medical and surgical relief to others as shall be imperative at the time of the accident;
(d) all reasonable expenses, other than loss of earnings, incurred by the Insured at this Company's request.

Section II of this Policy Does Not Apply:

(a) (1) to any business pursuits of an Insured, except, under Coverages E and F, activities therein which are ordinarily incident to nonbusiness pursuits, (2) to the rendering of any professional service or the omission thereof, or (3) to any act or omission in connection with premises, other than as defined, which are owned, rented or controlled by an Insured, but this subdivision (3) does not apply with respect to bodily injury to a residence employee arising out of and in the course of his employment by the Insured;
(b) under Coverages E and F, to the ownership, maintenance, operation, use, loading or unloading of (1) automobiles or midget automobiles while away from the premises or the ways immediately adjoining, except under Coverage E with respect to operations by independent contractors for non-business purposes of an Insured not involving automobiles owned or hired by the Insured, (2) watercraft owned by or rented to an Insured, while away from the premises, if with inboard motor power exceeding fifty horsepower, or if a sailing vessel with or without auxiliary power and twenty-six feet or more in overall length; (3) watercraft, other than a sailing vessel, while away from the premises and powered in whole or in part by an undeclared outboard motor owned by an Insured, or (4) aircraft; but, with respect to bodily injury to a residence employee, arising out of and in the course of his employment by the Insured, parts (1), (2) and (3) of this exclusion do not apply, and part (4) applies only while such employee is engaged in the operation or maintenance of aircraft;
(c) under Coverages E and F, to bodily injury or property damage caused intentionally by or at the direction of the Insured;
(d) under Coverages E and F, to bodily injury to any person (1) if the Insured has in effect on the date of the occurrence a policy providing workmen's compensation or occupational disease benefits therefor, or (2) if benefits therefor are in whole or in part either payable

SUPPLEMENTARY DEFINITIONS:

5. SUPPLEMENTARY DEFINITIONS:

(a) "**bodily injury**" means bodily injury, sickness or disease, including death resulting therefrom, sustained by any person;
(b) "**property damage**" means injury to or destruction of property, including loss of use thereof;
(c) **premises:** For purposes of Section II, the definition of "premises" appearing in the Basic Policy shall include: (1) all premises where the Named Insured or his spouse maintains a residence and includes private approaches thereto and other premises and private approaches thereto for use in connection with said residence, except business property and farms, (2) individual or family cemetery plots or burial vaults, (3) premises in which an Insured is temporarily residing, if not owned by an Insured, and (4) vacant land, other than farm land, owned by or rented to an Insured. Land shall not be deemed vacant following the commencement of any construction operations thereon unless such operations are being performed solely by independent contractors in connection with the construction of a one or two family dwelling for the Insured;
(d) "**business property**" includes (1) property on which a business is conducted, and (2) property rented in whole or in part to others, or held for such rental, by the Insured. The Insured's property shall not constitute "business property" because of (a) occasional rental of the Insured's residence, (b) rental in whole or in part to others of a one or two family dwelling usually occupied in part by the Insured as a residence, unless such rental is for the accommodations of more than two roomers or boarders per family occupying the dwelling, (c) rental of space in the Insured's residence for incidental office, school or studio occupancy, or (d) rental or holding for rental of not more than three car spaces or stalls in garages or stables;
(e) "**automobile**" means a land motor vehicle, trailer or semitrailer; but the term "automobile" does not include, except while being towed by or carried on an automobile, any of the following: any crawler or farm-type tractor, farm implement or, if not subject to motor vehicle registration, any equipment which is designed for use principally off public roads;
(f) "**midget automobile**" means a land motor vehicle of the type commonly referred to as a "midget automobile", "kart", "go-kart", "speedmobile" or by a comparable name, whether commercially built or otherwise;
(g) "**undeclared outboard motor**" means
(1) an outboard motor of more than twenty-four horsepower, or
(2) a combination of outboard motors of more than twenty-four horsepower in the aggregate and used with a single watercraft, if not declared and a premium charged therefor.

6. INSURANCE FOR NEWLY ACQUIRED OUTBOARD MOTORS:

Part (3) of Special Exclusion (b) does not apply to a watercraft powered by an undeclared outboard motor, ownership of which is acquired during the policy period by an Insured included within parts (1) or (2) of the definition of "Insured."

SPECIAL EXCLUSIONS

or required to be provided under any workmen's compensation or occupational disease law, but this subdivision (2) does not apply with respect to Coverage E unless such benefits are payable or required to be provided by the Insured;
(e) under Coverage E, to liability assumed by the Insured under any contract or agreement, but this exclusion as respects Insuring Agreement I (a) does not apply to (1) any indemnity obligation assumed by the Insured under a written contract directly relating to the ownership, maintenance or use of the premises or (2) liability of others assumed by the Insured under any other written contract;
(f) under Insuring Agreement I (a) of Coverage E, to property damage to property used by, rented to or in the care, custody or control of the Insured, or property as to which the Insured for any purpose is exercising physical control;
(g) under Coverage E, to sickness or disease of any residence employee unless prior to 36 months after the end of the policy period written claim is made or suit is brought against the Insured for damages because of such sickness or disease or death resulting therefrom;
(h) under Coverage F, to bodily injury to (1) any Insured included within part (1) and (2) of the definition of "Insured" or (2) any person, other than a residence employee, if such person is regularly residing on the premises including any part rented to such person or to others, or is on the premises because of a business conducted thereon, or is injured by an accident arising out of such business;
(i) under Coverage G, to loss (1) arising out of the ownership, maintenance, operation, use, loading or unloading of any land motor vehicle, trailer or semitrailer, farm machinery or equipment, aircraft or watercraft; or (2) of property owned by or rented to any Insured, any resident of the Named Insured's household or any tenant of the Insured; or (3) caused intentionally by an Insured over the age of 12 years.

Sections I and II are otherwise subject to the provisions set forth in the policy to which this form is attached.

APPENDIX B. HOMEOWNERS GENERAL RULES*

1. General Instructions.

The General Rules, rates and premiums contained herein shall govern the writing of the Homeowners Policy. The State Territorial Pages contain the basic premium and rate charts, and any applicable exceptions to the General Rules. The rules and rates of the appropriate bureau for each coverage shall govern in all cases not specifically provided for in these rules.

2. Eligibility.

a. A Homeowners Policy with Form 1, Form 2, Forms 3 and 4 or Form 5 attached may be written only for the owner-occupant of a dwelling which is used exclusively for private residential purposes (except as provided in Rule 2c) and which contains not more than two (2) families and with not more than two (2) boarders or roomers per family.

b. Except as provided in Rule 2a, a Homeowners Policy with only Form 4 (Residence Contents — Broad Form) attached may be issued only to:
   (1) the tenant (non-owner) of a dwelling or an apartment situated in any building; or
   (2) the owner-occupant of a dwelling or of a building containing an apartment who is not otherwise eligible for a Homeowners Policy under Rule 2a above;

   provided the residential premises occupied by the Insured is used exclusively for residential purposes (except as provided in Rule 2c) and is not occupied by more than one additional family or more than two boarders or roomers.

c. Incidental office, professional, private school or studio occupancy is permitted when the rules of the fire rating bureau permit such occupancy within a dwelling without additional charge for fire coverage.

d. A policy shall not be issued covering any property to which farm forms or rates apply under the rules of the fire bureau. In no event shall a policy be issued to cover any property situated on premises used for farming purposes unless farming conducted thereon is only incidental to the occupancy of the premises by the Insured as a dwelling, and farming is not the occupation of the Insured.

e. It is permissible to cover certain interests of a non-occupant, in the event of joint ownership of the dwelling, by attachment of Endorsement **HO-101** without additional premium.

f. When a two family dwelling is occupied by co-owners, each occupying separate and independent premises within the building, it is permissible to issue a Homeowners Policy to one of the two co-owner occupants of the dwelling and endorse the policy, using Endorsement **HO-101**, to cover the interest of the other co-owner in the building. A separate Homeowners Policy with Form 4 attached may then be issued to the second co-owner occupying the other apartment in the dwelling.

g. Subject to the preceding eligibility rules, a Homeowners policy may be written to cover a seasonal dwelling and such dwelling shall be designated as "Seasonal Dwelling" in the policy declarations. Unless otherwise provided in the State Territorial Pages seasonal dwellings shall be treated as specifically rated risks.

3. Tenants Coverage — Identification of Premises.

When a Homeowners Policy is written with only Form 4 (Residence Contents — Broad Form) attached, the policy declaration specifying the location of the premises covered shall identify by apartment number or other positive identification the premises actually occupied for residential purposes by the insured.

4. Policy Coverages — Description of Coverage.

The following is a general description of the coverage provided by the basic Homeowners forms. The policy, forms, endorsements and appropriate manual rules should be consulted for details.

a. Section I — Basic Physical Damage Coverages

(1) Form 1 — (Standard Form). Covers dwelling, appurtenant private structures, unscheduled personal property on and away from premises and additional living expense, against loss by fire, the usual Extended Coverage perils, and theft.

*(2) Form 2 — (Broad Form). Covers dwelling, appurtenant private structures, unscheduled personal property on and away from premises and additional living expense, against loss by fire, the usual Dwelling Broad Form perils, and theft.

(3) Form 3 — (Dwelling Special Form). Covers the dwelling, appurtenant private structures and additional living expense, against all risks of physical loss (with certain exceptions). This form can be used only in conjunction with Form 4 (Residence Contents – Broad Form).

*(4) Form 4 — (Residence Contents — Broad Form). Covers unscheduled personal property on and away from premises, additional living expense and the insured's interest in improvements and betterments, against loss by fire, the usual Dwelling Broad Form perils, and theft.

This form shall be used to provide coverage (a) for a tenant, or (b) in conjunction with the Dwelling Special Form to provide building and contents coverage for the owner-occupant, or (c) the owner-occupant of a building not otherwise eligible.

(5) Form 5 — (Comprehensive Form)

(a) Building Coverage — covers the dwelling, appurtenant private structures and additional living expense, against all risks of physical loss (with certain exceptions).

(b) Unscheduled Personal Property Coverage — covers unscheduled personal property both on and away from premises against all risks of loss (with certain exceptions).

*NOTE: Theft coverage under Forms 2 and 4 may be broadened by attachment of Extended Theft Coverage Endorsement **HO-103** at the applicable additional premium.

b. Section II — Basic Liability Coverages.

(1) Personal Liability — Covers payment on behalf of the Insured of all sums, subject to the stipulated limit, which he is legally obligated to pay as damages because of bodily injury, or damage to property, arising out of his residence premises or personal activities; including liability for damage to premises and house furnishings used by or in the care, custody or control of the Insured caused by fire, explosion and smoke.

(2) Personal Medical Payments — Covers medical and related expenses, subject to the stipulated limit, arising out of accidents to persons other than the Insured and residents of his home.

(3) Physical Damage to Property — Covers physical damage, subject to the stipulated limit, to property of others caused by an Insured regardless of the Insured's legal liability for such damage.

5. Mandatory Coverages.

a. It is required that coverages be written under Sections I and II of the Homeowners Policy for not less than the minimum limits set forth in Rule 7.

b. It is required that Section II of the policy include coverage for:

(1) all premises where the Named Insured or spouse maintains a residence;

(2) all residence employees of the Named Insured or spouse, not covered or required to be covered by Workmen's Compensation Insurance;

(3) all swimming or wading pools capable of being filled to a depth of 30 inches at any point.

6. Office, Professional, Private School or Studio Occupancies.

    a. When the Insured maintains an incidental office, professional, private school or studio occupancy in the dwelling, or in a separate structure on the premises, which otherwise meet the eligibility requirements, the appropriate declaration must be made on the first page of the policy. Endorsement **HO-105** must be attached and the limit of liability for Coverage C of Section I must be increased by an amount not less than 25% of the basic limit for Coverage C required by Rule 7 and the applicable additional premiums must be charged.

    b. When the Insured gives professional instruction, such as music, dancing, or similar instruction in the dwelling, employs no assistants and there has been no physical alteration of the dwelling to accommodate the occupancy, the increased amount for Coverage C of Section I may be waived. The liability exposure (Section II) must be covered using Endorsement **HO-105** for the additional premium indicated in the manual.

    c. When the Insured has permissible office, professional, private school or studio occupancy in a premises occupied by the Insured principally for residential purposes, other than on the described premises, the liability exposure (Section II) must be covered subject to the applicable premiums and forms.

7. Basic Limits of Liability Required.

    a. Forms 1, 2, or Form 3 with Form 4 attached.

        (1) The basic limits under Section I (Physical Damage) of the policy, expressed as percentages of the Limit of Liability on the dwelling, are as follows:

Coverage	Limit of Liability
A. Dwelling Building	Minimum Amount $8,000
B. Appurtenant Private Structures	10% of Limit on Dwelling
C. Unscheduled Personal Property	40% of Limit on Dwelling, with 10% of this amount, but not less than $1,000, applying to unscheduled personal property away from the premises
D. Additional Living Expense:	
Form 1	10% of Limit on Dwelling
Forms 2 or 3	20% of Limit on Dwelling

(2) The basic limits required under Section II are as follows:

    E. Personal Liability $25,000

    F. Personal Medical Payments $ 500 Each person

                                       $25,000 Each accident

    G. Physical Damage to property

           of others $ 250

(3) The basic limits of liability for Coverage B, C or D of Section I of this policy and E or F of Section II of the policy may be increased for an additional premium.

(4) It is permissible to reduce the basic limit of liability for Coverage C of Section I of the policy to an amount not less than 30% of the Limit of Liability on the dwelling building. The appropriate premium adjustment is indicated in the rate section of this manual.

(5) Basic limits of liability under Coverage C of Section I may not be reduced when Rule 6 (Office, Professional, Private School or Studio Occupancies rule) applies.

b. Form 4 (when not used in conjunction with Form 3).

(1) The basic limits required under Section I (Physical Damage) of the policy, expressed as percentages of the amount of insurance on unscheduled personal property, are as follows:

Limit of Liability	**Coverage**
C. Unscheduled Personal Property	Minimum amount $4,000 with 10% of this amount, but not less than $1,000, applying to unscheduled personal property away from the premises.
D. Additional Living Expense	20% of limit on unscheduled personal property.

(2) The basic limits under Section II are as follows:

    E. Personal Liability $25,000

    F. Personal Medical Payments $ 500 Each person

                                       $25,000 Each accident

    G. Physical Damage to property

           of others $ 250

(3) The basic limits of liability for Coverage E or F of Section II of the policy may be increased for an additional premium.

(4) The form also provides an optional extension of 10% of the amount of insurance on unscheduled personal property on premises to cover the Insured's interest in improvements and betterments.

c. Form 5.

(1) The basic limits under Section I (Physical Damage) of the policy, expressed as percentages of the Limit of Liability on the dwelling, are as follows:

Coverage	Limit of Liability
A. Dwelling	Minimum Amount $15,000
B. Appurtenant Private Structures	10% of Limit on Dwelling
C. Unscheduled Personal Property	50% of Limit on Dwelling
D. Additional Living Expense	20% of Limit on Dwelling

(2) The basic limits under Section II are as follows:

E. Personal Liability	$25,000
F. Personal Medical Payments	$ 500 Each person
	$25,000 Each accident
G. Physical Damage to property of others	$ 250

(3) The basic limits of liability for Coverage B, C or D of Section I of the policy and E or F of Section II of the policy may be increased for an additional premium.

8. Limits of Liability in Excess of Premium Charts.

Premiums for limits of liability in excess of those shown in the Premium Charts may be obtained from the Company.

9. Deductibles:

(a) **All Forms — Forms 1, 2, 3, 4 and 5 contain two deductible clauses —**

(1) Loss Deductible Clause No. I applies to loss caused by windstorm or hail to buildings, structures, and personal property in the open;

(2) Loss Deductible Clause No. 2 applies to loss caused by all perils under Section I except loss caused by windstorm or hail to buildings, structures and personal property in the open, and fire and lightning. With respect to Forms 2, 3 and 4, this deductible may be modified by attachment of "Modified Loss Deductible Clause No. 2" which makes the deductible applicable only to loss caused by certain enumerated perils.

(b) **Form 1 —**

(1) Loss Deductible Clause No. 2 may be eliminated in accordance with Basic Premium Charts.

(2) Loss Deductible Clause No. I may be eliminated if Loss Deductible Clause No. 2 has also been eliminated unless otherwise provided in the State Territorial Pages.

(c) **Forms 2, 3 and 4 —**
- (1) Loss Deductible Clause No. 2 may be eliminated in accordance with Basic Premium Charts.
- (2) Modified Loss Deductible Clause No. 2 may be used in lieu of Loss Deductible Clause No. 2 by attaching Endorsement **HO-141** to combined Forms 3 and 4, and Endorsement **HO-143** to Form 2 or Form 4 when used alone, in accordance with Basic Premium Charts.
- (3) Loss Deductible Clause No. 1 may be eliminated if Loss Deductible Clause No. 2 has been eliminated or Modified Loss Deductible Clause No. 2 is made applicable unless otherwise provided in the State Territorial Pages.
- (4) Unless otherwise provided in the State Territorial Pages, when a Homeowners Policy is written subject to Residence Contents—Broad Form MIC-4 and Loss Deductible Clause No. 2 has been either modified or eliminated, Loss Deductible Clause No. 1 may then be eliminated without charge.

(d) **Form 5 —** Unless otherwise provided in State Territorial Pages, the deductible amount of Loss Deductible Clauses No. 1 and No. 2 may be reduced from $100 to $50 by attachment of Endorsement **HO-145** and payment of appropriate additional premium. It is not permissible to eliminate either Loss Deductible Clause No. 1 or No. 2.

(e) Loss Deductible Clauses No. 1 and No. 2, as well as Modified Loss Deductible Clause No. 2 apply to each occurrence and decrease as the amount of the loss in excess of the deductible approaches $500 where the deductible is completely eliminated. When a $50 deductible applies, the Company is liable only when loss in each occurrence exceeds $50. When the loss is between $50 and $500, the Company will pay 111% of the loss in excess of $50, and when loss is $500 or more, the Loss Deductible Clause will not apply. When the $100 Loss Deductible Clause applies, the Company is liable only when loss in each occurrence exceeds $100. When the loss is between $100 and $500 the Company will pay 125% of loss in excess of $100 and when loss is $500 or more, the Loss Deductible Clause does not apply.

10. Additional Coverages.
The following are coverages which may be added to the Homeowners Policy at full manual premium unless otherwise provided for in this manual.

a. **Section I — Physical Damage.**
- (1) **Fire Department Service Charges.** Limits in excess of the $100 provided in the basic Homeowners Policy may be written at the applicable fire bureau rules and rates.

(2) **Demolition, Increased Costs Coverage.** If the rules of the fire rating bureau provide for a demolition endorsement, demolition time element endorsement, contingent liability from operation of building laws endorsement, or increased cost of construction coverage endorsement, it may be attached to the Homeowners Policy, subject to applicable fire bureau rules and rates.

(3) **Earthquake Damage Assumption.** If the rules of the fire rating bureau provide for the attachment of an Earthquake Damage Assumption Endorsement, such coverage may be included in the Homeowners Policy by attachment of Endorsement **HO-111** at the applicable additional premium shown in the rate section of this manual. When such endorsement is attached to the Homeowners Policy, it must apply to both building and unscheduled personal property insured under Section I. Except that with Form 5 such endorsement shall apply to building coverages only, because unscheduled personal property is covered against loss by earthquake in the basic form.

(4) **Physicians', Surgeons', Dentists' and Veterinarians' Outside Coverage.** (Use only on Forms 2 and 4 with Endorsement **HO-103** attached.) Theft coverage may be extended to cover surgical, medical or dental instruments, apparatus, medicines, drugs, or books, including the bag, kit or instrument case, while away from the Insured's office, subject to specific limits stated in the endorsement, by attachment of Endorsement **HO-113** at the applicable additional premium shown in the rate section of this manual. To provide similar coverage in conjunction with Form 5 see Rule 10c.

(5) **Money and Securities (Increased Limits) — Forms 1, 2, 4 and 5.** Increased limits on money, bullion, numismatic property, bank notes, and on accounts, bills, deeds, evidences of debt, letters of credit, notes other than bank notes, passports, railroad and other tickets, securities, and stamps including philatelic property, may be provided by attachment of Endorsement **HO-115** at the applicable additional premium shown in the rate section of this manual.

The limit on money etc. may be increased by an amount not exceeding $400 and the limit on securities, etc. may be increased by an amount not exceeding $500.

(6) **Unscheduled Jewelry, Watches and Furs (Increased Limits) — Form 5.** The special limit in Form 5 may be increased by an amount not exceeding $750, subject to a limit of $250 on any one article by attachment of Endorsement **HO-139.**

The additional premium shall be calculated using the applicable rate shown in the rate section of this manual applied to the amount of additional coverage.

(7) **Glass.** The Residence Glass Endorsement may be attached to the Homeowners Policy for the additional premium shown in the rate section of this Manual.

(8) **Appurtenant Private Structures.** An additional amount of insurance may be written on a specific outbuilding by attachment of Endorsement **HO-117** describing such outbuilding and stating a specific limit of liability thereon. The additional premium shall be calculated using the applicable rates shown in the rate section of this manual.

b. Section II — Liability.

(1) (a) **Farmers Comprehensive Liability Coverage.** When an Insured who is otherwise eligible for a Homeowners policy has farm liability (Section II) exposures, such exposures may be covered by attachment of Endorsement **HO-119** to convert the Personal Liability Coverage to a Farmer's Comprehensive Personal Liability Coverage. This endorsement may be used in connection with otherwise eligible risks having farm exposures except:

1. Farms where the principal purpose of the farm is to supply commodities for manufacturing or processing by the Insured for sale to others, such as creameries and dairies (but not dairy farms), farms operating freezing or dehydrating plants, or poultry factories. The word "processing" does not apply to the slaughtering and dressing of livestock or to such operations as bunching of vegetables or crating of berries.

2. Farms whose principal business is raising and using horses for racing purposes.

3. Incorporated farms.

(b) **Employer's Liability,** including employee's medical payments coverage—Liability coverage for farm employees of any Insured may be provided subject to the rules and rates filed by or on behalf of the Company. Farm employees employed in violation of law may be excluded by attachment of **HO-157** subject to the rules and rates filed by or on behalf of the Company.

(2) **Watercraft and Outboard Motors.** Watercraft and outboard motors not covered within the terms of Section II may be covered by Endorsement **HO-121** at the applicable additional premium shown in the rate section of this manual.

(3) **Business Pursuits.** Coverage for the liability of an Insured arising out of business activities, other than businesses of which the Insured is sole owner or in which he is a partner, may be provided by attachment of Endorsement **HO-123,** at the applicable additional premium shown in the rate section of this manual.

(4) **Additional Premises.** If the Named Insured or spouse owns additional one or two family residential premises rented to others, such premises may be covered by attachment of Endorsement **HO-125,** at the applicable additional premium shown in the rate section of this manual.

(5) **Non-Comprehensive Coverage.** It is permissible to provide a non-comprehensive liability coverage by attachment of Endorsement HO-127 to Form 4 (Residence Contents—Broad Form) to cover the liability of the owner-occupant of a three or four family dwelling. No other non-comprehensive liability endorsement shall be attached to the Homeowners Policy.

   c. Personal Articles Coverage. Floater coverage on certain classes of scheduled personal property may be provided by the attachment of a Personal Articles Floater Policy, subject to the forms, rates and rules filed by or on behalf of the Company.

   d. Workmen's Compensation coverage shall not be attached to the Homeowners Policy.

Rule 11. Rounding of Premium Rule

All Homeowners premiums shown in the premium box on the face of the policy, for each endorsement attached to the policy and for cancellations shall be carried to the nearest dollar. For this purpose an amount of fifty cents ($.50) or more shall be considered as a dollar. As respects cancellations requested by the Company, the return premium shall be carried to the next higher whole dollar.

12. Specifically Rated Risks.

Requests for premiums for specifically rated dwellings, as defined below, shall be submitted to the fire rating bureau by the Company or producer.

For the purpose of this rule specifically rated dwellings are defined as those dwellings which are specifically rated because of fire resistive construction or special construction features, and those dwellings which take special locality charges because of congestion or conflagration hazards. Dwellings shall not be considered specifically rated because of an individual exposure charge but such dwellings shall take the premium shown in the charts.

13. Secondary Locations.

   a. Same State or Territory. When the Insured owns and occupies, or occupies as tenant, one or more secondary locations situated in the same state as the principal location, such secondary location(s) may be insured under the Homeowners Policy issued to cover on the primary location by attaching Endorsement HO-131. All of the rules of this manual shall apply separately to the secondary location(s) except that the minimum limit of liability for Coverage A, Section I at a secondary location shall be $5,000.

   If the secondary location is not owned by the Insured, it is not permissible to cover the location using endorsement HO-131 when Form I is attached to the policy. In such cases a separate Homeowners Policy must be written as provided in paragraph b. below.

   b. Any State or Territory. A separate Homeowners Policy may be written covering secondary locations wherever located, which are otherwise eligible under the rules. When a separate Homeowners Policy is written covering the secondary location, all the rules in this manual shall apply: except that if the Company issuing such policy has also covered the primary location under a current Homeowners Policy the number of which is appropriately shown in the secondary location policy, then the rules are modified as follows:

(1) the minimum limit of liability for Coverage A, Section I, at the secondary location, shall be $5,000; and

(2) Section II (Liability) may be omitted from the policy covering the secondary location provided the policy is endorsed or otherwise amended to indicate that Section II coverage for the secondary location has been assumed in the Homeowners Policy covering the primary location.

c. Increased Coverage C Limits — Form 5 Only. The limit of 10% of Coverage C, Section I under Form 5 applicable to any secondary residence of the Insured may be increased by attachment of Endorsement **HO-129** for the appropriate additional premium shown in the rate section of this manual. Such additional premium applies separately for each additional secondary location where an increase of the Coverage C limit applicable thereto is desired.

14. Policy Period.

Premiums are stated for a term of three years. No policy shall be written for any other term except for the purpose of maintaining anniversary dates scheduled under a specific policy which is being replaced, in which case it is permissible to write a Homeowners Policy for an initial term of not less than two years and not more than three years at pro rata of the three year premium.

15. Interpolation of Premiums for Policy Amounts Not Shown on Premium Charts.

The premium for a policy amount, in excess of the minimum policy amount, not shown in the basic premium charts may be obtained by interpolation. The premium adjustment for reduction in Coverage C, Section I as permitted by these rules, and premiums for additional amounts or coverages for both Sections I and II of the policy may also be interpolated.

Method for Interpolation: A premium is desired for a policy amount of $16,000 which falls between $15,000 and $17,500 shown in the Chart. In other words, the desired amount is $1,000 in excess of the $15,000 shown.

(1) Policy Amounts Shown   Premiums Shown

    $17,500 $220

     15,000   200

    $ 2,500 (diff. in amounts) $ 20 (diff. in premiums)

(2) $\frac{\$\ 1,000\ \text{(additional amounts)}}{\$\ 2,500\ \text{(diff. in amounts)}}$ x $ 20 (diff. in premiums) = $8

(3) $ 200 (premium for $15,000)

        8 (premium for additional $1,000)

$ 208 (basic premium for $16,000)

NOTE: When the Premium is obtained by interpolation the limits for Coverages B, C and D, Section I should be revised in relation to the basic limit of liability on the dwelling. (See Rule 7)

16. Other Insurance.

Other insurance on the dwelling building described in the Declarations is not permitted except existing insurance for which credit is given in the policy.

When Form 4 is used alone, other insurance on property covered under Coverage C, Section I, is not permitted, except existing insurance for which credit is given in the policy.

17. Credit for Existing Insurance.

    a. Form 5. With respect to unscheduled personal property insured under Form 5, it shall be permissible to allow a credit for that portion of an existing Personal Property Floater Policy covering unscheduled property but only provided such existing policy shall have attached not less than 60 days prior to the effective date of the Homeowners Policy. When such credit is granted, Endorsement **HO-133** must be attached and the existing policy described therein.

    b. All Other Forms. It shall be permissible to allow credit for existing insurance covering the same insurable interest in the same property and against the same perils but only provided such existing policy shall have attached not less than 60 days prior to the effective date of the Homeowners Policy. Endorsement **HO-133** shall be attached to the Homeowners Policy and the existing specific insurance must be described therein. No credit shall be granted for any policy not included in the endorsement.

    c. The credit for existing insurance shall be calculated as follows:

        (1) Credit shall be given only to the extent that such coverage or perils are included in the Homeowners Policy;

        (2) When the Homeowners Policy contains a deductible(s) not contained in the existing insurance, existing insurance credits shall be calculated as if such existing insurance contained a deductible(s) equivalent, or as nearly equivalent as possible, to that in the Homeowners Policy;

        (3) The total credit for charges made for eliminating a deductible under one or more existing policies shall not exceed the charge made in the Homeowners Policy for elimination of an equivalent deductible;

        (4) The premium shall be developed at the current rates and rules applicable to such insurance if written separately by the company issuing the Homeowners Policy, multiplied by 80%;

        (5) Pro rate the premium so determined from the inception of the Homeowners Policy to the expiration of the existing insurance, or to the expiration of the Homeowners Policy, whichever may first occur;

        (6) No credit shall be granted for the amount of insurance that is in excess of the limit applicable to such coverage as set forth in the Homeowners Policy;

(7) Credit for existing insurance on specific appurtenant private structures, Additional Living Expense and Fire Department Service Charges may be allowed only to the extent that such coverages have been specifically included under the Homeowners Policy as provided in Rule 10a (8).

(8) In no event shall the total of all credits, as calculated above, exceed 80% of the Homeowners premium for such risk without credit for existing insurance.

The total pro rata existing insurance credit as calculated above and indicated on the endorsement shall be deducted from the total policy premium. No credit shall be allowed for existing Homeowners Policies; Comprehensive Dwelling Policies; and, except as provided in "a" above, "all risk" forms of policies covering personal property on an unscheduled basis. Credit may be allowed on a pro rata basis for scheduled items of personal property covered under "all risk" forms of policies to the extent that such items are scheduled under the Homeowners Policy, subject to the rates and rules filed by or on behalf of the insurer.

Rule 18.   Installment Payment of Premium

The premium for a policy may either be prepaid or payable in annual installments.

(a) If premiums for the Homeowners Policy are paid annually, the proper installment premium shall be determined as follows:

1. Multiply the three year prepaid premium by 35% to produce the D.P.P. annual premium, and round in accordance with Rule 11.

2. Multiply the rounded D.P.P. annual premium by three to produce the three year D.P.P. premium.

3. When credit for existing insurance is granted, the total existing insurance credit not exceeding three (3) years shall be deducted from the three year prepaid premium before applying the 35% factor in 1 above.

4. Insert the Deferred Premium Payment Premium obtained under 2 on the line of the policy entitled "Total premium if paid in installments". Insert the annual installment premiums as set forth in 1 on the line "At inception". This premium may be also repeated on the next line "At each or subsequent anniversary" if desired.

(b) In applying rule (a) above, the following simplified procedure may be used:

1. Compute the total net prepaid three year premium for the policy.

2. Determine the deferred payments for the three year prepaid premium using the Table of Deferred Payments in the state territorial pages.

(c) When changes occur during the term of the policy which result in changes in rate, limit, premium or additional coverages, the installment premiums shall be revised using **HO-135.**

(d) Additional premiums shall be calculated as shown in the following example:

Facts:

A policy with an inception date of January 1, endorsed the subsequent July 1, would require an additional premium of $54 if the endorsement were to be in effect for the full three year term.

Method:

$54.00   (3 year prepaid premium)
× ___35% (1 year D.P.P. factor)
$18.90
$19.00 (1 year D.P.P. premium due at each of next two installments—Rounded)

- -

$19.00   (annual installment)
× ___50% (pro-rata factor for last 6 months of current year)
$ 9.50
$10.00   (Cash amount due at endorsement's inception— Rounded)

(e) Return premium on short rate basis shall be computed as shown in the following example:

Facts:

Policy cancelled at end of 18 months. Three year prepaid premium = $200. Short rate factor = 52.6%.

Method:

$200.00   (3 year prepaid premium)
× ___35% (1 year D.P.P. factor)
$ 70.00   (1 year D.P.P. premium)
× ___3
$210.00   (3 year D.P.P. premium)

- -

100% — 52.6% = 47.4% —— Return premium factor
$210.00   (3 year D.P.P. premium)
× ___47.4% (Return premium factor)
$ 99.54   (Gross return premium)
$100.00   (Gross return premium—Rounded)
— ___70.00 (Unpaid installment)
$ 30.00   (Net return premium)

19. Additional Amounts or Coverages.

Amounts of insurance may be increased or additional coverages may be added after the inception date of the policy by attachment of Endorsement **HO-135** and any other required endorsements. The premium for such additional coverage or amount, unless otherwise specifically provided, shall be computed on a pro rata basis using the following formula:

$$\frac{\text{No. of Days to Expiration}}{1095} \times \text{rate (or premium)} = \text{Pro rata rate (or premium) to be used.}$$

Whenever an endorsement is attached requiring an additional charge, such charge shall be not less than $6.00.

20. Transfer or Assignment.

Insurance under a Homeowners Policy may be transferred to another location within the same state, provided the new location is eligible for coverage under a Homeowners Policy, by attachment of Endorsement **HO-135** and subject to any necessary adjustment of premium.

It shall be permissible to assign a Homeowners Policy from one Insured to a new Insured in the event of transfer of title of the dwelling covered under the Homeowners Policy by attachment of Endorsement **HO-135** and subject to any necessary adjustment of premium.

21. Cancellation.

It shall not be permissible to cancel any of the basic coverages in the policy unless the entire policy is cancelled.

If insurance is cancelled at the request of the Company, the earned premium shall be computed pro rata.

If insurance is cancelled at the request of the Insured the earned premium shall be computed on a short rate basis, using the standard short rate tables.

When credit for existing insurance has been granted under a Homeowners Policy which is being cancelled the return premium shall be calculated as follows:

(1) Determine Homeowners premium, including any installment charges, for the full term and based on the amounts, premiums and coverages in force at the time of cancellation, without any credit for existing insurance.

(2) Determine the unearned portion of the premium as produced under (1) based upon the unexpired term of the Homeowners Policy.

(3) Determine the unearned premium for specific insurance still in force and for which credit has been given, as follows:

   (a) Determine the number of days from inception of the Homeowners Policy to expiration of the specific policy or the Homeowners Policy whichever first occurs.

   (b) Divide the dollar amount of credit granted for the specific policy by the number of days produced under (a) to determine the cost per day.

   (c) Multiply the cost per day (b) by the number of days from the cancellation of the Homeowners Policy to the expiration of the specific policy to produce the unearned premium for the specific insurance.

(4) Deduct the amount produced under (3), plus any unpaid installments, from the amount produced under (2) to produce the return premium due under the Homeowners Policy.

Policies may be cancelled pro rata in the event of foreclosure of the mortgage on the insured real property.

22. Restriction of Individual Policies.

It is permitted, at the request of the Named Insured, to restrict an individual policy provided no reduction from the prescribed rate and minimum premium is allowed, if because of unusual circumstances or, exposures the policy otherwise would not be issued. Such requests shall be referred to the Company.

23. Change in Fire Protection Class.

Where there is a change in the Fire Protection Class which affects the premium group applicable to the Homeowners Policy, an adjustment in premium on the existing Homeowners Policy may be made in accordance with the rules of the fire rating bureau in connection with the specific change in protection class.

APPENDIX C. TERRITORIAL PAGES

PENNSYLVANIA*

PART I — EXCEPTIONS TO GENERAL RULES

Rule 2. Eligibility

The inclusion of the following additional paragraph to this rule:

h. A Homeowners policy shall not be issued covering any mobile home, trailer home, or house trailer whether or not set on blocks, foundations or otherwise made temporarily or permanently stationary.

Rule 9. Deductibles

Loss Deductible Clause No. I (Windstorm and Hail) is mandatory and may not be eliminated.

Rule 12. Specifically Rated Risks

The following paragraph is added to this rule:
"Any dwelling subject to the Pennsylvania Substandard Fire Insurance Rating Plan shall be treated as a specifically rated risk."

PART II — BASIC PREMIUM CHARTS
TERRITORIAL ZONES

Zone Ia—Adams, Berks, Cumberland, Dauphin, Franklin, Lancaster
(01)   Lebanon, Lehigh, Northampton and York.

Zone Ib—Bucks, Chester, Delaware and Montgomery.
(06)

Zone II—Bedford, Blair, Carbon, Centre, Clinton, Columbia, Fulton,
(02)   Huntingdon, Juniata, Lycoming, Mifflin, Monroe, Montour,
Northumberland, Perry, Pike, Schuylkill, Snyder and Union
Counties.

Zone III—Armstrong, Beaver, Bradford, Butler, Cambria, Cameron,
(03)   Clarion, Clearfield, Crawford, Elk, Erie, Fayette, Forest,
Greene, Indiana, Jefferson, Lackawanna, Lawrence, Luzerne,
McKean, Mercer, Potter, Somerset, Sullivan, Susquehanna,
Tioga, Venango, Warren, Washington, Wayne, Westmoreland
and Wyoming Counties.

Zone IV—City and County of Philadelphia.
(04)

Zone V—Allegheny County including the City of Pittsburgh.
(05)

PREMIUM GROUP CHARTS
Forms 1, 2, 3 with 4 and 5

Protection Class	(Protection Code)	Zone IA Br (Code) (3)	Fr (1)*	Zone IB Br (Code) (3)	Fr (1)*	Zone II Br (Code) (3)	Fr (1)*
B	(2)	1	1	1	1	1	3
C	(3)	1	1	1	1	1	3
D	(4)	1	1	1	1	1	3
E	(5)	2	3	2	3	4	5
F	(6)	3	4	3	4	5	6

Protection Class	Code	Zone III Br (Code) (3)	Fr (1)*	Zone V Br (Code) (3)	Fr (1)*
A	(1)	1	2	2	3
B	(2)	1	2	2	3
C	(3)	1	2	2	3
D	(4)	1	2	2	3
E	(5)	3	5	5	6
F	(6)	5	6	6	7

Protection Class	Code	Zone IV Br (Code) (3)	Fr (1)*
A	(1)	2	3

Aluminum or plastic siding over frame use Construction Code (5).

REQUIRED BASIC LIMITS OF LIABILITY
FORMS 1, 2 and 3 with 4

(See Rules 7 and 9 of General Rules)

						SECTION I		SECTION II		

COV. A	COV. B		COV. C		COV. D			COV. E	COV. F	COV. G
Described Dwelling	Appurtenant Private Structures		Unsched. Per. Prop. on the Premises	Unsched. Per. Prop. Away from the Premises	Additional Living Expense			Personal Liability	Personal Medical Payments	Physical Damage to Property of Others
					Form 1	Form 2				
* $ 5,000	$ 500		$ 2,000	$1,000	$ 500	$ 1,000		$25,000	$500	$250
* 6,000	600		2,400	1,000	600	1,200		25,000	500	250
* 7,000	700		2,800	1,000	700	1,400		25,000	500	250
8,000	800		3,200	1,000	800	1,600		25,000	500	250
9,000	900		3,600	1,000	900	1,800		25,000	500	250
10,000	1,000		4,000	1,000	1,000	2,000		25,000	500	250
11,000	1,100		4,400	1,000	1,100	2,200		25,000	500	250
12,000	1,200		4,800	1,000	1,200	2,400		25,000	500	250
13,500	1,350		5,400	1,000	1,350	2,700		25,000	500	250
15,000	1,500		6,000	1,000	1,500	3,000		25,000	500	250
17,500	1,750		7,000	1,000	1,750	3,500		25,000	500	250
20,000	2,000		8,000	1,000	2,000	4,000		25,000	500	250
22,500	2,250		9,000	1,000	2,250	4,500		25,000	500	250
25,000	2,500		10,000	1,000	2,500	5,000		25,000	500	250
27,500	2,750		11,000	1,100	2,750	5,500		25,000	500	250
30,000	3,000		12,000	1,200	3,000	6,000		25,000	500	250
32,500	3,250		13,000	1,300	3,250	6,500		25,000	500	250
35,000	3,500		14,000	1,400	3,500	7,000		25,000	500	250
37,500	3,750		15,000	1,500	3,750	7,500		25,000	500	250
40,000	4,000		16,000	1,600	4,000	8,000		25,000	500	250
42,500	4,250		17,000	1,700	4,250	8,500		25,000	500	250
45,000	4,500		18,000	1,800	4,500	9,000		25,000	500	250
47,500	4,750		19,000	1,900	4,750	9,500		25,000	500	250
50,000	5,000		20,000	2,000	5,000	10,000		25,000	500	250

A policy may be issued for an amount in excess of $50,000 on Coverage A. The additional limits on the coverages for each $5,000 mulitple are as follows:

COV. A	COV. B	COV. C	COV. D	COV. E	COV. F	COV. G
$ 5,000	$ 500	$ 2,000 On Prem.	$ 200 Off Prem.	{$ 500** {$1,000***	— —	— —	— —

*Secondary Dwellings Only.
**Form 1.
***Forms 2, 3 with 4.

REQUIRED BASIC LIMITS OF LIABILITY
FORM — 5

	SECTION I			SECTION II		
COV. A	COV. B	COV. C	COV. D	COV. E	COV. F	COV. G
Described Dwelling	Appurtenant Private Structures	Personal Property	Additional Living Expense	Personal Liability	Personal Medical Payments	Physical Damage to Property of Others
$15,000	$1,500	$ 7,500	$3,000	$25,000	$500	$250
17,500	1,750	8,750	3,500	25,000	500	250
20,000	2,000	10,000	4,000	25,000	500	250
22,500	2,250	11,250	4,500	25,000	500	250
25,000	2,500	12,500	5,000	25,000	500	250
27,500	2,750	13,750	5,500	25,000	500	250
30,000	3,000	15,000	6,000	25,000	500	250
32,500	3,250	16,250	6,500	25,000	500	250
35,000	3,500	17,500	7,000	25,000	500	250
37,500	3,750	18,750	7,500	25,000	500	250
40,000	4,000	20,000	8,000	25,000	500	250
42,500	4,250	21,250	8,500	25,000	500	250
45,000	4,500	22,500	9,000	25,000	500	250
47,500	4,750	23,750	9,500	25,000	500	250
50,000	5,000	25,000	10,000	25,000	500	250

A policy may be issued for an amount in excess of $50,000 on Coverage A. The additional limits on the coverages for each $5,000 mulitple are as follows:

COV. A	COV. B	COV. C	COV. D	COV. E	COV. F	COV. G
$5,000	$500	$2,500	$1,000	....	....	....

REQUIRED BASIC LIMITS OF LIABILITY
FORM — 4

SECTION I			SECTION II		
COV. C		COV. D	COV. E	COV. F	COV. G
Unscheduled Personal Property on the Premises	Unscheduled Personal Property Away from the Premises	Additional Living Expense	Personal Liability	Personal Medical Payments	Physical Damage to Property of Others
$ 4,000	$1,000	$ 800	$25,000	$500	$250
5,000	1,000	1,000	25,000	500	250
6,000	1,000	1,200	25,000	500	250
7,000	1,000	1,400	25,000	500	250
8,000	1,000	1,600	25,000	500	250
9,000	1,000	1,800	25,000	500	250
10,000	1,000	2,000	25,000	500	250
11,000	1,100	2,200	25,000	500	250
12,000	1,200	2,400	25,000	500	250
13,000	1,300	2,600	25,000	500	250
14,000	1,400	2,800	25,000	500	250
15,000	1,500	3,000	25,000	500	250

For amounts in excess of $15,000 on Coverage C, the additional limits on the coverages for each $1,000 multiple are as follows:

COV. C	COV. D	COV. E	COV. F	COV. G
$1,000 on Premises / 100 off Premises	$200.	....	....	

BASIC PREMIUM GROUP — 1

Three Year Prepaid Premium

Loss Deductible Clauses Applicable

Cov. A Dwelling	FORM 1 No. 1 and No. 2	FORM 1 No. 1	FORM 2 No. 1 and No. 2	FORM 2 Nos. 1 and Mod. 2	FORM 2 No. 1	FORM 3 with 4 No. 1 and No. 2	FORM 3 with 4 Nos. 1 and Mod. 2	FORM 3 with 4 No. 1
$ 8,000	58	70	63	79	85	68	87	96
9,000	59	73	66	84	91	71	93	103
10,000	61	76	69	89	97	75	99	110
11,000	62	79	71	93	102	77	104	116
12,000	65	83	73	97	107	80	109	122
13,500	69	89	78	105	116	86	118	132
15,000	72	95	81	111	123	90	126	141
17,500	80	106	89	124	138	99	141	159
20,000	87	117	99	139	155	111	159	179
22,500	96	130	108	153	171	121	175	198
25,000	102	140	117	167	187	132	192	217
27,500	114	155	129	184	206	145	211	239
30,000	121	166	138	198	222	156	228	258
32,500	129	178	148	213	239	167	245	278
35,000	134	187	156	226	254	177	261	296
37,500	150	206	172	247	277	194	284	322
40,000	157	217	181	261	293	205	300	341
42,500	165	229	192	277	311	217	318	362
45,000	172	240	201	291	327	227	334	381
47,500	181	252	209	304	342	237	350	399
50,000	188	263	219	319	359	249	367	419
Each add'l $5,000 up to $125,000-add	16	23	18	28	32	22	33	38

BASIC PREMIUM GROUP — 2

Three Year Prepaid Premium

Loss Deductible Clauses Applicable

Cov. A Dwelling	FORM 1 No. 1 and No. 2	FORM 1 No. 1	FORM 2 No. 1 and No. 2	FORM 2 Nos. 1 and Mod. 2	FORM 2 No. 1	FORM 3 with 4 No. 1 and No. 2	FORM 3 with 4 Nos. 1 and Mod. 2	FORM 3 with 4 No. 1
$ 8,000	61	73	67	83	89	72	91	100
9,000	64	78	71	89	96	76	98	108
10,000	67	82	74	94	102	80	104	115
11,000	69	86	75	97	106	81	108	120
12,000	71	89	78	102	112	85	114	127
13,500	76	96	85	112	123	93	125	139
15,000	78	101	88	118	130	97	133	148
17,500	87	113	98	133	147	108	150	168
20,000	95	125	108	148	164	120	168	188
22,500	105	139	119	164	182	132	186	209
25,000	113	151	129	179	199	144	204	229
27,500	125	166	143	198	220	159	225	253
30,000	133	178	154	214	238	172	244	274
32,500	142	191	163	228	254	182	260	293
35,000	150	203	173	243	271	194	278	313
37,500	165	221	192	267	297	214	304	342
40,000	174	234	202	282	314	226	321	362
42,500	183	247	212	297	331	237	338	382
45,000	191	259	224	314	350	250	357	404
47,500	201	272	235	330	368	263	376	425
50,000	210	285	245	345	385	275	393	445
Each add'l $5,000 up to $125,000-add	19	26	21	31	35	25	36	41

BASIC PREMIUM GROUP — 3

Three Year Prepaid Premium

Loss Deductible Clauses Applicable

Cov. A Dwelling	FORM 1 No. 1 and No. 2	FORM 1 No. 1	FORM 2 No. 1 and No. 2	FORM 2 Nos. 1 and Mod. 2	FORM 2 No. 1	FORM 3 with 4 No. 1 and No. 2	FORM 3 with 4 Nos. 1 and Mod. 2	FORM 3 with 4 No. 1
$ 8,000	66	78	73	89	95	78	97	106
9,000	69	83	76	94	101	81	103	113
10,000	73	88	80	100	108	86	110	121
11,000	75	92	81	103	112	87	114	126
12,000	78	96	85	109	119	92	121	134
13,500	83	103	92	119	130	100	132	146
15,000	86	109	96	126	138	105	141	156
17,500	98	124	108	143	157	118	160	178
20,000	107	137	120	160	176	132	180	200
22,500	117	151	132	177	195	145	199	222
25,000	127	165	143	193	213	158	218	243
27,500	141	182	159	214	236	175	241	269
30,000	151	196	171	231	255	189	261	291
32,500	161	210	183	248	274	202	280	313
35,000	170	223	193	263	291	214	298	333
37,500	188	244	214	289	319	236	326	364
40,000	194	254	226	306	338	250	345	386
42,500	209	273	238	323	357	263	364	408
45,000	218	286	251	341	377	277	384	431
47,500	230	301	263	358	396	291	404	453
50,000	240	315	275	375	415	305	423	475
Each add'l. $5,000 up to $125,000-add	22	29	24	34	38	28	39	44

BASIC PREMIUM GROUP — 4

Three Year Prepaid Premium

Loss Deductible Clauses Applicable

Cov. A Dwelling	FORM 1 No. 1 and No. 2	FORM 1 No. 1	FORM 2 No. 1 and No. 2	FORM 2 Nos. 1 and Mod. 2	FORM 2 No. 1	FORM 3 with 4 No. 1 and No. 2	FORM 3 with 4 Nos. 1 and Mod. 2	FORM 3 with 4 No. 1
$ 8,000	72	84	78	94	100	83	102	111
9,000	76	90	84	102	109	89	111	121
10,000	80	95	89	109	117	95	119	130
11,000	82	99	91	113	122	97	124	136
12,000	87	105	96	120	130	103	132	145
13,500	93	113	104	131	142	112	144	158
15,000	99	122	111	141	153	120	156	171
17,500	111	137	126	161	175	136	178	196
20,000	123	153	139	179	195	151	199	219
22,500	135	169	154	199	217	167	221	244
25,000	146	184	167	217	237	182	242	267
27,500	161	202	183	238	260	199	265	293
30,000	172	217	196	256	280	214	286	316
32,500	183	232	211	276	302	230	308	341
35,000	195	248	223	293	321	244	328	363
37,500	212	268	244	319	349	266	356	394
40,000	224	284	257	337	369	281	376	417
42,500	236	300	272	357	391	297	398	442
45,000	248	316	285	375	411	311	418	465
47,500	260	331	300	395	433	328	441	490
50,000	272	347	314	414	454	344	462	514
Each add'l. $5,000 up to $125,000-add	24	31	29	39	43	33	44	49

BASIC PREMIUM GROUP — 5
Three Year Prepaid Premium

Loss Deductible Clauses Applicable

Cov. A Dwelling	FORM 1 No. 1 and No. 2	FORM 1 No. 1	FORM 2 No. 1 and No. 2	FORM 2 Nos. 1 and Mod. 2	FORM 2 No. 1	FORM 3 with 4 No. 1 and No. 2	FORM 3 with 4 Nos. 1 and Mod. 2	FORM 3 with 4 No. 1
$ 8,000	78	90	85	101	107	90	109	118
9,000	82	96	90	108	115	95	117	127
10,000	88	103	96	116	124	102	126	137
11,000	90	107	99	121	130	105	132	144
12,000	94	112	105	129	139	112	141	154
13,500	103	123	113	140	151	121	153	167
15,000	109	132	121	151	163	130	166	181
17,500	123	149	138	173	187	148	190	208
20,000	136	166	153	193	209	165	213	233
22,500	150	184	169	214	232	182	236	259
25,000	165	203	184	234	254	199	259	284
27,500	180	221	202	257	279	218	284	312
30,000	193	238	218	278	302	236	308	338
32,500	206	255	234	299	325	253	331	364
35,000	219	272	247	317	345	268	352	387
37,500	239	295	270	345	375	292	382	420
40,000	253	313	286	366	398	310	405	446
42,500	266	330	302	387	421	327	428	472
45,000	280	348	318	408	444	344	451	498
47,500	294	365	333	428	466	361	474	523
50,000	307	382	349	449	489	379	497	549
Each add'l $5,000 up to $125,000-add	27	34	31	41	45	35	46	51

BASIC PREMIUM GROUP — 6
Three Year Prepaid Premium

Loss Deductible Clauses Applicable

Cov. A Dwelling	FORM 1 No. 1 and No. 2	FORM 1 No. 1	FORM 2 No. 1 and No. 2	FORM 2 Nos. 1 and Mod. 2	FORM 2 No. 1	FORM 3 with 4 No. 1 and No. 2	FORM 3 with 4 Nos. 1 and Mod. 2	FORM 3 with 4 No. 1
$ 8,000	84	96	93	109	115	98	117	126
9,000	90	104	99	117	124	104	126	136
10,000	96	111	106	126	134	112	136	147
11,000	100	117	111	133	142	117	144	156
12,000	106	124	117	141	151	124	153	166
13,500	115	135	129	156	167	137	169	183
15,000	124	147	140	170	182	149	185	200
17,500	141	167	158	193	207	168	210	228
20,000	156	186	177	217	233	189	237	257
22,500	173	207	195	240	258	208	262	285
25,000	188	226	214	264	284	229	289	314
27,500	207	248	234	289	311	250	316	344
30,000	222	267	253	313	337	271	343	373
32,500	238	287	272	337	363	291	369	402
35,000	253	306	288	358	386	309	393	428
37,500	269	325	307	382	412	329	419	457
40,000	285	345	325	405	437	349	444	485
42,500	300	364	344	429	463	369	470	514
45,000	316	384	362	452	488	388	495	542
47,500	332	403	380	475	513	408	521	570
50,000	348	423	399	499	539	429	547	599
Each add'l $5,000 up to $125,000-add	32	39	37	47	51	41	52	57

BASIC PREMIUM GROUP — 7
Three Year Prepaid Premium

Loss Deductible Clauses Applicable

Cov. A Dwelling	FORM 1 No. 1 and No. 2	FORM 1 No. 1	FORM 2 No. 1 and No. 2	FORM 2 Nos. 1 and Mod. 2	FORM 2 No. 1	FORM 3 with 4 No. 1 and No. 2	FORM 3 with 4 Nos. 1 and Mod. 2	FORM 3 with 4 No. 1
$ 8,000	92	104	99	115	121	104	123	132
9,000	98	112	107	125	132	112	134	144
10,000	105	120	114	134	142	120	144	155
11,000	109	126	120	142	151	126	153	165
12,000	116	134	127	151	161	134	163	176
13,500	127	147	140	167	178	148	180	194
15,000	138	161	151	181	193	160	196	211
17,500	156	182	173	208	222	183	225	243
20,000	174	204	192	232	248	204	252	272
22,500	192	226	213	258	276	226	280	303
25,000	210	248	234	284	304	249	309	334
27,500	231	272	257	312	334	273	339	367
30,000	249	294	277	337	361	295	367	397
32,500	267	316	297	362	388	316	394	427
35,000	284	337	317	387	415	338	422	457
37,500	302	358	338	413	443	360	450	488
40,000	320	380	358	438	470	382	477	518
42,500	338	402	377	462	496	402	503	547
45,000	356	424	399	489	525	425	532	579
47,500	375	446	419	514	552	447	560	609
50,000	392	467	440	540	580	470	588	640
Each add'l. $5,000 up to $125,000-add	36	43	41	51	55	45	56	61

PENNSYLVANIA

FORM 5 COMPREHENSIVE FORM — BASIC PREMIUM CHART

$100 Deductible Section I Perils Except Fire and Lightning

Three Year Prepaid Premiums

PREMIUM GROUPS

Cov. A Dwelling	1	2	3	4	5	6	7
$15,000	269	279	290	300	314	331	345
17,500	290	301	315	327	343	361	380
20,000	311	323	339	353	371	393	413
22,500	333	348	365	381	401	425	447
25,000	353	370	388	405	428	456	481
27,500	371	390	410	430	454	484	512
30,000	391	412	435	454	481	514	544
32,500	412	432	458	480	510	545	577
35,000	430	453	480	503	534	573	609
37,500	452	478	506	532	565	606	644
40,000	478	505	535	562	598	642	682
42,500	501	528	561	590	628	675	717
45,000	523	552	588	617	658	708	753
47,500	545	578	615	647	688	741	789
50,000	568	601	641	674	718	774	824
For each add'l. $5,000 up to $125,000—add	45	48	53	55	60	65	70
Cov. C ea. add'l. $1,000 incr. add CONTS. AMT.							
$7,500-10,000	21	21	22	22	22	22	22
10,001-20,000	12	12	15	15	15	16	17
Excess of 20,001	9	9	10	10	11	11	12

PENNSYLVANIA
FORM 4 RESIDENCE CONTENTS — BROAD FORM — BASIC PREMIUM CHART

Basic Premium Chart for Residence Contents — Broad Form
$50 Deductible Section 1 Perils Except Fire and Lightning
Three Year Prepaid Premiums

(Policy Amounts)

Annual Fire and E.C. Contents Rates:	$4,000	$5,000	$6,000	$7,000	$8,000	$9,000	$10,000	$11,000	$12,000	$13,000	$14,000	$15,000	Add each add'l. $1,000
To — $.184	51	56	61	66	71	79	84	89	94	99	104	109	5
$ .185 — .214	54	59	64	72	77	85	90	95	100	105	110	118	5
.215 — .254	57	62	70	75	83	91	96	104	109	114	122	127	5
.255 — .294	60	65	73	81	89	97	105	110	118	126	131	139	8
.295 — .334	63	71	79	87	95	103	111	119	127	135	143	151	8
.335 — .374	66	74	82	93	101	112	120	128	136	147	155	163	8
.375 — .414	72	77	88	99	107	118	129	137	148	156	164	175	11
.415 — .464	75	83	94	105	116	127	138	146	157	168	179	187	11
.465 — .514	78	89	100	111	122	136	147	158	169	180	191	202	11
.515 — .564	81	92	106	117	131	145	156	170	181	195	206	217	11
.565 — .614	87	98	112	126	140	154	168	179	193	207	218	232	14
.615 — .674	90	104	118	132	146	163	177	191	205	222	233	247	14
.675 — .744	96	110	124	141	158	175	189	206	223	237	251	268	17
.745 — .824	102	116	133	153	170	187	204	221	241	258	272	289	17
.825 — .914	108	125	145	165	182	202	222	242	259	279	296	316	20
.915 — 1.004	114	134	154	177	197	220	240	260	280	303	323	343	20
1.005 — 1.094	123	143	166	189	212	235	258	281	304	324	347	370	23
1.095 — 1.184	129	152	175	201	227	250	276	299	325	348	371	397	26
**1.185 — 1.264	138	161	187	213	239	268	294	320	346	372	398	424	26
*For apartment premises add to basic premium	3	3	3	3	4	4	5	5	5	6	6	6	—
Add for Philadelphia	12	15	18	18	21	21	24	24	27	27	30	30	—
Add for Allegheny	9	9	12	12	12	15	15	18	18	18	21	21	—
Add for Mod. Loss Ded. #2	12	13	14	15	16	17	18	19	20	21	22	23	1.00
Add to Elim. Loss Ded. #2	15	16	17	18	19	23	24	25	26	27	31	32	1.75

NOTES: *Apartment premises means a premises in any building normally occupied by more than four families.
***If the annual Fire and Extended Coverage rates for contents exceed $1.264, apply to Company for premium.

PART III — RATE SECTION

Loss Deductible Clauses — Form 5 Only

Basic Premiums for Form 5 contemplate a $100 deductible applicable to all perils of Section I only, except fire and lightning. This deductible may be reduced to $50 for an increased premium of 10% of the Basic Premium subject to a minimum premium of $30 or a maximum premium of $150. If the $50 Deductible Clause is desired endorsemenr **HO-145** must be attached.

Money and Securities (Increased Limits)

Increased limits for these items may be obtained by the attachment of **HO-115** at a three-year prepaid premium per $100 of coverage of:

Form	Money	Securities, etc.
1, 2 and 4 (Personal Theft)	$10.00	$ 8.00
2 and 4 (Extended Theft)	16.00	12.00
5	7.00	5.00

Physicians', Surgeons' and Dentists' Outside Coverage

This coverage may be provided by the attachment of **HO-113** and the additional three-year prepaid premium per $100 of coverage as follows:

With Deductible Clause #2 applicable	$ 4.00
In all other cases	5.00

This coverage shall be subject to a minimum premium of $20 when Loss Deductible Clause No. 2 applies and a minimum premium of $27 when Loss Deductible Clause No. 2 is waived or modified.

Additional Residence Employees

The basic premium contemplates not more than two full time residence employees. If there are more than two such employees, additional premium shall be charged in accordance with the table shown below:

CHARGE FOR EACH RESIDENCE EMPLOYEE IN EXCESS OF TWO

Liability Limit in the Policy	MEDICAL PAYMENTS LIMIT $500	$1,000
$ 25,000	$ 7	$10
50,000	8	11
100,000	9	12
200,000	10	13
250,000	11	14
300,000	12	15

Employees whose time of employment is not more than half of the customary full time, or to whom the workmen's compensation exclusion applies as set forth in Section II of the policy under the caption "Exclusions", shall be disregarded.

Watercraft

Private watercraft not covered under the terms of the basic form may be covered by attachment of **HO-121** and for the following additional three-year prepaid premiums:

LIABILITY AND MEDICAL PAYMENTS COVERAGES

| Limit of Liability | INBOARD MOTOR BOATS AND SAILBOATS | | | | | | | | | OUTBOARD MOTORS | |
| | UNDER 16 MPH | | | 16-30 MPH | | | OVER 30 MPH | | Sailboats No Aux. 26 to 40 ft. Inc. | More than 24 HP and less than 50 HP | 50 HP and over. |
	Less than 26 ft.	26 to 40 ft.	Over 40 ft.	Less than 26 ft.	26 to 40 ft.	Over 40 ft.	Less than 26 ft.	26 to 40 ft.			
$ 25,000	$32	$ 85	$166	$67	$134	$250	$166	$250	$67	$13	$24
50,000	37	97	191	77	154	287	191	287	77	16	28
100,000	42	110	216	87	174	325	216	325	87	18	32
200,000	48	127	249	101	201	375	249	375	101	20	36
250,000	51	135	266	107	214	400	266	400	107	22	39
300,000	55	144	282	114	228	425	282	425	114	23	41
Inc. Lim. Med. Pay. $ 1,000	4	10	20	8	16	30	20	30	8	4	6

Notes: (1) Sailboats 26 to 40 feet inclusive equipped with Auxiliary Power are classed as Motor Boats.
(2) For boats not described above, coverage is not available under the Homeowners policies.
(3) For higher limits, submit for rating.
(4) Limits of liability on above must be the same as limits in the basic policy.
(5) This coverage cannot be added annually but must be written to expiration of the policy. Inboard motor boats and sail boats only (not applicable to outboard motors) — if written until policy expiration, it is permissible to limit the coverage to the navigation period of each year. Submit to Company for appropriate rates.
(6) Where two or more outboard motors are regularly used together in connection with any single watercraft owned by the Insured, the horsepower of all such outboards shall be accumulated for rating purposes. Where two or more outboard motors are not regularly used together, rate each separately.
(7) The rates applicable in the state in which the Insured's initial residence premises is located shall apply except that if the Insured owns another premises where he maintains a residence and operates his boat principally from such other premises, the rates applicable in the state where the latter premises are located shall apply.

Appurtenant Private Structures (Increased Limits)

Additional limits on specific Appurtenant Private Structures may be provided by attachment of **HO-117** at the 3 year prepaid rates per $100 shown below, regardless of deductibles:

Prot. Class	Form 1	Form 2	Forms 3 & 5
A Brick B Brick Phila. Area A Brick Phila. Area B Brick	.35	.40	.45
A Frame B Frame C Brick D Brick Phila. Area A Frame Phila. Area B Frame	.40	.45	.50
C Frame D Frame E Brick F Brick	.45	.50	.55
E Frame F Frame	.55	.60	.65

Additional Living Expense (Increased Limits)

The limit for Additional Living Expense may be increased at the rates shown for increased amounts of Coverage B — Appurtenant Private Structures, where Forms 1, 2, 3 with 4, and 5 are involved, and at the bureau dwelling contents rates when Form 4 (Tenants) is involved.

Unscheduled Jewelry and Fur (Increased Limits) — Form 5 Only

When it is desired to increase the limit for unscheduled jewelry and furs under Form 5 the three-year rate per $100 of coverage shall be:

$100 Deductible Basis	$3.25
$ 50 Deductible Basis	$4.86

Glass

When the Residence Glass Endorsement is attached the additional three-year prepaid premium shall be $9.00.

Coverage C — (Increased Limits)

(a) Forms 1, 2, 3 and 4.

The limit for Coverage C may be increased at the additional three year prepaid premium of $7.00 per $1,000.

(b) Form 5 — See Basic Premium Chart.

Coverage C — (Decreased Limits)

The limit for Coverage C under all forms except Form 5 may be decreased to not less than 30% of the limit of Coverage A at the three-year credit of $4.00 per thousand.

Incidental Office Occupancies by the Insured

A. When the Insured has permissible office, business, etc. occupancy in the described dwelling endorsement **HO-105,** must be attached and an additional three-year prepaid premium calculated as follows:

1. Calculate the basic premium for additional amount of coverage at the premium indicated for increased amounts of Coverage C.

2. Add to the foregoing the appropriate charge from the following table:

Limit of Liability	Three-year premium, not including Medical Payments for Office Occupancy
	Described Dwelling
$ 25,000	$26
50,000	27
100,000	29
200,000	32
250,000	33
300,000	35

If Medical Payments are to be included for office occupancy add the following:

$ 500	$ 6
1,000	13

Notes: (1) Limits of liability above must be the same as limits in the basic policy. When increased limits are thus required it is first necessary to increase the liability limits on the basic policy.

(2) Submit to Company for Medical Payment charges on incidental day nurseries or nursery schools.

B. When the Insured gives professional instructions such as music, dancing, etc. as set forth under paragraph (b) of Rule 6 the additional liability exposure charge to be made shall be the single charge for an additional one family dwelling owned and occupied by the Insured.

C. When the Insured has permissible office, professional, private school or studio occupancies in an additional one or two family dwelling not on the described premises, but where he also maintains a dwelling for residential purposes, the liability exposure may be covered at the rates filed by or on behalf of the Company. This includes such permissible occupancies which are located in an apartment maintained by the Insured as tenant principally for dwelling purposes and occupied by not more than two families.

Earthquake Damage Assumption Endorsement

If the Earthquake Damage Assumption Endorsement **HO-111,** is attached to the policy, the following additional three-year prepaid rates per $100 of Coverage A shall be charged.

	THREE YEAR RATES PER $100			
	Eq. Zone II		Eq. Zone III	
Form	Frame	All Others	Frame	All Others
1, 2, 3 with 4 attached	.13	.19	.06	.13
5	.08	.12	.04	.08
4 (Coverage C Only)	.09	.14	.05	.09

Zone II: Bucks, Chester, Delaware, Montgomery, Philadelphia.

Zone III: Balance of state.

Extended Theft — Forms 2 and 4 only.

If the Extended Theft Coverage Endorsement **HO-103** is attached the additional three-year prepaid premium shall be as follows:

	Zones Ia, II & III	Zone Ib	Zone IV	Zone V
With Loss Deductible Clause No. 2	$10.00	*$12.00	$20.00	$14.00
In all other cases	20.00	*$24.00	40.00	29.00

Note: **Secondary Locations** — If the primary and secondary locations are covered under the same or separate policies in the same company, the Extended Theft charge shall be that applicable to the highest rated location. Otherwise, the applicable theft charge must be made for each location. In all cases, **HO-103** must be attached to each policy.

Business Pursuits—Section II

The coverages on comprehensive personal liability and medical payments may be extended by endorsement to cover business pursuits of eligible Insureds listed below. This coverage does not apply to businesses of which the Insured is sole owner or in which he is a partner, nor to bodily injury to or sickness, disease or death of any fellow employee of the Insured. The business classifications with the premium group applicable thereto are set forth below:

Premium Groups

Clerical Office Employees — defined as those employees whose duties are confined to keeping the books or records, conducting correspondence, or who are engaged wholly in office work where such books or records are kept or where such correspondence is conducted, having no other duty of any nature in or about the employee's premises. This classification applies only to persons who are employed exclusively in separate buildings or on separate floors of buildings or in departments on such floors which are separated from all other work places of the employer by structural partitions and within which no work is performed other than clerical office duties as above defined.

A

* Corrected.

	Premium Groups
Salesmen, Collectors or Messengers—no installation demonstration or servicing operations.	A
Salesmen, Collectors or Messengers—including installation, demonstration or servicing operations.	B
Teachers—athletic, laboratory, manual training, physical training and swimming instruction, excluding liability for corporal punishment of pupils.	C
Teachers—not otherwise classified, excluding liability for corporal punishment of pupils.	D
Teachers—liability for corporal punishment of pupils.	E

(Note: Additional premium for this coverage must be added to premium for above classification C or D.)
Occupations not otherwise classified ....Submit to Company

BUSINESS PURSUITS

Additional Premiums (3 Year Prepaid)

Liability Limit in Policy	(Premium Groups)				
	A	B	C	D	E
$ 25,000	$3	$5	$ 9	$4	$ 7
50,000	4	6	11	4	8
100,000	4	7	12	5	9
200,000	5	8	14	6	10
250,000	5	9	15	6	11
300,000	5	9	16	7	12

Medical Payments Limits					
$ 500	$1	$3	$ 5	$2	
1,000	2	6	10	4	

Notes: (1) For higher limits on liability and medical payments, refer to Company.

(2) Liability and medical payments limits in connection with business pursuits must be the same limits as the basic policy.

PENNSYLVANIA

ADDITIONAL THREE-YEAR PREPAID PREMIUMS

FOR INCREASED LIMITS OR ADDITIONAL RESIDENCE PREMISES (SECTION II)

Limit of Liability	INITIAL RESID. PREMISES		EACH ADD'L RESIDENCE PREMISES OCCUPIED BY INSURED		EACH ADD'L RESID. PREM. RENTED TO OTHERS*				INITIAL FARM PREMISES		EACH ADD'L FARM PREMISES OCCUPIED OR RENTED		ACREAGE CHARGES				
					One Family Terr.		Two Family † Terr.										
	$500 Med. Pay.	$1,000 Med. Pay.	$500 Med. Pay.	$1,000 Med. Pay.	02	01 & 03-13	02	01 & 03-13	$500 Med. Pay.	$1,000 Med. Pay.	$500 Med. Pay.	$1,000 Med. Pay.	over 160 to 240 acres	over 240 to 320 acres	over 320 to 400 acres	over 400 to 500 acres	over 500 to 1000 acres
25,000	—	7	8	11	16	9	24	18	23	30	14	17	3	5	8	11	22
50,000	4	11	10	13	19	11	28	20	31	38	16	19	4	6	9	13	25
100,000	8	15	11	14	21	12	32	23	38	45	18	21	4	7	10	14	28
200,000	14	21	12	15	24	14	36	26	49	56	21	24	5	8	12	16	33
250,000	17	24	13	16	26	15	39	28	54	61	22	25	5	9	13	17	35
300,000	20	27	14	17	28	16	41	30	59	66	23	26	5	9	13	19	37

* FOR MEDICAL PAYMENTS ADD:
  $ 500 — $3
  1,000 — 6

† Territory 02 — Pittsburgh
01 & 03-13 — Remainder of State

Animal Collision — $8

Secondary Locations

Forms 1, 2, 3 with 4 attached, and 5

Secondary locations may be insured as permitted by the General Rules. If the secondary locations for Forms 1, 2 or 3 with 4 attached requires a dwelling limit from $5,000 to $7,000 or as respects Form 5 if the dwelling limit is from $5,000 to $12,500, use Basic Premium Chart — Secondary Locations.

In computing the total premium for the policy or coverage at the first location add the applicable charge for additional residence premises occupied by Insured from Page R-7. The secondary location should be entered on the appropriate declaration in the policy face. In computing the total premium for the coverage at the second location, determine the applicable premium to be charged from the Basic Premium Chart in the state in which the secondary location is situated. To recognize duplication of coverage the following premium credit shall be subtracted from the premium applicable to the secondary location:

Forms 1, 2, 3 with 4 attached and Form 5 — $21

EXAMPLE

	THREE-YEAR PREPAID PREMIUMS
Basic Homeowners Premium Described Dwelling	$123
Add'l residence premises charge	$ 8
Total	$131
Basic Homeowners Premium Secondary Dwelling	$ 90
Less Secondary Dwelling Duplication of Coverage Credit	—$ 21
Total	$ 69
Net Basic Homeowners Premium for both Dwellings	$200

Form 5 — Coverage C only

The limit of liability for Coverage C at secondary locations may be increased by attaching Endorsement **HO-129** and the payment of an additional three year prepaid premium. This additional premium shall be found on the Basic Premium Chart for Form 5 for increased limits for Coverage C using the appropriate increment for the applicable premium group in the state in which the secondary location is situated.

SECONDARY LOCATIONS

Three Year Prepaid Premium — Loss Deductible Clauses Applicable

BASIC PREMIUM GROUP — 1

Cov. A Dwelling	FORM 1		FORM 2			FORM 3 with 4		
	No. 1 and No. 2	No. 1	No. 1 and No. 2	Nos. 1 and Mod. 2	No. 1	No. 1 and No. 2	Nos. 1 and Mod. 2	No. 1
$ 5,000	50	58	54	64	68	58	71	78
6,000	54	63	57	69	74	61	76	84
7,000	55	66	59	73	79	63	80	89

BASIC PREMIUM GROUP — 2

Cov. A Dwelling	FORM 1		FORM 2			FORM 3 with 4		
	No. 1 and No. 2	No. 1	No. 1 and No. 2	Nos. 1 and Mod. 2	No. 1	No. 1 and No. 2	Nos. 1 and Mod. 2	No. 1
$ 5,000	53	61	57	67	71	61	74	81
6,000	56	65	60	72	77	64	79	87
7,000	58	69	64	78	84	68	85	94

BASIC PREMIUM GROUP — 3

Cov. A Dwelling	FORM 1		FORM 2			FORM 3 with 4		
	No. 1 and No. 2	No. 1	No. 1 and No. 2	Nos. 1 and Mod. 2	No. 1	No. 1 and No. 2	Nos. 1 and Mod. 2	No. 1
$ 5,000	55	63	59	69	73	63	76	83
6,000	60	69	63	75	80	67	82	90
7,000	62	73	68	82	88	72	89	98

BASIC PREMIUM GROUP — 4

Cov. A Dwelling	FORM 1		FORM 2			FORM 3 with 4		
	No. 1 and No. 2	No. 1	No. 1 and No. 2	Nos. 1 and Mod. 2	No. 1	No. 1 and No. 2	Nos. 1 and Mod. 2	No. 1
$ 5,000	60	68	65	75	79	69	82	89
6,000	65	74	69	81	86	73	88	96
7,000	67	78	74	88	94	78	95	104

BASIC PREMIUM GROUP — 5

Cov. A Dwelling	FORM 1		FORM 2			FORM 3 with 4		
	No. 1 and No. 2	No. 1	No. 1 and No. 2	Nos. 1 and Mod. 2	No. 1	No. 1 and No. 2	Nos. 1 and Mod. 2	No. 1
$ 5,000	64	72	67	77	81	71	84	91
6,000	68	77	73	85	90	77	92	100
7,000	73	84	79	93	99	83	100	109

BASIC PREMIUM GROUP — 6

Cov. A Dwelling	FORM 1		FORM 2			FORM 3 with 4		
	No. 1 and No. 2	No. 1	No. 1 and No. 2	Nos. 1 and Mod. 2	No. 1	No. 1 and No. 2	Nos. 1 and Mod. 2	No. 1
$ 5,000	67	75	73	83	87	77	90	97
6,000	73	82	80	92	97	84	99	107
7,000	78	89	86	100	106	90	107	116

BASIC PREMIUM GROUP — 7

Cov. A Dwelling	FORM 1		FORM 2			FORM 3 with 4		
	No. 1 and No. 2	No. 1	No. 1 and No. 2	Nos. 1 and Mod. 2	No. 1	No. 1 and No. 2	Nos. 1 and Mod. 2	No. 1
$ 5,000	72	80	77	87	91	81	94	101
6,000	78	81	84	96	101	88	103	111
7,000	84	95	92	106	112	96	113	122

FORM 5 — $100 Deductible Section I Perils Except Fire and Lightning

Cov. A Dwelling	BASIC PREMIUM GROUPS						
	1	2	3	4	5	6	7
$ 5,000	158	160	164	165	170	173	178
7,500	176	180	187	191	198	206	212
10,000	228	233	241	245	255	263	271
12,500	247	256	265	273	284	306	317

NOTE: To find premiums for higher limits, refer to basic premium charts.

CONTINUOUS RENEWAL PLAN

A Homeowners Policy with Forms 1, 2, 3 with 4, 4 or 5 attached may be written under the Continuous Renewal Plan for a term of three, six or twelve months. The policy may be continued for successive terms upon payment of the required premium to the Company on or before the inception date of each successive term.

The premium for a one year term shall be 35% of the three year prepaid premium. The premium for a six or three month term shall be pro rata of this one year term premium plus fifty cents ($.50) per payment.

The Homeowners Continuous Renewal Plan requires the use of:

(1) the Homeowners Policy—Continuous Renewal Plan, Edition April 1961 C.R.P., or

(2) the standard Homeowners Policy with the Homeowners Continuous Renewal Plan Amendatory Endorsement **HO-155** attached.

EXCEPTIONS TO GENERAL RULES UNDER THIS PLAN

GR-11—Rounding Rule

The premium for a policy written under the Continuous Renewal Plan for a twelve month term shall be carried to the nearest dollar. For this purpose an amount of fifty cents ($.50) or more shall be considered as a dollar.

The premium for a term of three months or six months is based on this twelve month term premium and is not subject to the further application of the rounding rule.

GR-14

(a) **Policy Period**—A Homeowners Policy under the Continuous Renewal Plan may be issued only for a term of three, six or twelve months. Such policy may then be extended for successive terms upon payment of the then current extension premium to the company prior to expiration.

(b) **Continuation of Policy Period**—The extension premium shall be based upon the then prevailing premiums and rates, and the then current editions of the forms must be substituted if revised during the previous policy term.

GR-17—Credit for Existing Insurance

It is not permissible to grant credit for existing insurance when a Homeowners policy is written under this plan.

GR-19—Additional Amounts or Coverages

Amounts of insurance may be increased or additional coverages may be added after the inception date of the current policy term by attachment of Endorsement **HO-135** and any other required endorsements. The premium shall be pro rata of the then current annual Continuous Renewal Plan premium.

GR-21—Cancellation

It shall not be permissible to cancel any of the basic coverages in the policy unless the entire policy is cancelled.

If insurance is cancelled at the request of the Company, the earned premium shall be computed pro rata of the premium charged for the current policy period.

If insurance is cancelled at the request of the Insured, the earned premium shall be computed short rate of the premium charged for the current policy period using the Continuous Renewal Plan short rate table.

Policies may be cancelled pro rata in the event of foreclosure of the mortgage on the insured real property.

SHORT RATE TABLE
For use only with the
HOMEOWNERS CONTINUOUS RENEWAL PLAN

Days in Force	3 mos. Term	6 mos. Term	12 mos. Term
1	20	10	5
2	22	11	6
3-4	24	12	6
5-6	28	14	7
7-8	32	16	8
9-10	36	18	9
11-12	40	20	10
13-14	44	22	11
15-16	48	24	12
17-18	50	25	13
19-20	52	26	13
21-22	54	27	14
23-25	56	28	14
26-28	58	29	15
29-31	60	30	15
32-34	62	31	16
35-37	64	32	16
38-40	66	33	17
41-43	68	34	17
44-46	70	35	18
47-49	72	36	18
50-52	74	37	19
53-55	76	38	19
56-58	78	39	20
59-61	80	40	20

Days in Force	3 mos. Term	6 mos. Term	12 mos. Term
62-64	82	41	21
65-67	84	42	21
68-70	86	43	22
71-73	88	44	22
74-76	90	45	23
77-79	92	46	23
80-82	94	47	24
83-85	96	48	24
86-88	98	49	25
89-92	100	50	26
93-96		53	27
97-100		56	28
101-104		59	30
105-108		62	31
109-112		64	32
113-116		66	33
117-120		68	34
121-124		70	35
125-128		72	36
129-132		74	37
133-136		76	38
137-140		78	39
141-144		80	40
145-148		82	41
149-152		84	42

Days in Force	6 mos. Term	12 mos. Term
153-156	86	43
157-160	88	44
161-164	90	45
165-168	92	46
169-172	94	47
173-176	96	48
177-180	98	49
181-184	100	50
185-188		51
189-192		53
193-196		54
197-200		56
201-204		57
205-208		59
209-212		60
213-216		62
217-220		63
221-224		65
225-228		66
229-232		67
233-236		68
237-240		69
241-244		70
245-248		71
249-252		72

Days in Force	12 mos. Term
253-256	72
257-260	74
261-264	75
265-268	76
269-272	77
273-276	78
277-280	79
281-284	80
285-288	81
289-292	82
293-296	83
297-300	84
301-304	85
305-308	86
309-312	87
313-316	88
317-320	89
321-324	90
325-328	91
329-332	92
333-336	93
337-340	94
341-344	95
345-348	96
349-352	97
353-356	98
357-360	99
361-365	100

CREDIT CARD AND DEPOSITORS FORGERY COVERAGE

A Homeowners Policy with Forms 1, 2, 3 with 4, 4 or 5 attached may be extended to provide credit card and depositor forgery coverage by the attachment of Endorsement **HO-64** and the payment of the additional 3 year prepaid premium as follows:

Limit of Liability	Three year Prepaid Premiums
$ 1,000	$ 8.00
2,500	13.00
5,000	18.00
7,500	22.00
10,000	24.00

Notes: (1) Where coverage is added during the policy term, such charge shall not be less than $6.

(2) Credit card and depositor forgery coverage is not subject to a deductible.

(3) For limits in excess of $10,000, refer to Company.

APPENDIX D. DEFERRED PREMIUM PAYMENT PLAN*

TABLE OF DEFERRED PAYMENTS

The following tables permit ready calculation of the three year Deferred Premium as well as the amount due each year. The D.P.P. premiums were obtained by taking 35% of the rounded prepaid three year premium to arrive at the annual payment. The annual payment is rounded and then multiplied by 3 to produce the D.P.P. three year term premium.

Prepaid Premium	D.P.P. Premium	Annual Payment	Prepaid Premium	D.P.P. Premium	Annual Payment	Prepaid Premium	D.P.P. Premium	Annual Payment
$ 40- 41	$ 42	$ 14	$153-155	$162	$ 54	$268-269	$282	$ 94
42- 44	45	15	156-158	165	55	270-272	285	95
45- 47	48	16	159-161	168	56	273-275	288	96
48- 49	51	17	162-164	171	57	276-278	291	97
50- 52	54	18	165-167	174	58	279-281	294	98
53- 55	57	19	168-169	177	59	282-284	297	99
56- 58	60	20	170-172	180	60	285-287	300	100
59- 61	63	21	173-175	183	61	288-289	303	101
62- 64	66	22	176-178	186	62	290-292	306	102
65- 67	69	23	179-181	189	63	293-295	309	103
68- 69	72	24	182-184	192	64	296-298	312	104
70- 72	75	25	185-187	195	65	299-301	315	105
73- 75	78	26	188-189	198	66	302-304	318	106
76- 78	81	27	190-192	201	67	305-307	321	107
79- 81	84	28	193-195	204	68	308-309	324	108
82- 84	87	29	196-198	207	69	310-312	327	109
85- 87	90	30	199-201	210	70	313-315	330	110
88- 89	93	31	202-204	213	71	316-318	333	111
90- 92	96	32	205-207	216	72	319-321	336	112
93- 95	99	33	208-209	219	73	322-324	339	113
96- 98	102	34	210-212	222	74	325-327	342	114
99-101	105	35	213-215	225	75	328-329	345	115
102-104	108	36	216-218	228	76	330-332	348	116
105-107	111	37	219-221	231	77	333-335	351	117
108-109	114	38	222-224	234	78	336-338	354	118
110-112	117	39	225-227	237	79	339-341	357	119
113-115	120	40	228-229	240	80	342-344	360	120
116-118	123	41	230-232	243	81	345-347	363	121
119-121	126	42	233-235	246	82	348-349	366	122
122-124	129	43	236-238	249	83	350-352	369	123
125-127	132	44	239-241	252	84	353-355	372	124
128-129	135	45	242-244	255	85	356-358	375	125
130-132	138	46	245-247	258	86	359-361	378	126
133-135	141	47	248-249	261	87	362-364	381	127
136-138	144	48	250-252	264	88	365-367	384	128
139-141	147	49	253-255	267	89	368-369	387	129
142-144	150	50	256-258	270	90	370-372	390	130
145-147	153	51	259-261	273	91	373-375	393	131
148-149	156	52	262-264	276	92	376-378	396	132
150-152	159	53	265-267	279	93	379-381	399	133

TABLE OF DEFERRED PAYMENTS

Prepaid Premium	D.P.P. Premium	Annual Payment	Prepaid Premium	D.P.P. Premium	Annual Payment	Prepaid Premium	D.P.P. Premium	Annual Payment
$382-384	$402	$134	$525-527	$552	$184	$668-669	$702	$234
385-387	405	135	528-529	555	185	670-672	705	235
388-389	408	136	530-532	558	186	673-675	708	236
390-392	411	137	533-535	561	187	676-678	711	237
393-395	414	138	536-538	564	188	679-681	714	238
396-398	417	139	539-541	567	189	682-684	717	239
399-401	420	140	542-544	570	190	685-687	720	240
402-404	423	141	545-547	573	191	688-689	723	241
405-407	426	142	548-549	576	192	690-692	726	242
408-409	429	143	550-552	579	193	693-695	729	243
410-412	432	144	553-555	582	194	696-698	732	244
413-415	435	145	556-558	585	195	699-701	735	245
416-418	438	146	559-561	588	196	702-704	738	246
419-421	441	147	562-564	591	197	705-707	741	247
422-424	444	148	565-567	594	198	708-709	744	248
425-427	447	149	568-569	597	199	710-712	747	249
428-429	450	150	570-572	600	200	713-715	750	250
430-432	453	151	573-575	603	201	716-718	753	251
433-435	456	152	576-578	606	202	719-721	756	252
436-438	459	153	579-581	609	203	722-724	759	253
439-441	462	154	582-584	612	204	725-727	762	254
442-444	465	155	585-587	615	205	728-729	765	255
445-447	468	156	588-589	618	206	730-732	768	256
448-449	471	157	590-592	621	207	733-735	771	257
450-452	474	158	593-595	624	208	736-738	774	258
453-455	477	159	596-598	627	209	739-741	777	259
456-458	480	160	599-601	630	210	742-744	780	260
459-461	483	161	602-604	633	211	745-747	783	261
462-464	486	162	605-607	636	212	748-749	786	262
465-467	489	163	608-609	639	213	750-752	789	263
468-469	492	164	610-612	642	214	753-755	792	264
470-472	495	165	613-615	645	215	756-758	795	265
473-475	498	166	616-618	648	216	759-761	798	266
476-478	501	167	619-621	651	217	762-764	801	267
479-481	504	168	622-624	654	218	765-767	804	268
482-484	507	169	625-627	657	219	768-769	807	269
485-487	510	170	628-629	660	220	770-772	810	270
488-489	513	171	630-632	663	221	773-775	813	271
490-492	516	172	633-635	666	222	776-778	816	272
493-495	519	173	636-638	669	223	779-781	819	273
496-498	522	174	639-641	672	224	782-784	822	274
499-501	525	175	642-644	675	225	785-787	825	275
502-504	528	176	645-647	678	226	788-789	828	276
505-507	531	177	648-649	681	227	790-792	831	277
508-509	534	178	650-652	684	228	793-795	834	278
510-512	537	179	653-655	687	229	796-798	837	279
513-515	540	180	656-658	690	230	799-801	840	280
516-518	543	181	659-661	693	231	802-804	843	281
519-521	546	182	662-664	696	232	805-807	846	282
522-524	549	183	665-667	699	233	808-809	849	283

BIBLIOGRAPHY

Bibliography

BOOKS

APPLEMAN, EARLE. *Inland Marine Insurance.* New York: McGraw-Hill Book Co., Inc., 1934.

BACKMAN, JULES. *Surety Rate-Making.* New York: The Surety Association of America, 1948.

BENNETT, WALTER H. *The History of the National Association of Insurance Agents.* Cincinnati: The National Underwriter Co., 1954.

BICKELHAUPT, DAVID L. *Transition to Multiple-Line Insurance Companies.* Homewood, Illinois: Richard D. Irwin, Inc., 1961.

BREARLEY, HARRY CHASE. *The History of the National Board of Fire Underwriters.* New York: F. A. Stokes Co., 1916.

BYE, RAYMOND T. *Principles of Economics.* 5th ed. New York: Appleton-Century-Crofts, Inc., 1956.

————. AND HEWETT, W. W. *The Economic Process.* New York: Appleton-Century-Crofts, Inc., 1952.

DEAN, A. F. *The Philosophy of Fire Insurance.* Vol. I. Edited by W. R. Townley. Chicago: Edward B. Hatch, 1925.

DENENBERG, H. S., *et. al. Risk and Insurance* (Englewood Cliffs, N. J.: Prentice-Hall, Inc.), 1964.

FELLER, W. *An Introduction to Probability Theory,* Vol. I. New York: John Wiley and Sons, Inc., 1957.

GOLDBERG, SAMUEL. *Probability: An Introduction.* Englewood Cliffs, N. J.: Prentice-Hall, Inc., 1960.

HAMMOND, W. R. AND HARTMAN, G. R. (eds.). *Insurance Accounting Fire and Casualty.* Philadelphia: Chilton Co., 1965.

HARDY, E. R. *The Making of the Fire Insurance Rate.* New York: Spectator Co., 1926.

KIMBALL, SPENCER L. *Insurance and Public Policy.* Madison, Wisconsin: The University of Wisconsin Press, 1960.

KULP, C. A. *Casualty Insurance.* Rev. ed. New York: The Ronald Press Co., 1942.

――――. *Casualty Insurance.* 3d ed. New York: The Ronald Press Co., 1956.

LONGLEY-COOK, L. H. *An Introduction to Credibility Theory.* New York: Casualty Actuarial Society, 1962.

MARSHALL, R. M. *Workmen's Compensation Insurance Rate Making.* New York: Casualty Actuarial Society, 1961.

MAYERSON, ALLEN. *Introduction to Insurance.* New York: The Macmillan Co., 1962.

McGILL, DAN M. *Life Insurance.* Homewood, Illinois: Richard D. Irwin, Inc., 1967.

MEHR, R. J., AND CAMMACK, E. *Principles of Insurance.* 3rd ed. Homewood, Illinois: Richard D. Irwin, Inc., 1961.

MICHELBACHER, G. E. *Multiple-line Insurance.* New York: McGraw-Hill Book Co., Inc., 1957.

MOWBRAY, A. H., AND BLANCHARD, R. H. *Insurance.* 5th ed. New York: McGraw-Hill Book Co., Inc., 1961.

PFEFFER, IRVING. *Insurance and Economic Theory.* Homewood, Illinois: Richard D. Irwin, Inc., 1956.

PIERCE, JOHN E. *Development of Comprehensive Insurance for the Household.* Homewood, Illinois: Richard D. Irwin, Inc., 1958.

RIEGEL, R., AND MILLER, J. S. *Insurance Principles and Practices.* 4th ed. Englewood Cliffs, N. J.: Prentice-Hall, Inc., 1959.

RODDA, WILLIAM H. *Fire and Property Insurance.* Englewood Cliffs, N. J.: Prentice-Hall, Inc., 1956.

――――. *Inland Marine and Transportation Insurance.* 2nd ed. Englewood Cliffs, N. J.: Prentice-Hall, Inc., 1958.

SAWYER, E. W. *Comprehensive Liability Insurance.* New York: The Underwriter Printing and Publishing Co., 1943.

SCHUBERT, GLENDON. *The Public Interest.* Glencoe, Illinois: The Free Press of Glencoe, Illinois, 1960.

SNIDER, H. W., (ed.). *Readings in Property and Casualty Insurance.* Homewood, Ill.: Richard D. Irwin, Inc., 1959.

WEINTRAUB, SIDNEY. *Price Theory.* New York: Pitman Publishing Co., 1949.

WILLIAMS, ARTHER C. *Price Discrimination in Property and Liability Insurance.* (University of Minnesota Studies in Economics and Business, No. 19.) Minneapolis: University of Minnesota Press, 1959.

ARTICLES AND PERIODICALS

BENBROOK, PAUL. "The Advantages of Calendar-Accident Year Experience and the Need for Appropriate Trend and Projection Factors in the Determination of Automobile Liability Rates," *Automobile Insurance Rate Making* (1961), p. 59.

BEST, A. M. "Rating the Financial Structure of Insurance Companies," *Readings in Property and Casualty Insurance*, Edited by H. W. Snider (1959), pp. 80–83.

BORCH, KARL. "Some Elements of a theory of Reinsurance," *The Journal of Insurance*, Vol. 28, No. 3 (Sept. 1961), p. 42.

BRAINARD, CALVIN H. "A Comparison and Integration of Economic and Actuarial Explanations of Life Insurance Premium Computations," *The Journal of Insurance*, Vol. 30, No. 2 (June 1963), p. 257.

BUFFINTON, P. G. "The Low Value Risk," *Proceedings of the Casualty Actuarial Society*, Vol. 49, No. 92 (1962), p. 119.

CAHILL, JAMES. "Multiple Line Underwriting," *Proceedings of the Casualty Actuarial Society*, Vol. 36, No. 66 (November 18, 1949), p. 4.

CARLSON, THOMAS O. "Observations on Casualty Insurance Rate-Making Theory in the United States," *Proceedings of the Casualty Actuarial Society*, Vol. LI (1964), pp. 283–85.

———. "Rate Regulation and the Casualty Actuary," *Proceedings of the Casualty Actuarial Society*, Vol. 38, Part 1, No. 69 (May, 1951), p. 16.

———. "Trends in Casualty Insurance Rate Making," *The Journal of Insurance*, Vol. 30, No. 1 (March, 1963), p. 20.

COLLINS, JOSEPH F. "Rate Regulation in Fire and Casualty Insurance," *Examination of Insurance Companies*, Vol. 5 (1955), p. xviii.

DIEMAND, J. A. "Developments in Comprehensive Property-Casualty Insurance (Multiple Line Underwriting)," *Journal of the American Association of University Teachers of Insurance*, Vol. 13, No. 1 (March, 1946), pp. 57–58.

DONOVAN, JAMES B. "Rate Regulation Revisited," *Insurance and Government*. Edited by C. C. Center and R. M. Heins (1962), p. 291.

DORWEILER, PAUL. "Notes on Exposures and Premium Bases," *Automobile Insurance Rate Making* (1961), p. 34.

DUNHAM, F. G., JR. "Loss Constants," *Best's Insurance News* (Fire and Casualty Edition), Vol. 63, No. 9 (Jan. 1963), p. 20.

GOULD, WILLIAM C. "Insurance Examinations—History and Development," *Examination of Insurance Companies*, Vol. II, p. xv.

HALE, CLAYTON G. "A Comprehensive Policy," *The Spectator* (December 11, 1930), p. 28 ff.

HARRIS, RAYMOND. "Provisions of the New York Insurance Law Affecting the Organization, Licensing, and Corporate Procedure of Insurers Under Sections 40–46," *Examination of Insurance Companies*, Vol. II, p. 61.

HARWAYNE, FRANK. "Workmen's Compensation Insurance Rates," *Examination of Insurance Companies*, Vol. 5 (1955), p. 12.

HEINS, RICHARD M. "Liquidations of Insurance Companies," *Insurance and Government* (1962), pp. 237–68.

HOBBS, CLARENCE W. "State Regulation of Insurance Rates," *Proceedings of the Casualty Actuarial Society*, Vol. XI, No. 24 (June, 1925), p. 221.

HOUSTON, DAVID B. "The Equivalence of the Pure Premium and the Loss Ratio Methods of Ratemaking," *The Review of Insurance Studies*, III, No. 2 (Summer, 1956), pp. 72–75.

———. "Risk Insurance, and Sampling," *The Journal of Risk and Insurance*, Vol. 31, No. 4 (Dec., 1964), pp. 511–38.

HUNT, FREDERIC J. "Homeowners—The First Decade," *Proceedings of the Casualty Actuarial Society*, Vol. 49, No. 91 (May, 1962), p. 12.

HURLEY, ROBERT L. "A Credibility Framework for Gauging Fire Classification Experience," *Fire Insurance Rate Making and Kindred Problems* (1960), p. 124.

INTER-REGIONAL INSURANCE CONFERENCE. "Basic Principles—Rate Level Adjustments," *Fire Insurance Rate Making and Kindred Problems* (1960), p. 155.

JOHNSON, G. CARTER. "An Analysis of the Supplemental Contract," *The Insurance Post* (Aug. 1935).

KIDD, J. M. "Multiple Line Underwriting Outside the U. S. A.," *Readings in Property and Casualty Insurance*, Edited by H. W. Snider (1959), p. 117.

KIMBALL, SPENCER L. "The Goals of Insurance Law: Means vs. Ends," *The Journal of Insurance*, Vol. 29, No. 1 (March, 1962), pp. 19–20.

LONGLEY-COOK, L. H. "All Lines Insurance," *Proceedings of the Conference of Actuaries in Public Practice*, Vol. XIII, p. 278.

———. "Notes on Some Actuarial Problems of Property Insurance," *Fire Insurance Rate Making and Kindred Problems* (1960), p. 89.

———. "Trends in Property Insurance Rate Making," *The Journal of Insurance*, Vol. XXX, No. 1 (March, 1963), p. 25.

——— AND PRUITT, D. M. "Law of Large Numbers," *Readings in Property and Casualty Insurance*, Edited by H. W. Snider (1959), p. 298.

MAGRATH, J. J. "New York Insurance Rating Law and Rating Organizations," *Examination of Insurance Companies*, Vol. 5 (1955), p. 266.

MAYS, M. W. "Significant Contrasts and Comparisons between Life Insurance and the Various Property and Casualty Insurance Fields," *Readings in Property and Casualty Insurance*, Edited by H. W. Snider (1959), p. 38.

MANES, ALFRED. "Insurance, Principles, and History," *Encyclopedia of the Social Sciences*, Vol. 8 (1935), p. 95.

MANSFIELD, BURTON. "Shall We Abandon the American Restrictions Upon the Classes of Insurance Written by (A) A Company Doing Direct Writing, and (B) A Company Doing Reinsurance?," *Proceedings of the National Convention of Insurance Commissioners* (1914), pp. 150–51.

McCULLOUGH, ROY C. "Insurance Rates in the Courts," *The Insurance Law Journal*, No. 461 (June, 1961), p. 423.

McCONNELL, M. H. "A Casualty Man Looks at Fire Insurance Rate Making," *Fire Insurance Rate Making and Kindred Problems* (1960), p. 37.

MORRILL, THOMAS C. "Forces Underlying Trend Toward All Lines Insurance," *All Lines Insurance*. Edited by Dan M. McGill (1960), p. 4.

"New Rating Approach for HO Gaining Acceptance: MLIRB," *Insurance Advocate* (July 17, 1965), p. 5.

"New Standard Provisions for Personal Liability," *The Eastern Underwriter*, Vol. XLIV (January 8, 1943), pp. 28–29.

PARKER, KENT H. *Weekly Underwriter*, Vol. 188, No. 7 (Address at 6th Annual Arizona Insurance Day, February 8, 1963), p. 16.

PERLET, HARRY F. "Multi-Peril Developments," *No. 52 National Underwriter* (Address before Joint Meeting of District of Columbia Association of Insurance Agents and Managers Association) (December 29, 1961), pp. 2, 17.

———. "Multi-Peril Trends," *Proceedings of the Thirteenth Annual Insurance Conference*, No. C-148 (March 8, 1962), p. 143.

———. "Rate Making in Multiple Line Insurance," *Property and Liability Insurance Hand Book* edited by John D. Long and Davis W. Gregg.

Proceedings of the National Association of Insurance Commissioners, various years.

Proceedings of the National Convention of Insurance Commissioners (1914) p. 19.

SIMON, LEROY J. "Merit Rating Myths and Mysteries," *Automobile Insurance Rate Making* (1961), p. 182.

———. "Statistical Support for Adequate Rates," *Best's Insurance News* (Fire and Casualty Edition), Vol. 67, No. 3 (July, 1966), p. 1166.

SNIDER, H. WAYNE. "Inland Marine Rating and Rate Regulation," *The Journal of Insurance*, Vol. 30, No. 1 (March, 1963), p. 77.

SOHMER, HAROLD. "Fire and Allied Lines Insurance Rates," *Examination of Insurance Companies*, Vol. 5 (1955), p. 169.

WALTON, JR., T. E. "How Homeowners Policies Benefit Producers As Well As Policyholders," *Eastern Underwriter* (December 12, 1952), p. 73.

WINTER, WILLIAM D. "The Multiple-Line Concept," *Examination of Insurance Companies*, Vol. I (1953), p. 536.

PUBLIC DOCUMENTS

ALFORD, NEWALL, JR. *Opinion in the Matter of New York Fire Insurance Rating Organization: National Bureau of Casualty Underwriters; Inland Marine Insurance Bureau Hearing Pursuant to Section 186 of the Insurance Law Relating to Homeowners Policies.* New York Insurance Department, August 28, 1962. (Mimeographed.)

GEORGIA INSURANCE DEPARTMENT, *et al. Report of Examination of South-Eastern Underwriters Association*, December 31, 1957.

German Alliance Insurance Company v. *Lewis*, 233 U. S. 389, 58L. Ed. 1011, 345, Ct. 612 (1914).

ILLINOIS INSURANCE DEPARTMENT. *Report of Convention Examination of Mill and Elevator Rating Bureau*, June 30, 1958.

———. *Report of Convention Examination of Transportation Insurance Rating Bureau*, June 30, 1954. Also Oct. 10, 1956.

———. *Report of Examination of Western Underwriters Association*, May 15, 1958.

Matter of the Independent Filing of the Insurance Company of North America, et al. Confirmed in the *Matter of Cullen v. Bohlinger*, 284 App. Div. 963. Leave to appeal to Court of Appeals denied, 308 N. Y. 886, 308 N. Y. 1049, Appeal dismissed, 350 U. S. 803.

NEW YORK INSURANCE DEPARTMENT. *Report on Examination of Allied Line's Association*, June 9, 1952.

———. *Report on Examination of the Explosion Conference*, 1933 to 1945.

———. *Report on Examination of the Inland Marine Insurance Bureau*, September 1, 1961.

———. *Report on Examination of Inter-Regional Insurance Conference*, May 1, 1962.

———. *Report on Examination of the Mutual Insurance Rating Bureau*, August 15, 1955.

————. *Report on Examination of the National Bureau of Casualty Underwriters*, April 15, 1954.

New York Insurance Law, Art. VIII, Sec. 180, Subsec. 2.

RHODE ISLAND INSURANCE DEPARTMENT. *Report on Examination of the Factory Mutual Rating Bureau*, December 31, 1961.

STATE OF NEW YORK. *Intermediate Report of the Joint Legislative Committee on Housing*. Legislative Document No. 60, 1922.

————. *Report of the Joint Committee of the Senate and Assembly of the State of New York Appointed to Investigate Corrupt Practices in Connection with Legislation, and the Affairs of Insurance Companies, Other Than Those Doing a Life Insurance Business*. Assembly Document No. 30, 134th sess. (1911).

————. *78th Annual Report of the Superintendent of Insurance*, Part I (1937).

15 U. S. C. 1011–15 (1945).

U.S. SENATE, SUBCOMMITTEE ON ANTI-TRUST AND MONOPOLY OF THE COMMITTEE ON THE JUDICIARY. *Hearings on the Insurance Industry*. 85th and 86th Cong., 1958–60.

————. *The Insurance Industry: Insurance: Rates, Rating Organizations, and State Regulation*. Report No. 831, 87th Cong., 1st sess., 1961.

UNPUBLISHED MATERIAL

"Agreement of consolidation between Interbureau Insurance Advisory Group and Multiple Peril Rating Organization under name of Multi-Peril Insurance Conference" (April 18, 1957), p. 4.

BECKWITH, R. M. Manager, Inter-Regional Insurance Conference. (Letter to Roy C. McCullough, Manager, MPIRO, January 14, 1955.)

BOHLINGER, ALFRED J. "The Prospect for Multiple-Peril Underwriting.' Address before the New York Chapter of the National Insurance Buyers Association, Inc., New York, May 24, 1951. (Mimeographed.)

BURBACH, LOUIS R. "Multiple Line Package Insurance," pp. 5–6. Address before the Mutual Insurance Advisory Association, New York, November 14, 1950. (Mimeographed.)

CARLSON, THOMAS O. "Multiple-Line Underwriting." Address before the Pacific Northwest Insurance Seminar, Seattle, Washington, March 26, 1952. (Mimeographed.)

CONICK, H. C. "Multiple Line Insurance." Address before the Southwest Chapter of the Society of Chartered Property and Casualty Underwriters, Dallas, Texas, November 3, 1950. (Mimeographed.)

DINEEN, ROBERT E. "The Battle of the Bureaus." Address before the New York State Association of Agents, Inc., Syracuse, May 9, 1950. (Mimeographed.)

EASTERN UNDERWRITERS ASSOCIATION. "History and Development, Mandatory $50 Loss Deductible Clause, Windstorm and Hail Perils-Extended Coverage Endorsement." July, 1955.

HOBBS, CLARENCE W. "The Powers of Casualty Insurance Companies." Address before 161st Meeting of the Insurance Society of New York, December 6, 1921. (Mimeographed.)

IIAG. Explanatory Material, Comprehensive Dwelling Policy, New York (n.d.), p. 3.

LANGE, ROLAND H. "Report to the First Annual Meeting of the Multi-Peril Insurance Conference," October 16, 1957. (Mimeographed.)

LONGLEY-COOK, L. H. "Development and Rating of Package Policies." Address before All Industry Lucheon, Pacific Northwest Chapter, Chartered Property Casualty Underwriters, Seattle, Washington, October 24, 1961. (Mimeographed.)

MALONEY, JOHN R. "Welcoming Address." Given before 45 Annual Convention of the California Association of Insurance Agents, November 17, 1952.

McCULLOUGH, ROY C. "Multiple-Line Insurance and Its Value to the Insuring Public." Address before the First Annual Baltimore Insurance Day, Baltimore, Maryland, February 4, 1954. (Mimeographed.)

————. "Multiple Line Rates and Rating." Address before Insurance Regulation Institute, East Lansing, Michigan, February 11, 1958. (Mimeographed.)

MULTI-LINE INSURANCE RATING BUREAU. "Filing: MLIRB H65-3, Maine."

————. "Minutes, First Annual Meeting," Oct. 14, 1964.

————. "Report of General Manager," Oct. 14, 1965.

MPIRO. "Constitution," June 30, 1953, p. 2.

————. "Minutes, Executive Committee Meeting," January 14, 1954.

————. "Minutes, Rating Committee for Dwellings," July 24 and August 1, 1952, January 14, 1953.

————. "Minutes, Special Meeting," April 8, 1953.

————. "Report of Householders" Comprehensive Dwelling Policy.

————. "Report of Rating Committee for Dwelling Policies," January 29, 1953.

————. "Statement of Principles," June 30, 1953, p. 3.

MULTI-PERIL INSURANCE CONFERENCE. "Report of the Dwelling Committee." (n.d.)

NIASA. "Personal Lines Statistical Plan," effective Jan. 1, 1966.

NYFIRO. "Filing Letter November 22, 1961," p. 4.

O'MAHONEY, SENATOR JOSEPH C. "Competition vs. Collectivism," p. 8. Address before Sixth Annual Meeting of the National Association of Independent Insurers, Chicago, November 2, 1950.

SPECIAL SUBCOMMITTEE OF THE EXECUTIVE COMMITTEE OF THE BOARD OF FIRE UNDERWRITERS OF THE PACIFIC. "Report on Dwelling House Forms and Rates," March 11, 1943. (Mimeographed.)

STODDARD, FRANCIS R. "The History of Acquisition Costs in New York." (n.d.)

"Summary of: Proposals for Multiple-Line Underwriting, Problems Involved and Conclusions." (A statement authorized and approved by Insurance Executives Association and Casualty and Surety Executives, June 3, 1944.)

WOOD, HENRY. Letter of September, 1946, to Senator McCarran quoted in "Insurance as Interstate Commerce: The First Two Years." New York: Lawyers Press, Inc. Pamphlet.

OTHER SOURCES

CHARLES, A. CHALMERS. *Historical Background and Definition of Inland Marine Insurance.* New York: Insurance Institute of America, 1939.

HEDGES, J. E., AND MCMASTERS, C. V. *The Effects of Public Law Fifteen on the Local Insurance Agent.* Bloomington: Indiana University Bureau of Business Research, Study No. 34, January, 1952.

ILLINOIS INSPECTION BUREAU. *Advisory Rules.* From 1910 to 1967.

————. *The Extended Coverage Endorsement* (Feb., 1938).

INLAND MARINE INSURANCE BUREAU. *Forms-Rules-Rates, PPF-6*, page reprinted July, 1950.

KIMBALL, SPENCER L. "Problems in Regulation of Insurance." (Transcript of a Panel during the 55th Annual Meeting of the National Association of Attorneys General, July 10, 1961), pp. 16–17.

KIMBALL, S. L., AND CONKLIN, W. *The Montana Insurance Commissioner.* Ann Arbor: The University of Michigan Law School, 1960.

Standard Classification of Occupancy Hazards. 3d ed. rev. New York: National Board of Fire Underwriters, 1958.

1961 Annual Report. Insurance Company of North America, Philadelphia, Pa., p. 2.

1962 Annual Report. Reliance Insurance Company, Philadelphia, Pa., p. 5.

————. Letter to the author from Robert B. Taylor, Assistant to General Manager, IMIB, August 20, 1963.

————. Letter to the author from Robert C. Hayden, Assistant Manager, New York Fire Insurance Rating Organization, October 4, 1963.

INDEX

Index

This book has been set in 10 point Modern, leaded 3 points, and 9 point Modern, leaded 2 points. The chapter numbers are in 14 and 24 point Craw Clarendon and the chapter titles are in 18 point Craw Clarendon. The size of the type page is 24 by 41½ picas.